Matters of
CONSEQUENCE

Critical Eschatological Issues
Impacting Endtime Preparation

DR. RICK YOUNG

authorHOUSE®

AuthorHouse™
1663 Liberty Drive
Bloomington, IN 47403
www.authorhouse.com
Phone: 1 (800) 839-8640

Author Photos by R. P. Allen

Published by AuthorHouse   02/21/2018

ISBN: 978-1-5462-2864-6 (sc)
ISBN: 978-1-5462-2863-9 (e)

Library of Congress Control Number: 2018901813

Print information available on the last page.

Any people depicted in stock imagery provided by Getty Images are models, and such images are being used for illustrative purposes only.
Certain stock imagery © Getty Images.

This book is printed on acid-free paper.

Scripture taken from The Holy Bible, King James Version. Public Domain

Scripture quotations marked NASB are taken from the New American Standard Bible®, Copyright © 1960, 1962, 1963, 1968, 1971, 1972, 1973, 1975, 1977, 1995 by The Lockman Foundation. Used by permission.

"Behold, I have told you in advance" (Matthew 24:25).
— JESUS THE MESSIAH

This book is dedicated to the Lord Jesus Christ.

CONTENTS

PART I: PRE-TRIBULATIONALISM

PART II: PRE-DETERMINARIANISM

PART III: BABYLONIALISM

PREFACE

It is the glory of God to conceal a matter... (Proverbs 25:2).

This is a work on preparing Christians, the Body of Christ, for what may lay ahead for us. Numerous passages in both the Old and New Testaments of the Bible indicate a particularly severe period of human history before the return of Jesus Christ, our Lord. In fact, Jesus Himself declared, "For then there will be a great tribulation, such as has not occurred since the beginning of the world until now, nor ever will. Unless those days had been cut short, no life would have been saved" (Matthew 24:21-22). For anyone, then, living in the days preceding Christ's return, the Endtimes, thought, if not action, should be made towards preparing for such an event.

This leads us to the most basic issue of preparation. There is a standard axiom in emergency preparation and management: "Hope for the best, *but*, prepare for the worst." Indeed, the scriptural counterpart of the second half of the axiom is found in Proverbs 22:3, "The prudent sees the evil and hides himself, but the naïve go on, and are punished for it" (see also Proverbs 27:12).

In 2008, as a direct result of my Masters capstone project and resulting thesis, I was led to create the Bible-based Emergency Preparation Ministry to prepare Christians for the Endtime events depicted in Scripture. Though it was greeted with some open-mindedness, for the most part, it was heralded as unnecessary. The arguments to support the, often open and hostile, rejection consistently stemmed from three deeply held beliefs. Though I would patiently try to persuade, these beliefs were so entrenched that no amount of evidence could convince.

The mistake in my rebuttal, I came to realize, was that I was trying to dissuade the listener from their long-held beliefs (a near impossible task) as a prerequisite to getting them to see their need for preparation. The truth, I have come to see, is that their beliefs don't need to be changed; the person just needs to see the *possibility* of the worst-case scenario, which places them in dire jeopardy, should their current belief be proved wrong by future events.

This writing, then, is not an *apologetic*. Its intent is not to change one's mind from one set of beliefs to another. Its intent is to clearly set a worst-case scenario before the reader, and demonstrate the need to prepare for that worst-case, all the while current beliefs being maintained. It is hoped taking this approach should prove less antagonistic.

The key for the reader is the opening quote from Proverbs: "It is the glory of God to conceal a matter." Humility dictates that none of us "know it all." God has withheld information from us (see Revelation 10:4 as an example). This information is not the basics of the Gospel, which must be understood for justification; they are other issues for which the Church has "debated" (often vehemently) amongst herself during this, the Church Age.

Once one acknowledges that these issues may actually be being seen "through a glass darkly," the possibility of seeing other outcomes becomes less intrusive. From there, preparation becomes a viable alternative. That is my hope.

In order to keep a focused approach, though there are probably many objections to the need for preparation that can be made, I have found there are three consistent ones. They are held so tight-fisted by their advocates that it has proved near impossible to discuss without causing a rift. Yet, these three, if their adherents are found to be wrong, place them in the gravest of danger.

That is because they are unaware that their tightly-held beliefs have placed themselves in the *worst* worst-case scenario. As an act of Christian love, in fulfillment of the New Commandment (John 13:34), this writing has been undertaken.

Finally, it should be noted that although I have a 3-year Advanced Bible Study Certification from a well-known conservative Christian University, a program I sometimes refer to as, borrowing from cola advertisements, "seminary lite," as well a Masters from another conservative Christian University, my background is not theological. I have spent over 28 years in

Federal law enforcement, 21 of them as a criminal investigator, attaining the position of senior special agent. My approach, then, to much of what is to be presented here is from that investigative training and experience. Yes, the issues are theological, but the approach to them is not that of a seminarian. For that I make no apologies. My hope is that this method is seen as "refreshing," not intrusive. More, that it will help individuals see past "theology" to the very practical need for preparation.

My very firm belief is that when Jesus said, "Behold I have told you in advance" (Matthew 24:24), He did so for a reason… that we prepare for the events He was describing.

So let it be.

Allen Richard "Rick" Young

INTRODUCTION

A. PURPOSE

1. Concept Background

Since approximately 1988 this writer has been involved in teaching eschatology and its practical application. Drawing from his over 28-year military and law enforcement background, where preparation for battle, dangerous arrests, etc., were essential to survival, he has taken to heart the words of Jesus, "Behold, I have told you in advance" (Matthew 24:25), as a call to preparation for Endtime events.

Prior *informal* approaches to that preparation, given during his Bible studies or sermons, became *formal* as part of his matriculation at Philadelphia Biblical University (now, Cairn University), Langhorne, PA. In fulfillment of the Master Degree requirements, a capstone project and subsequent thesis developed the "Endtime Crisis Management Ministry: An Eschatological Christian Ministry."

The focus of the ministry concept was to be through its *Active Training* session, a methodology developed by Mel Silberman and presented in his book of the same title.[1] The principle elements developed for that presentation were

1.) An exploration of the history of Divine judgment: identifying key Old Testament passages to establish *why* God judges and *how* that judgment was carried out.

---

[1] Mel Silberman, *Active Training: A Handbook of Techniques, Designs, Case Examples, and Tips* (San Francisco: Jossey-Bass Publishers, 1998).

2.) A look at the current condition of the United States and comparing it with the reasons for Divine judgment expressed in the Old Testament: Is God's judgment of America a possibility? A probability?

3.) If Divine judgment is possible/probable, what are the steps necessary to prepare? Noting that a human being is composed of body, soul, and spirit (1st Thessalonians 5:23b), each of these elements are addressed separately.

4.) A guide to develop an individually constructed plan for identified, necessary preparation.

2. Ministry Creation

On November 1, 2007, The Bible-based Emergency Preparation Ministry was incorporated in the state of New Jersey as a Non-Profit, Faith Based Initiative organization to provide "Bible-based spiritual and physical aid in emergency preparation." The ministry "brings emergency preparation techniques, provided by sources such as the Red Cross and the U.S. Department of Homeland Security, into a Bible-based context for faith-based response to emergency pre-planning and management."[2]

Since its creation, presentations, providing the information listed above, have supplied a Bible-based, faith-based perspective to emergency pre-planning and management. This has been done informally at churches and small groups through Bible studies, and formally, at church and conference settings.

It is this writer's direct observation that where once this ministry was, at best, shunned, at worst, openly rejected, with the current disintegration of world and national conditions, it is becoming more and more accepted. There is a demonstrated growing awareness of the need to be prepared. It is anticipated that, as the events of Matthew 24, et al, continue to increase in number and intensity, acceptance, if not embracement, of this ministry will occur.

3. The Problem

---

[2] See the ministry website, www.BibleEmergencyPreparation.org

In spite of the growth of the acceptance of, and comprehension of the need for, this ministry, there are three significant developments that are working to undermine it. At this point, it is important to again note that a human being is made of body (physical), soul (psychological), and spirit (spiritual) (1st Thessalonians 5:23).

The first issue of contention deals with the eschatological concept of the Rapture. Specifically, the issue deals with the timing of that event. In regards to preparation, it is centered in the failure to be willing to prepare physically and psychologically.

As background to this issue, Scripture indicates that before Jesus returns to the earth (Acts 1:11), those who are "in Christ," i.e. Christians, will be removed from the world to join Him in the sky (1st Corinthians 15:51-52; 1st Thessalonians 4:15-17). This is commonly referred to as the Rapture. The timing of this event is not evident in the Bible, which has led to four fundamental views on that timing. These will be discussed in-depth later, but for overview purposes they are listed here.

1.) **Pre-tribulation**: the Church will be removed *before* the events of the Book of Revelation.

2.) **Mid-tribulation**: the Church will be removed in the *middle* of the events of Revelation.

3.) **Pre-Wrath**: similar to Mid-tribulation, the Church will be removed before the Wrath of God events of the Book of Revelation occur (principally, at and after chapter 8, and definitely before chapter 15); this may be near to, but not exactly at, the middle.

4.) **Post-Tribulation**: the Church will be removed just prior to the return of Christ in Revelation 19.

With these in mind, it can easily be seen that the Mid-, Pre-Wrath, and Post-tribulation adherents would immediately understand the need for preparation. Experiencing some, or all, of the events of Revelation virtually demands it!

The problem is with the Pre-tribulational view. If the Church is removed prior to all the events of Revelation, adherents of this view see no need to prepare physically and psychologically (of the soul) for those Endtime events. "Don't worry," they almost universally say, "we're out-of-here before *any* of this occurs." To be fair, they do see the need to remain spiritually prepared if, for no other reason, then to be "alert," as required by Matthew 24:42; 25:13, amongst other passages.

It is this writer's experience that this view is *entrenched* in the minds of Pre-tribulationalists. Though Scripture does not overtly define the timing of the Rapture, and, hence, all these views are theory, Pre-tribulationalists see their view *as fact*. In the Literature Review (below) response to this will be discussed. It should be noted that much of that literature could be seen, in part or whole, as being written in "high theology terms" not easily understood by the laity.

Notwithstanding, the concern for this writer is that, if a Pre-tribulational Rapture does *not* occur, Pre-tribulationalists are virtually, completely unprepared for the catastrophic Endtime events described in Scripture. Being thus blindsided, the devastating effect this will have on their faith, much less their well-being, cannot be, and should not be, ignored. It is anticipated wholesale abandonment of their faith may result. For pastors as well as laity.

Further, just when a Christian's pastor will be most needed for support, trust in Pre-tribulational pastors, who were obviously "wrong," will no doubt hit an all-time low. For those few who are still able, this will render them ineffective at a time when they will be most needed.

It is this writer's strongly held view that a gentle, but concise laity-held perspective (i.e. not over-burdened in "theology" and theological terms), needs to be created that will guide the Pre-tribulationalist to understand his or her view *is theory*. Although done firmly, it should hold to an attitude of grace demonstrating that preparation needs to be made for a worst-case scenario (the concept of which is discussed below).

The point-of-view is from that of the Titanic evacuation: The first contingent of lifeboats went only partially filled because the need was not adequately made known. Had that need been expressed properly *at the outset*, more lives would have been saved.

It is the intent of this writer to save lives by systematically presenting the weaknesses of the current Pre-tribulational theory. In doing this, it is hoped the Pre-tribulationalist will see the need to re-think his or her position relative to physical and psychological preparation, where, currently, no need is seen.

The second issue of this writing deals with the eschatological concept of the Millennial Kingdom. This issue is relative to the need for the individual to prepare *spiritually*.

Certain Christians are of the belief that "he who began a good work in you will perfect it until the day of Christ Jesus" (Philippians 1:6). The stated claim is that true Christians will *absolutely* persevere in their faith until the end of their life, or if they are alive at the time of the Rapture, until that moment. There is an undercurrent in their belief that, having been "chosen" by God, they are not directly responsible to be concerned about their spiritual condition *per se*, much less its relation to preparation for the catastrophic Endtime events. "Don't worry," they almost universally say, "God alone will take care of my spiritual condition; it's been pre-destined. Having been 'chosen,' I can't possibly 'fall away.'"

The eschatological problem here is that the Holy Spirit through the Apostle Paul makes it clear otherwise, even in spite of being "The Chosen": "[T]he Spirit explicitly says that in later times some will fall away from the faith" (1st Timothy 4:1). Jesus was even more dire: "[A]t that time *many* will fall away..." (Matthew 24:10; emphasis added). To confirm this perspective, and to determine the cause(s) for departing the faith will be the second objective of this writing.

As seen in the Literature Review (below) adherents who proport that one *cannot* fall away also hold to the teaching that such a person was never a Christian to begin with. It is necessary to explore whether this is true, as well as look at the ancillary beliefs associated with this perspective. If these are wrong perceptions, misled Christians might be run astray spiritually during the calamitous Endtime events, the very time they need to be rock solid in their faith.

Worse, rejection of saved individuals who have fallen away because they are viewed as "never saved to begin with," invites a "shooting of the wounded" as saved, but fallen, individuals are rejected when they are, in fact, in need of assistance the most. The spiritual impact here could be devastating!

Further, as explored in Literature Review, such a wrongful understanding of Scripture will have drastic consequences relative to the eschatological concept of the Kingdom of God which, this writing will explore, most directly refers to the Thousand Year reign of Jesus Christ on the earth, often referred to as the Millennial Kingdom. It is believed by this writer that direct harm can be done to a person's spiritual well-being in regards to that Kingdom as a result of this misunderstanding of being "chosen."

With all of this in mind, a second objective will be the attempt to safeguard the spiritual lives of believers who hold to an absolute perseverance, et al, theology as it impacts an Endtime perspective. This will be done by clearly presenting that view's weaknesses.

The final issue deals with the eschatological Endtime Babylon. It is completely independent of one's view on the timing of the Rapture or theological persuasion to the perseverance of the saints. It deals with the role the United States of America plays in the Endtimes, an understanding *vital* to American Christians... and those Americans who will undergo the events of Revelation. This issue will impact all three elements of preparation: physical, psychological, and spiritual.

In this writer's Masters thesis (and project), a critical understanding of a pre-Great Tribulation judgment of America was postulated, and then supported by evidence. (Portions of this are contained in the Literature Review, below).

The essence of the worst-case scenario (again, described more fully below in the Literature Review) was that the worst case would, indeed, be a Divine judgment of America. In fact, many eschatological scholars believed the removal of the United States as a world power would cause the ensuing power vacuum that was necessary to help enable the Antichrist to ascend to power. This perspective was used in this writer's ministry presentations to establish credibility for the need for preparation, even amongst Pre-tribulationalists, because such divine judgment was seen to pre-date the Rapture.

The driving rational behind all of this was "What could be worse than Divine judgment?" The universal response was always, "Nothing!" Hence, the *worst*-case scenario.

But, what if there *was* something worse?

In post-Masters personal study, this writer has identified something worse. In fact, it is so obvious, it has rendered him significantly embarrassed in not seeing it before. Revelation 18 states clearly, "Give back to her [Babylon, v. 2] *double...*" (v. 6). Endtime Babylon receives a *double portion* of Divine wrath. This *has* to be the *worst* worse-case.

In conjunction with this, additional personal study has identified literature which begins to lay an evidentiary foundation that America might be Endtime Babylon. This needs to be further explored and reported. If there is enough credible evidence, Americans must be alerted in order to better guide them to prepare: For the unsaved to accept Jesus as Savior *now*; for the saved, to be better prepared to deal with the contingency America *is* Endtime Babylon. Survival will depend on it, if for no other reason, then that they are not blindsided as evil continues to rise – and reign – in the United States.

Added to the concept of being blindsided, and thus increasing its impact, as demonstrated in the Literature Review, the existing accepted belief is that the Endtime Babylon is a risen New Roman Empire. Christians are looking for that event to occur as a signal to them the rise of the Antichrist is at hand, i.e. confirmation they are in the Endtimes.

The problem is, if they are looking towards Rome... they just might be looking in the wrong direction. This could easily decrease their ability to survive if Endtime Babylon were rising somewhere else, i.e., right below their very feet.

This writing will attempt to so alert them.

B. REVIEW OF LITERATURE

1. Pre-tribulationalism

As a preface to this section, in order to identify matters concerning Bible interpretation (hermeneutics), the principles that will be applied are discussed here. These principles are taken from the books of Bernard Ramm, *Protestant Biblical Interpretation*; Earl D. Radmacher, general editor of the *Nelson NKJV Bible*, (where those principles are discussed in that book's "Forward"); Robert H. Stein, *A Basic Guide to Interpreting the Bible*; and Roy B. Zuck, *Basic Bible Interpretation*. In summary, they are:

1.) The Word of God interprets itself; it is self-defining
2.) The Word of God is to be taken literally
3.) The "plain sense" meaning is the prevalent understanding
4.) The best understanding, especially in a word study, is that in the original Hebrew and Greek

Other reference material includes the books of Warren Baker and Eugene Carpenter, *The Complete Word Study Dictionary Old Testament*; Jerry Falwell, Edward E. Hindson, and Woodrow M. Kroll, *Liberty Bible Commentary*; James I. Packer, Merrill C. Tenney and William White, Jr., *The Bible Almanac*; James Strong, *Strong's Exhaustive Concordance of the Bible*; and W. E. Vine, *An Expository Dictionary of New Testament Words*. These provide commentary where needed and help define terms and concepts.

A review of the following authors and their works have identified key themes central to the issues being reviewed. They include: 1) an historical overview of Eschatology, including current prevailing attitudes towards the timing of the Rapture and the existence of a 1,000-year reign of Christ on earth (the Millennium). These include, but are not be limited to:

+ Paul N. Benware, *Understanding End Times Prophecy*;
+ Wayne Grudem, *Making Sense of the Future*;

- Tim LaHaye, *The Beginning of the End*, (and with reference to his *Left Behind* Series and *Revelation: Illustrated and Made Plain*;
- Hal Lindsey, *The Late Great Planet Earth*;
- Jim McKeever, *Christians Will Go Through The Tribulation: And How to Prepare for It*;
- Dwight J. Pentecost, *Things to Come: A Study in Biblical Eschatology*;
- Marvin Rosenthal, *The Pre-Wrath Rapture of the Church*;
- Charles C. Ryrie, *The Ryrie Study Bible: New American Standard Translation* and *The Basis of the Premillennial Faith*;
- Jack Van Impe, *11:59 and Counting* and *Your Future: An A-Z Index to Prophecy*;
- Geerhardus Vos, *Biblical Theology* and *The Kingdom and the Church*;
- John F. Walvoord, *The Rapture Question*.

Pre-tribulationalism is defined in most of these quintessential, and highly regarded, works, and is expressed therein by its most ardent supporters. The following issues have been identified from these writings and will be directly addressed in this writing:

1.) The Blessed Hope (Titus 2:13)
2.) The Thessalonian Rapture Concern (2nd Thessalonians 2:1-2)
3.) The Day of the Lord (2nd Thessalonians 2:2-5, et al)
4.) The Doctrine of Imminence (Matthew 24:42, et al)
5.) Kept from the Hour of Testing (Revelation 3:10)
6.) Not Appointed Us to Wrath (1st Thessalonians 5:9)
7.) A Firm Covenant (Daniel 9:24-27)

These seven components are the core of Pre-tribulationalism. If they are found to have identifiable weaknesses, then that view of the timing of the Rapture comes into question. As such, a foundation is laid for even the Pre-tribulationalist to see the need for preparation; the intent of addressing this issue of eschatology. (Note: it is not this writer's intent to discredit the persons of Pre-tribulationalist authors and advocates, but merely to show that view's weaknesses in order to get its adherents to, at the least, consider the need for preparation).

Of particular interest to this writer is the last issue, "A Firm Covenant."

A review of *Barnes Notes on Daniel*, by Albert Barnes, with a copyright date of 1881, (yes, **eighteen** eighty-one!) states, "[T]he 'he' of verse 27 [previously quoted] refers to the Messiah… for there can be no doubt that it is the same person which is mentioned in the phrase 'he shall confirm the covenant with many.'"[3] Acceptance of this understanding would mean, as Barnes implies, that there are only 3½ years left on God's prophetic timeline. Henry H. Halley in his world-renowned *Halley's Bible Handbook*, with an original copyright date of 1927, agrees with this dating: "[W]ithin 3½ years Jesus was crucified, that is, 'in the midst of the one week,' [i.e. Daniel's 70th week] 'the Anointed One' was 'cut off…' "[4]

The concept that the "he" of verse 27 is the *Messiah*, and that there are only 3½ years remaining on God's prophetic timeline is rejected by *every* author cited above regarding this Pre-tribulational subject. Whether that author is Pre-, Mid-, Pre-Wrath, or Post-tribulational in their view on the timing of the Rapture, they are *all* in agreement that the "he" of verse 27 is the *Antichrist*, and that the *entire* 7-year period of Daniel's 70th week still remains. Which group is correct? This is critical: a wrongful understanding of this crucial Endtime event, and to whom it is referring, could have devastating effects in regards to preparation… for the unprepared.

This issue simply *must* be explored in detail! And is in this writing.

2. Pre-determinarianism

It should be noted that many of the references in the Pre-tribulationalism Literature Review above will also be used relative to this issue. In addition, the following authors have been identified:

+ Donald Grey Barnhouse, *The Invisible War* and *Revelation*;
+ Lewis Sperry Chafer, *Satan: His Motives and Methods*;
+ Arlen L. Chitwood, *Salvation of the Soul*;
+ Joseph C. Dillow *Reign of the Servant Kings: A Study of Eternal Security and the Significance of Man*;

---

[3] Albert Barnes, *Barnes' Notes on the Book of Daniel* (New York: R. Worthington, 1881), 413.

[4] Henry H. Halley, *Halley's Bible Handbook* (Grand Rapids, MI: Zondervan Publishing House, 1927, 24th ed., 1965).

- Robert Govett, *Entrance Into The Kingdom* and *Govett On Revelation*;
- Wayne Grudem, *Systematic Theology*;
- Watchman Nee, *The King and the Kingdom of Heaven*;
- J. Dwight Pentecost, *Thy Kingdom Come*;
- Earl D. Radmacher, *Salvation*;
- J. A. Seiss, *The Apocalypse: Letures on the Book of Revelation*;
- R. C. Sproul, *Chosen By God*;
- Gary T. Whipple, *Shock & Surprise Beyond The Rapture* and *The Matthew Mysteries*.

Grudem and Sproul, in particular, look at the issue of perseverance of "The Chosen," a key element of Pre-determinarianism, in detail. Linked with that issue are those of total depravity, limited atonement, irresistible grace, and unconditional election. Because these other elements are so totally intertwined with the issue of perseverance, the concepts of each will be explored. The following have been identified from these writings and will be directly addressed:

1.) The issue of "election" (Ephesians 1:4, et al)
2.) Overcomers (Revelation 2:7, 11, 17, 26, 29; 3:5-6, 12-13, 21-22).
3.) The "Bride" (Revelation 21:9, et al)
4.) Perseverance: The Faithful (Revelation 19:11, 13; 17:14)
5.) The Inheritance (Titus 3:6-7, et al)
6.) Total Depravity (John 16:8; Romans 10:13; Acts 2:21, etc.)
7.) The Universal Call (John 1:29; 3:16; 2nd Corinthians 5:19, et al)
8.) God's Sovereignty (Romans 9)
9.) The Act of Faith (Hebrews 11:1, et al)

The review of the above concepts will be a prelude to exploring how a wrongful understanding of each of these issues places one in jeopardy in relation to the 1,000-year Messianic Kingdom, the Kingdom of God.

The key to this understanding is seeing there are three separate issues in relation to this Kingdom (see below). Unfortunately, more often than not, the three are "lumped together" as if one concept. As J. Sidlow Baxter, (amongst many of the other cited authors), explained:

When John and our Lord came preaching, "Repent ye; for the kingdom of heaven is at hand," they were referring to something publicly understood, namely, the long-promised Messianic kingdom which was the grand subject of Old Testament prophecy.... When our Lord interviewed Nicodemus (John 3) He spoke at once of the "kingdom of God" as a concern already familiar to Nicodemus' mind....

If by the "kingdom of heaven" our Lord meant the *Gospel*, as we now commonly use that word, meaning "the grace of God which bringeth salvation" to all who by faith appropriate the atonement of Christ, He would have been unintelligible, unless He had first explained that He meant this. For the Gospel of Calvary is "good news" of personal salvation to individual men and women everywhere ("whosoever"), not the proclamation of a "kingdom"...[5]

The Gospel and Kingdom of God, though inter-related, are, these authors argue, separate entities. Further, with the statement in 1st Corinthians 15:24-26 that the kingdom is handed over ("delivered up") to the Father after the 1,000-year Millennium, the Word of God implies this as well.[6]

Hence, it is argued that the Gospel, the Kingdom, and the Eternal State are three separate issues. Entrance then into salvation (justification; the Gospel), the Kingdom (sanctification, which they argue is conditional), and the Eternal State (glorification) have separate components.

Should their perspective prove true, and this writing will pursue looking into this, the worst-case scenario for those who believe they cannot fall away is that they are wrong. This places them in serious jeopardy should Scripture make it clear one *can* fall away.[7] And this falling away might have a serious impact on placement in the Kingdom: This writing will demonstrate loss suffered at the Bema Seat (1st Corinthians 3:10-15) will include loss of

---

[5] J. Sidlow Baxter, *The Strategic Grasp of the Bible* (Grand Rapids, MI: Zondervan Publishing House, 1968), 234, 235.

[6] Note also in this Corinthian passage, the issue of death being destroyed; this doesn't happen until after the final judgment (cf. Revelation 20:7 and 11-14).

[7] For example, see 1st Timothy 4:1 and Matthew 24:10, amongst others.

being able to rule and reign with Christ during, at the least, His Millennial Kingdom (i.e. a *non*-overcomer; see Revelation 2:26-27; 3:21).

The current belief by some Christians that they will face no consequences for their actions since they are "saved" – because they are "chosen" and, therefore, simply cannot fall away – could place them in the precarious position of, as Whipple writes, being "shocked and surprised beyond the Rapture"![8]

For the sake of those "in Christ," this issue cannot be ignored. Having been made aware of this, how can one fulfill the New Commandment (John 15:12, 17) by turning away, disregarding it, and not alerting others? It certainly can't be ignored if one is involved in a ministry to prepare Christians for what is coming in the future!

For that reason, it is addressed in this writing.

3. Babylonialism

A. Background

The primary function of the Bible-based Emergency Preparation Ministry is to prepare Christians for the eschatological events preceding Jesus' Second Advent which are presented in the Bible. In regards to any organization that is involved in such pre-planning, secular as well as religious, a predominant core issue is, again, that of the worst-case scenario.

Ian I. Mitroff with Gus Angus observed in *Managing Crises Before They Happen* (2001), "The best form of crisis management is preparation for a major crisis before it has occurred."[9] Steven Fink in his *Crisis Management* directed that the question which needed to be asked was: " 'What is the

---

[8] Gary T. Whipple, *Shock & Surprise Beyond The Rapture* (Hayesville, North Carolina: Schoettle Publishing Company, 1992), Title. It is this writer's sad personal experience that *many* Christians are oblivious to the up-coming, future judgment at the Bema Seat after their Rapture or resurrection as expressed in 1st Corinthians 3:10-15.

[9] Ian I. Mitroff, with Gus Anagnos, *Managing Crises Before They Happen: What Every Executive and Manager Needs to Know About Crisis Management* (New York: American Management Association, 2001), 40.

worst thing that could happen?' and then prepare accordingly."[10] Peter Schwartz, President of the Global Business Network, writing in his *The Art of the Long View: Planning for the Future in an Uncertain World* makes it more personal, "What if our worst nightmare took place?"[11]

The worst-case concept is based on the belief that if one prepares for the worst, anything less demanding becomes more manageable. The opposite is equally as true: anything more demanding, because one is *un*prepared, becomes less manageable. As Bruce T. Blythe, CEO of Crisis Management International, Inc. noted in his book *Blindsided*, "There is little possibility of effective response without thoughtful preparedness."[12] And, obviously, less prepared when undergoing a Divine judgment would place one in an extremely dire position.

With the need to determine the worst-case scenario, this ministry identified the judgement of the United States by Almighty God as, by far, *the* worst. Further, to demonstrate the need by all Christians for preparation for such an event (actually series of events), the worst case developed was framed on such judgment to occur even before a Pre-tribulational Rapture. Hence, even Pre-tribulationalists should take note of being inclined towards the need for preparation.

This view was based on writings of Pre-tribulational eschatologists. Over 45 years ago, Hal Lindsay wrote in his acclaimed book on the Endtimes, *Late Great Planet Earth* (1970), "... according to the prophetic outlook the United States will cease being a world leader of the West... [Based on Daniel 7] it is certain that the leadership of the West must shift to Rome, in its revived form, and if the U.S. is still around at that time, it will not be the power it now is."[13] Tim LaHaye, co-author of the renowned *Left Behind* Series, holds a similar view. Writing in 1984, LaHaye stated in his book *The Coming Peace in the Middle East* (1984), a book on the false

---

[10]   Steven Fink, *Crisis Management: Planning for the Inevitable* (New York: American Management Association, 1986), 36.

[11]   Peter Schwartz, *The Art of the Long View: Planning for the Future in an Uncertain World* (New York: Doubleday Publishers, 1996), xv.

[12]   Bruce T. Blythe, *Blindsided: A Manager's Guide to Catastrophic Incidents in the Workplace* (New York: Penguin Putnam, Inc., 2002), 4.

[13]   Hal Lindsey, with C.C. Carlson, *The Late Great Planet Earth* (Grand Rapids, MI: Zondervan Publishing House, 1970), 95-96.

peace surrounding the rise of the Antichrist, "it is not difficult to predict the future of America... we will be[come] a fifth-rate power."[14]

What if they are wrong? What if America isn't completely removed? What if the United States of America is, in fact, the Endtime Babylon? The reason this would be the worst worst-case scenario is, as previously stated, that nation, whomever she turns out to be, will receive a *double* portion of God's wrath![15]

It becomes critical, then, to pursue an investigation into available information which might point to the fact America *is* Endtime Babylon.

B. ANALYSIS

Scripture states clearly that Satan is the ruler of this world: "The whole world lies in the power of the evil one" (1st John 5:19). And his *modus operandi* is that of lies (deceit) and murderer: "[T]he devil was a murder from the beginning, and... there is no truth in him... he is a liar, and the father of lies" (John 8:44). Regarding the Endtimes, we are told Satan will give his authority to the Antichrist who himself will have "authority over every tribe and people and tongue and nation" (Revelation 13:7, cf. vv. 4-5). If we are, indeed, living in the Endtimes, what should be looked for are indicators that an evil power is at work which uses lies (and murder) as instruments in creating a one-world government.

Before he became saved, Christian author Gary H. Kah was once an inside member of the plot for a one-world government. In his book *En Route to Global Occupation*, he stated:

> During the early 1980s, I was on the fast track of a successful government career, which took me around the world dealing with American embassies, foreign governments officials, international business leaders, and, at times, member of the press and media...from Taiwan to Israel to the Soviet Union....
> Through my travels and job-related contacts, I became aware of plans being laid worldwide for the establishment of a one-world

---

14   Tim LaHaye, *The Coming Peace in the Middle East* (Grand Rapids, Michigan: Zondervan Publishing House, 1984), 172.

15   Revelation 18:6.

government, most frequently referred to by insiders as the New World Order."[16]

Kah goes on to lay out the covert, systematic attempt by unseen, power-mad forces to create a one-world government. His conclusion is chilling: ""I am convinced that America's purpose in the overall plan was to lay the necessary groundwork for the world government; and then, having accomplished this mission, to lead humanity to the threshold, if not actually into, the New World Order."[17]

Before one quickly labels him as a "conspiracy theorist" and discards Kah as a mad man, writings by noted Christian authors, many acknowledged (Pre-tribulational) eschatological scholars, support Kah's findings. These include, in part, Salem Kirban in *Satan's Angels Exposed*; Dave Hunt in *Peace, Prosperity and the Coming Holocaust: The New Age Movement in Prophecy*; Donald S. McAlvany in *Toward A New World Order*; Texe Marrs in *Millenium: Peace, Promises, and the Day They Take Our Money Away*; and Grant R. Jeffrey in *Prince of Darkness: Antichrist and the New World Order*, amongst others.

There is much "overlap" between these works, each providing the same information, but in a different "style." Yet, if a matter is confirmed on the testimony of two or three witnesses (Deuteronomy 17:6; 2nd Corinthians 13:1), then, certainly, there is credibility when there are half-a-dozen or more. In unison, these authors clearly identify a sinister plot occurring "just below the surface," i.e. *in deceit*, to create a one-world government that will include the United States of America.

As Kirban quotes from their own writings, they will do this with their allegiance "maintained in the purity of the Luciferian doctrine."[18] The thrust of this attempt to create a one-world government is to produce a political (and economic) system whereby there is a ruling elite, made up of a small, limited number of individuals, who are committed to Satan, and bring this about for his glory... and their benefit. The rest of the world's population will

---

[16]   Gary H. Kah, *En Route To Global Occupation: A High Rankin Government Liaison Exposes the Secret Agenda for World Unification* (Lafayette, Louisiana: Huntington House Publishers, 1992), 6.

[17]   Ibid., 62.

[18]   Salem Kirban, *Satan's Angels Exposed* (Chattanooga, Tennessee: AMG Publishers, 1980), 161.

be enslaved, to do the elite's bidding. Control will be through intimidation and killings. This is an exact description of the Antichrist's rule being fulfilled in Revelation 13.

Further, authors William T. Still in *New World Order: The Ancient Plan of Secret Societies*, Des Griffin *in Fourth Reich of the Rich*, Dennis L. Cuddy in his books *The Globalists: The Power Elite Exposed* and *Now is the Dawning of the New Age New World Order*, Tal Brooke in *When The World Will Be As One: The Coming New World Order in the New Age*, Roy Allan Anderson in *The New Age Movement and the Illuminati 666*, Antony C. Sutton in *America's Secret Establishment: An Introduction to the Order of the Skull & Bones*, and Jim Marrs, a respected investigative journalist, in *Rule By Secrecy: The Hidden History that Connects the Trilateral Commission, the Freemasons, and the Great Pyramids*, trace the historical activities *within the United States* to create this one-world government. A most recent look at this is Michael D. Fortner's book, *The Fall of Babylon the Great America*. Again, there is "overlap," but this creates a more than "double portion" of witnesses, a scriptural requirement to confirm a matter.

All of these authors implicate the United States as being part of, if not integral and central to, a Luciferic scheme to create a one-world government. They demonstrate that scheme has been occurring over the centuries through ancient, and recent, secret societies, who, again by their own writings, place their allegiance to (hence, worship of) Satan. They trace the progression of these Satanic-led societies from the Garden of Eden to our present day. Consistently they show that the semi-overt writings and covert activities of groups such as the Freemasons, the Illuminati, the Council on Foreign Relations, the Trilateral Commission, etc., coupled with the New Age Movement (in its many forms) and the extremely wealthy international bankers (who have a *love* of money; cf. 1st Timothy 6:9-10) are working systematically to create this one-world government with the United States as its front runner.

In regards to the international bankers, Doug Clark in *The Greatest Banking Scandal in History*, Howard S. Katz in *The Paper Aristocracy: America's Money System*, and Christian author Grant R. Jeffery in *Final Warning: Economic Collapse and the Coming World Government* provide strong evidence of these bankers' involvement in creating this one-world government... especially through the activities of "Wall Street."

As one looks at the growing evil within the world—and within the United States—and sees the now overt attempt at creating a one-world order, it is hard to ignore the evidence presented by the above cited authors. Further, Christians, being led by the current "popular" eschatology of today, are told to look toward Europe for a revived "Rome" from which the Antichrist arises. From the evidence presented by these authors, again, many of them Christian, there is strong evidence those who are looking towards "Rome" are looking in the wrong direction. This would, then, leave them less prepared and open to being blindsided. And for American Christians, the peril is increased by their being unaware of what is actually going on in their nation.

One observation: the intent of this part of the writing will be to make Christians aware of these nefarious activities linked to Satan. It will not be to confirm this beyond a reasonable doubt (the cited authors have written volumes to attempt just that), but to establish enough credible evidence to confirm a need for seeing this as being an integral part of the worst worst-case scenario – and cause them to prepare accordingly.

C. METHODOLOGY

1. Background: Crisis Forecasting

Crisis forecasting is the proactive identification of events that may adversely impact a person or group. When applied in the areas of the military or law enforcement it is called an *intelligence operation*.

At the outset it is important to understand that there is a difference between crisis management and disaster management, though there is some overlap in response techniques, especially when the crisis leads to horrific outcomes. Generally, though, a disaster is defined as a natural or "Act of God" harmful event (or series of events), such as a hurricane (or one that makes multiple landfalls). In contrast, a crisis is defined as a "man-made" adverse event.[19] (Please note the response to the devastation caused by Hurricane Andrew, a disaster, would be different than that of Bristol-Meyers executives trying to head-off the Tylenol poisoning scare, a crisis.) To avoid any misunderstanding between these two terms and, thus, be more all-inclusive, government agencies usually define these as *Emergency Management*.

Having provided the accepted definitions, the Bible-based Emergency Preparation Ministry modifies those terms by taking the view that a *crisis* is that portion of an event or series of connected events, whether natural or man-made, when the event(s) itself is actually occurring. A *disaster* is the *outcome* of a crisis, which can be one of two occurrences: a negative outcome, hence, *true disaster*, or a positive outcome, which is an *averted disaster*. Thus, when the Titanic struck the iceberg and began to sink, a crisis had occurred; when it actually sunk it became a disaster. Note the response during the Titanic's crisis – trying to keep the ship afloat and save as many passengers and crew as possible – was different to the response once it became a disaster – assisting the survivors.

With that as background, it should be noted the essence of strategic crisis forecasting is the creation of the "worst-case" scenario: What is the

---

19   Mitroff and Anagnos, 6.

worst thing that could happen?[20] In effect, a good crisis scenario envisions how the unthinkable can and will occur. It is for this event that one should prepare. In this way, if something *less* than worst-case occurs, you are *more* than prepared.

Unfortunately, the main barrier to crisis forecasting – as well as crisis management in general – is that of denial.[21] Far too many people, *far* too many decision-makers, mouth the cliché, "It can't happen to us." As a result, they conclude it is a waste of time, energy, and resources to identify and prepare for crises associated with their lives... or livelihoods. Yet, it has been demonstrated that decision-makers who have merely *thought* about the worst-case scenario are better prepared to react when that crisis actually occurs. The fact they anticipated the unthinkable *in some form* keeps them from being blindsided and, thus, paralyzed in the midst of the chaos.[22]

That is not to say the crisis forecast must be accepted in total – because it can never be made totally foolproof. While it should be used to help make sound decisions, it should not enslave the decision-maker: There is *always* a trade-off in using crisis forecasting information; as inherent in any activity where there is the element of risk. The crisis forecast, though, helps provide insights that can be gained *before* the emergency, thus significantly assisting decision-makers in weighing outcomes with ensuing risks – and guiding them to viable decisions.[23]

2. Analysis

With this understanding of crisis forecasting in mind, the approach to this writing is to employ accepted forecasting techniques and couple them with this writer's training and experience in both military and law enforcement intelligence operations. The object is to provide pertinent information to the target groups identified previously, i.e., Pre-tribulationalists, who believe they will experience *none* of the Endtime events described in Matthew 24, the Book of Revelation, et al; advocates

---

[20]   Fink, 36.

[21]   Mitroff and Anagnos, 8, 46-47; cf. Schwartz, 36.

[22]   Blythe, 111.

[23]   Schwartz, 49; cf. Fink, 83-85.

of Pre-destinarianism, being "chosen," those who promote guaranteed perseverance in their Christian walk, *never* able to fall away from it; and, lastly, American Christians, those who live in this nation and believe it is not mentioned in the Bible, nor involved in Endtime events. This information is intended to show the weakness of their belief(s) and demonstrate that this weakness can, ultimately, place them in a situation where they are unprepared for Endtime events. By making them aware, thus giving them an opportunity to prepare, their survivability should be increased.

To accomplish this, material from the books cited in the Literature Review and Bibliography have been used to show the current belief systems of each group. Specifically, those beliefs will be shown by taking them from *the writings of their own advocates.* These issues were identified in the Literature Review as numbered line items. Each is analyzed in a separate chapter using an intelligence operation approach, where contrary information has been provided to show the weakness of each tenet of that belief. Once the weakness is established, a worst-case scenario is developed that should cause the reader to draw their own conclusion that preparation for Endtime events *is not optional*—and should be undertaken as soon as possible.

With that in mind, it is important to again state this writing is *not* an apologetic, i.e., an attempt to sway those with opposing views to change their minds. Its purpose is a practical look at eschatology in order to develop a worst worst-case scenario from which appropriate plans can be made that will increase survivability in body, soul (*psuche*, psychological), and spirit.

If individual Christians can objectively view the weaknesses in their own eschatological theology presented here, this should drive them to realize they might be blinded to, and therefore need to come to the realization of, the existence of a worst worst-case scenario. To accomplish this purpose of making them so aware, in addition to material gained from the cited books, Internet sources have been used to reinforce, or, when necessary, update that material.

Further, to ascertain the extent of the need for the people of each of these groups, a Christian Belief Assessment Survey was conducted. The survey has helped confirm the validity of the concerns raised. In so doing, required necessary response to those concerns has been developed within this writing.

All of these efforts, research, survey, and its results have been combined here to further show the need for preparation. This writer wholeheartedly agrees with what Jesus has said, "Behold, I have told you in advance."

His statement, coupled with the issues raised in this writing, makes the responsibility for preparation now ours.

PART I

PRE-TRIBULATIONALISM

INTRODUCTION

Now faith is the assurance of things hoped for... (Hebrews 11:1).

This verse in the book of Hebrews clearly defines belief in terms of hope. It is the *assurance* of something for which a person hopes. Webster defines the verb hope as, "to long for with the expectation of fulfillment; to expect with desire."[24] Hope, then, is a desired expectation awaiting fulfillment.

The Greek New Testament noun for hope is *elpis*, which reinforces this definition. *Elpis* is described by Vine's *An Expository Dictionary of New Testament Words* as, "favorable and confident expectation."[25] The point here is that one can see by both definitions, hope is something that is *not* 100% guaranteed; it is an *expectation*.

Faith, on the other hand, is guaranteed. Notice, "faith is the *assurance...*" The Bible states clearly that we *know* we are children of God because His Spirit testifies to our spirit (Romans 8:16; see also 1st John 4:13; 5:13). As a result, we are *assured* of our salvation: "that you may *know...*" John writes in his first epistle.

Because God has withheld a full accounting of his dealings with mankind regarding events preceding the return of His Son (see the discussion on Revelation 10:3-4, below), we cannot say with full assurance that we have been given *every* detail of the events that will happen. In fact, the on-going debate by men and women of strong, committed faith in Jesus

---

[24]   Henry Bosely Woolf, ed., *Webster's New Collegiate Dictionary* (Springfield, Massachusetts: G. & C. Merriam Company, 1975), 551.

[25]   M. E. Vine, *An Expository Dictionary of New Testament Words* (Nashville, Tennessee: Royal Publishing, Inc., 1939), 562.

Christ about the timing of the Rapture indicates how that event's exact moment has been veiled by God.

This is clearly seen in that there exists *no* verse that says with absolute certainty the precise timing of Christ's return for His church. This is not the case with salvation: "Believe in the Lord Jesus Christ and you shall be saved..." (Acts 16:31) is precise, quickly understandable, and clearly not open to debate. If the timing of the Rapture were as apparent as this, there would be no doubt as to the timing of this issue.

This leads to an unmistakable conclusion: Though we have *faith* – complete assurance, because Scripture says so – that the Rapture will occur, the best one can say of his or her view on the Rapture's timing is that they *hope* for it in the way they perceive it. Hope, because that viewpoint has not been confirmed, thus assured, by a precise, clear, *specific* verse or passage in Scripture.

This raises a concern regarding those individuals who assert that the Holy Spirit confirms to their spirit that there will be a Pre-tribulational Rapture. An unease is caused by the fact that, if God has not placed this direct confirmation in His Word, such an assertion then becomes extra-Biblical. Of such activities cults are born. The increase in seducing spirits "in the later times" (1st Timothy 4:1; see also 2nd Corinthians 11:14) needs to be taken very seriously here.

Again, there is nothing wrong with a *hope* in a Pre-tribulational Rapture. But an attempt to make it absolute *fact*—any attempt—does not fit with Scripture. The best one can say, then, if they are being truly honest, is that "this is what I see," and have the humility to understand no one can say he or she has a "lock" on it. Again, if the timing of the Rapture were that clear, there would be no debate at all.

This leads us to the heart of the issue of preparation for Endtime events: As previously expressed, there is a standard axiom in emergency preparation and management: "Hope for the best, *but*, prepare for the worst." The scriptural counterpart of the second half of the axiom is, again, found in Proverbs 22:3, "The prudent sees the evil and hides himself, but the naïve go on, and are punished for it" (see also Proverbs 27:12).

If, as we have seen here, scripturally the best one can do is hope for a Pre-tribulational Rapture, then wisdom dictates that Christians should prepare for the worst case: That we might have to endure the Great

Tribulation, or, at the least, some portion of it. Yet, such a perspective on preparation is rarely the case in today's Church, especially churches within the United States. This could prove disastrous if the hoped-for Rapture does not precede any significant tribulation events.

With this said, it, thus, seems extremely wise to address the issues of preparation, and especially look at the worst worst-case: *hard* persecution; the life-or-death type. Scripture plainly states that is what is to be faced by those undergoing Endtime tribulation.

So, the axiom is repeated: Hope for the best, but... *prepare for the worst.* From Proverbs 22:3, it seems scripturally wise to do so.

Unfortunately, the vast majority of those who believe in a Pre-tribulational Rapture have never considered that preparation.

CHAPTER 1

THE BLESSED HOPE

*...looking for the blessed hope and the appearing of the glory of our
great God and Savior, Christ Jesus (Titus 2:13).*

One of the four primary "cornerstone" passages within Pre-Tribulationalism
is that of the Blessed Hope. Titus 2:13 is a verse to which reference is made
for not only the timing of the Rapture—before the Great Tribulation—but
also as a proof-text for the doctrine of Imminence (discussed subsequently).
For these reasons it is a fitting place to begin.

The most succinct position description of the Blessed Hope is in
the writings of Paul N. Benware, a graduate of the Dallas Theological
Seminary (Th.M.) and Grace Theological Seminary (Th.D.), and, at the
time of his writing, a professor of Bible and Theology at Moody Bible
Institute in Chicago. Benware writes in *Understanding End Times Prophecy:
A Comprehensive Approach*:

> ... (I)n the context of righteous living Paul says that we should
> be "looking for the blessed hope and the appearing of the glory
> of our great God and Savior, Christ Jesus..." Christians are
> reminded to have a glad expectancy as they anticipate "the
> blessed hope," the glorious appearing of the Lord Himself.
> This is the proper anticipation, not the terrible days of the
> Tribulation, which certainly would not be viewed by anyone as

a blessed hope. Paul's accompanying exhortation to godly living makes sense only if the Lord's return is imminent.[26]

Noted Christian author Tim LaHaye, co-author of the renowned *Left Behind* Series, in his book *The Beginning of the End*, agrees:

> Titus 2:13 speaks of Christians as the Second Coming of Christ "looking for that blessed hope, and the glorious appearing of the great God and our Savior Jesus Christ." The blessed hope is a reference to the Rapture of the Church—the cause for great rejoicing by the Church.[27]

As you can see from Benware's statement, he also provides the generally-held Pre-Tribulational reason for considering the Blessed Hope as an occurrence that precedes the Rapture and ties it to the other foundational issue of Imminency. Let us analyze the *entire* epistle to Titus to see if this is a correct understanding.

✦ ✦ ✦ ✦ ✦ ✦

> Paul, a bond-servant of God, and an apostle of Jesus Christ, for the faith of those chosen of God and the knowledge of the truth which is according to godliness, in the hope of eternal life, which God, who cannot lie, promised long ages ago… to Titus, my true child in common faith… (Titus 1:2,4).

In doing a basic investigative *who, what, when, where,* and *why* (the 5-Ws) we see that the author of the letter (*what*) is the apostle Paul (*who*). The timing (*when*) of the letter is judged by Biblical scholars as being roughly AD 65, and it is written to Titus who then was in Crete (*who* and *where*). Paul states clearly the reason for the letter (*why*): "for the faith of those chosen of God" (i.e. *Christians,* of whom Titus was one). The *Ryrie Study Bible* confirms this by stating in its note to this verse: "Paul was commissioned

---

[26]   Paul N. Benware, *Understanding End Times Prophecy: A comprehensive Approach* (Chicago: Moody Press, 1995), 178.

[27]   Tim LaHaye, *The Beginning of the End* (Wheaton, Illinois: Tyndale House Publishers, 1972), 24.

to further the faith of God's elect so that they might acquire full knowledge of Christian truth."[28]

There are two points of particular importance to our analysis of the Blessed Hope contained in this epistle's opening. The first is that Paul provides his perspective of Christian hope at the outset of the letter: "...the hope of eternal life" (v. 2).

The question that needs to be asked here is: What elements make up Paul's perspective? Does he view Christian Hope as temporal, existing in time, or is it "long distance," viewed as something beyond this current age? Does his view apply to the whole Church, or is it relegated to just a select portion?

This is Paul's "first mention" of hope within the letter and, therefore, it sets the foundation from which he will exposit "hope." Any change of this initial view *would require compelling evidence*: One would expect Paul to provide his reasons for changing his focus. Additionally, as Paul wraps-up the letter with the exact same wording, "the hope of eternal life" (3:7), not only is a Second Witness provided, but one would expect *everything* in between to hold to that viewpoint—unless there was evidence to the contrary. The "internal integrity" of the letter would require it.

With this insight as background, let's look at Titus 2:13. First of all, is there any direct evidence that specifically says this is reference to the Rapture? As an example, in 2nd Thessalonians we have such a direct statement: "...with regard to the coming of our Lord Jesus Christ, and our gathering together to Him" (2:1). Here in 2nd Thessalonians is distinct wording that indicates this passage concerns the Rapture.

Having searched the entire epistle of Titus, there is, in fact, no similar wording. To overtly state that the Blessed Hope is about the Rapture from information provided in the Titus letter is *pure speculation*, because there is no direct evidence—no direct statement—in the passage to substantiate it. Benware's (and other Pre-Tribulational scholars) reasons to the contrary, apart from *Scriptural evidence*, there is no justification to assume this is speaking about the Rapture.

Having raised the challenge about identifying evidence that the Blessed

---

[28]   Charles C. Ryrie, *The Ryrie Study Bible: New American Standard Translation* (Chicago: Moody Press, 1978), 1831.

Hope is the Rapture, it is fair to inquire if there is evidence that it is *not*. Stated positively, is there evidence that the Blessed Hope is something else, something other than the Rapture?

First of all, there is the previously identified issue of Paul's initial viewpoint of Christian Hope given in verses 1:2 and 3:7. In both instances his view is *not* temporal, it is that of the "eternal." Because the Rapture occurs during this present age, i.e. "in time," this view of hope would exclude the Rapture. Additionally, the wording "for those chosen of God" would *include the* entire *Church*, thus also excluding the Rapture which pertains to only a portion of the Church (see 1st Thessalonians 4:15-17). As there is absolutely *no* evidence to show Paul changes his view of hope from the eternal to the temporal, as given in verses 1:2 and 3:7. Therefore, in relation to verse 2:13, this is *strong* evidence that he is not discussing the temporal Rapture. What then *is* he discussing? The evidence, as we will now see, exists in the verse itself.

Every Pre-Tribulational scholar looks at verse 2:13, which, again, states "Looking for the blessed hope and the appearing of the glory of our great God and Savior, Jesus Christ," and links the two separate elements, (1) the blessed hope, with (2) the appearing of Jesus, using the conjunction "and" as their rationale. Look again at Benware, "Christians are reminded to have a glad expectancy as they anticipate 'the blessed hope,' the glorious appearing of the Lord Himself."[29]

Hal Lindsey in his "bestselling book of the 1970s decade," *The Late Great Planet Earth* (1970), also states, "Someday... Jesus Christ is coming to take away all those who believe in Him.... It will be the ultimate trip.... [called] the 'Rapture'... Here is the real hope for the Christian, the 'blessed hope' for true believers."[30]

If you quickly scan the verse, such a conclusion seems perfectly correct. The two *are* linked together by the conjunction "and," giving credence that this is a correct understanding. But look at the verse again. In the original Greek, correctly presented word-for-word in the NASV, the object of the "appearing" in *not* Jesus, but *His glory*: "the appearing of the glory... of

---

[29] Benware, 178.

[30] Hal Lindsey, with C.C. Carlson, 137, 138.

Jesus." From an evidentiary viewpoint this is a *huge* difference, as we are about to see.

When is the glory of Jesus Christ revealed? This is *the* paramount question because Pre-Tribulational scholars time the Blessed Hope as occurring before the Great Tribulation. To answer that question, we need to look at the second point of importance contained in Paul's opening to Titus. Paul equates Christian hope to the word "eternal," a word that points to something beyond our current age. How is Christian hope defined within the New Testament? Does it uphold this perspective? Basically, what is the Doctrine of Christian Hope?

Let's lay some ground rules. In studying Scriptural doctrines, Biblical scholars have identified verses where the subject is actually stated, and then reviewed each passage to see if there is information there that can be used to develop a broad view of the topic—a *doctrine* of it. An example is Satan. To answer the 5-Ws simply identify each verse in Scripture where Satan is so named and see if that verse or passage provides answers to these basic questions.

There is, however, other "supporting verses"—verses where the name "Satan" may not be so stated, but where there is strong indication the information applies to him. Ezekiel 28, where the individual being cited was "in Eden, the garden of God," (v. 13), can hardly be the king of Tyre (v. 12). From Daniel 10:13-14 we know that there are demonic forces behind the earthly Gentile governments. Scholars, therefore, have (rightfully) identified this passage in Ezekiel as being the spiritual force behind the king of Tyre, Satan (see also Isaiah 14). Using these same principles of direct and applicable supporting verses, let's look at Christian Hope.

The majority of the books of the New Testament were penned by Paul, Peter, and John. If each provides information on Christian Hope, we will have, at the least, three witnesses to its doctrine. Let's look first at John as he is the writer of a Gospel, the Gospel which portrays Jesus Christ as the Son of God (regarding this, see especially the Introduction to the Gospel of John in the *Life Application Bible*[31]), *and* the author of the Book of Revelation, a book that identifies when Christ appears.

---

[31] Bruce M. Metzger, ed., *Life Application Bible: New Revised Standard Version* (Iowa Falls, Iowa: World Bible Publishers, Inc, 1990), 1814.

> Beloved, now we are children of God, and it has not appeared
> as yet what we shall be. We know that, when He appears, we
> shall be like Him, because we shall see Him just as He is. And
> everyone who has this hope fixed on Him purifies himself, just
> as He is pure (1ˢᵗ John 3:2-3).

Anyone see the word *appear* in relation to Jesus? The word *hope?* Do
you see the *exact* similarity with Titus 2:13? What does John say? "When
He appears, we shall be like Him...and everyone who has this hope..." To
whom does this hope apply; a portion of the Church or *everyone* of us? "...
now we are children of God." The strong indication is that of *every* Christian.
When does it occur? *At His appearing.* And, finally, what is the Christian
Hope? *That we shall be like Him.* This is all *direct evidence,* and clearly
stated. No speculation. No assumptions. So, in keeping with our previous
questioning, is this temporal or eternal? It is most definitely eternal.

Let's turn now to Peter:

> Blessed be the God and Father of our Lord Jesus Christ, who
> according to His great mercy caused us to be born again to a
> living hope through the resurrection of Jesus from the dead, to
> obtain an inheritance which... will not fade away... reserved for
> you in heaven (1ˢᵗ Peter 1:3-4).

Peter opens his first epistle, "Peter, an apostle of Jesus Christ... to
those who are chosen according to the foreknowledge of God the Father"
(1:1,2). Though he names specific provinces in verse 1, it can be argued the
inclusion of 1ˢᵗ Peter in Scripture makes it applicable to all "who are chosen."
To whom, then, does this hope apply; a portion of the Church or *everyone*
of us? *"Reserved for you"* (i.e. *every* Christian). Is this a temporal or eternal?
"...*will not fade away.*" The implication is clearly eternal. And, again, what
is the Christian Hope, this time called a *living* hope? That we "*obtain an
inheritance.*" Peter does not link Christian Hope with the Rapture, but with
the eternal reward for our faithfulness, the inheritance.

It is important to note that the original Greek word used here is
kleronomia, literally "heirship,"[32] "that which is passed on from father to

---

32 James Strong, *Strong's Exhaustive Concordance of the Bible* (Nashville, Tennessee: Abingdon Press, 1890), #2817.

son."[33] Why is that so important? Because of the Greek word for "heir" is *kleronomos*, "one who obtains an inheritance."[34] Note the same word root. Titus 3:7, which was quoted earlier, more fully states:

...we might be made heirs according to the hope of eternal life.

The issue of *heir* and, thus, *inheritance* is an unmistakable theme contained within the Titus epistle. Verse 2:13 speaks directly to that very issue—*and only that issue*—and thus an important clue to its understanding.

So, what *is* this inheritance linked to hope and eternal life? Let's return to the writer of Titus, Paul, who also states:

[There is a] mystery which has been hidden from the past ages and generations, but has now been manifested to His saints, to whom God willed to make known what is the riches of the glory of this mystery... which is Christ in you, *the hope of glory* (Colossians 1:26-27; emphasis added).

Again, to whom does this hope apply; a portion of the Church or *everyone* of us? "*...to His saints.*" This has to be *all* Christians. When does it occur? Paul doesn't say here (but, see below). And, what is that Christian Hope? "*Christ in you, the* hope *of glory.*" He confirms this in Romans:

For whom He foreknew, He also predestined to become conformed to the image of His Son (8:29a).

And how is that image, at least in part, manifested? Let Jesus tell us:

"As you Father are in me, and I am in you, may they also be in us... The glory that you have\ given me I have given to them... I in them" (John 17:21,22,23).

Peter echoes Jesus and Paul:

Grace and peace be multiplied to you in the knowledge of God and of Jesus our Lord; seeing that His divine power has

---

[33] Vine, 589.

[34] Ibid.

granted us everything pertaining to life and godliness, through the true knowledge of Him who called us by His own glory and excellence. For by these He granted to us His precious and magnificent promises in order that by them you might become partakers of the divine nature (2nd Peter 2-4a).

How does Peter describe "conformed to the image of His Son" and "Jesus in us"? He states clearly: We are *partakers of the divine nature.* Notice also that we have been "granted everything pertaining to life." This description is *eternal* life (see John 17:3)... which is again linked to "His own glory," further supporting Paul's view written in Titus.

Putting this all together, if we let Scripture interpret Scripture, *the blessed, and living, hope* is the *inheritance* which is part of *eternal life,* that is, the *knowing of God the Father and His Son Jesus* in such a deep, personal, intimate way. In this, then, we actually *partake of the divine nature* resulting in *visible glory* for us, *His glory...* and this *forever!*

Can these passages be so misunderstood as to believe they relate to something other than this? More importantly to our discussion, does "hope" presented in Scripture have *anything* to do with the Rapture... or its timing? It clearly does not.

As a closing thought, we need to answer the *when,* i.e. the timing, of Titus 2:13. Paul makes that perfectly clear:

> When Christ, who is your life, is revealed, then you also will be revealed with Him in glory (Colossians 3:4).

Our Second Witness is contained in the previously cited verse of 1st John:

> ...when He appears, we shall be like Him (3:2).

When is Christ revealed from heaven? Revelation 19:11-16 makes that perfectly apparent: *after* the judgments, when Jesus returns to set up His kingdom. We will see this further substantiated when we analyze 2nd Thessalonians, "The Thessalonian Rapture Concern," as we see the consistency of this view.

One final aside on Colossians 3:4: It is offered that Christ is our *eternal* life. This helps bring full-circle the thought of "hope of eternal life" given in

Titus 1:2 and 3:7, and further links the (blessed) hope with the appearing of Christ's glory spoken of in 2:13.

Do you see why the "appearing of the glory…of Jesus" is so important? This verse is *not* highlighting Jesus' appearance; it is focusing on *His glory* appearing. This tells us the blessed hope—which is that we will be glorified too—*is linked to His glory being seen*. And the conjunction "and" links each Christian to this glory. Just as the verses presented above confirm.

Relying on Scripture—and not conjecture—there is absolutely no other way to rightly divide this verse. The "blessed hope" simply doesn't apply to a Pre-tribulational Rapture. That view of the timing of the Rapture, then, is significantly weakened with its removal as a proof text.

Closing thought: If Jesus tarries another thousand years, *a delay assuring those of us living today are all dead by then,* will you want the Blessed Hope to be the Rapture… or our inheritance?

CHAPTER 2

THE THESSALONIAN
RAPTURE CONCERN

> Now we request you, brethren, with regard to the coming of our Lord
> Jesus Christ, and our gathering together to Him, that you may not
> be quickly shaken from your composure or be disturbed either by a
> spirit or a message or a letter as if from us… (2nd Thessalonians 2:1-2).

A second primary "cornerstone" passage within Pre-Tribulationalism is that
of the Thessalonian concern regarding the Rapture. Well-known author
John F. Walvoord, then a president of Dallas Theological Seminary with a
Th.D. from that institution in Systematic Theology, states the position in
his book *The Rapture Question*:

> The situation described in 2 Thessalonians 2 *indicates* that the
> teaching that the church would go through the Tribulation was
> already being advanced by certain teachers whom Paul opposed
> in this passage…. Here in 2 Thessalonians 2 it becomes evident
> that there were already those who taught that the church would
> go through the Tribulation, or as it is described here, the day
> of the Lord…. [However], the passage clearly *implied* that Paul
> had taught them that they would not enter the day of the Lord
> and that the Rapture would come before the final persecutions
> of the saints.[35]

---

[35] John F. Walvoord, *The Rapture Question* (Grand Rapids, Michigan: Zondervan
Corporation, 1979), 238, 239; emphasis added.

Please especially note Walvoord uses the words *indicates* and *implied* regarding his conclusions drawn from this passage. Without an actual direct statement that this relates to the Rapture, which is never presented, these conclusions cannot be taken, then, as *facts*; they are merely his *assumptions*. Assumptions, we shall soon see, that are not Scriptural.

> Paul and Silvanus and Timothy to the church of the Thessalonians... I Paul, write this greeting with my own hand... (2nd Thessalonians 1:1; 3:16).

Let's again do a basic investigative *who, what, when, where,* and *why.* The author of the letter is the apostle Paul (*what* and *who*), though the indication of verse 3:16 is that another, no doubt Timothy or Silvanus, actually penned it. The timing (*when*) of the letter is judged by Biblical scholars as being roughly AD 50, or about 15 years before the letter to Titus. It was written to the church at Thessalonica (*who* and *where*). The *why* will become clear as we analyze the letter.

> We ourselves speak proudly of you among the churches of God for your perseverance and faith in the midst of all your persecutions and afflictions. This is a plain indication of God's righteous judgment so that you may be considered worthy of the kingdom of God, for which indeed you are suffering. (1:4-5).

Obviously, the Thessalonians are suffering and one of the reasons (*why*) Paul writes this letter is to provide encouragement ("we speak proudly of you"). As part of that encouragement he then addresses why they suffer.

> For after all it is only just for God to repay with affliction those who afflict you, and to give relief to you who are afflicted and to us as well when the Lord Jesus shall be revealed from heaven with His mighty angels in flaming fire, dealing out retribution to those who do not know God and to those who do not obey the gospel of our Lord Jesus Christ... when He comes to be

glorified in His saints on that day and to be marveled at among all who have believed—for our testimony to you was believed. To this end also we pray for you always that our God may count you worthy of your calling... (1:6-11a).

Paul explains that by allowing themselves to be afflicted by the unsaved ("those who do not know God..."), the believers at Thessalonica are proving the afflicters' evil condition —actually being unsaved, and thus an enemy of God (James 4:4)—and thus providing "evidence" for Jesus when He sits in judgment of them. Note that all of this sets the stage for what will be said in chapter 2 that immediately follows.

But first, let's take a further look at what is said here in chapter 1. Note that "when the Lord Jesus shall be revealed from heaven... [is] when He comes to be glorified in His saints *on that day.*" This ties in *exactly* with what we just saw in the previous chapter regarding the letter to Titus. Both the event itself, expressed here, and its timing, fit in perfectly with the conclusion the Blessed Hope is in regards to our coming inheritance, the glorification of the saints—including these Thessalonica believers (who, by the way, are currently deceased and, no doubt, are now not interested in the Rapture, but in their inheritance).

This leads us to our first observation: Where in chapter 1 is there a mention of the Rapture or its timing? It is important to note, there is none.

From the issues of encouraging the Thessalonians (the *why*), Paul then immediately goes into chapter 2—which in the original letter was *not* separated by chapter numbers. Thus, we must keep in mind this remains a continuation, a building upon, chapter 1. If read without the chapter separations it is seen as a continuing thought.

> Now we request you, brethren, with regard to the coming of our Lord Jesus Christ, and our gathering together to Him, that you may not be quickly shaken from your composure or be disturbed either by a spirit or a message or a letter as if from us, to the effect that the day of the Lord has come (2:1-2).

Every Bible scholar, regardless of their view on the timing of this "gathering to Him," acknowledges this as being the Rapture. So, though there is no mention of the Rapture in chapter 1, we now answer the question as to the timing of the Rapture here at the beginning of chapter 2.

Ignoring, for the moment, the chapter separations and seeing this as one continuous thought, what conclusions can be drawn for the *timing* of this event? "The coming of our Lord Jesus Christ" (2:1) is "when the Lord Jesus shall be revealed from heaven" (1:7). There is simply no other way to interpret this.

When is Jesus revealed..."dealing out retribution" (1: 8)—i.e., *not* "secretly" in the clouds, but openly where "all shall see Him" (Matthew 24:30b)? We saw *when* in our analysis of Titus: near the end of the Book of Revelation in 19:11-16, when He returns in judgment (Matthew 16:27).

And what happens concurrent to this "coming"? "...*our gathering together to Him*." What, then, is the *only* conclusion that can be drawn without violating the internal integrity of this letter? Paul, in the very same sentence, links "the coming of the Lord Jesus" with "our gathering together to Him" with "the day of the Lord."

If you read verses 1 and 2 without any pre-conceived prejudice, *and just let the witness' testimony speak for itself*, it is *impossible*, without violating the integrity of the statement, to draw any other conclusion:

> Now we request you, brethren, (1) with regard to the coming of our Lord Jesus Christ, and (2) our gathering together to Him, that you may not be quickly shaken... that (3) the day of the Lord has come.

Before we go on, we need to go back and look at some of the elements raised by Walvoord.

> The situation described in 2 Thessalonians 2 *indicates* that the teaching that the church would go through the Tribulation was already being advanced by certain teachers whom Paul opposed in this passage...

Where *anywhere* in this letter is it stated, or, of less evidentiary value, implied or *indicated*, that Paul opposed the teaching that the church would go through the Tribulation? (For that matter, where is the word "tribulation" at all?)

Paul states *directly* that he opposed the teaching "that the day of the Lord had come." If there is no evidence to the contrary, the issue that this is regarding the Great Tribulation is *pure speculation*. Walvoord's statement is completely ungrounded in this letter, and by extension, thus not Scriptural.

> Here in 2 Thessalonians 2 it becomes *evident* that there were already those who taught that the church would go through the Tribulation, or as it is described here, the day of the Lord…

"It becomes evident" is not factual. One must ask: *Where* is the "evidence." Nowhere in this passage is it stated the Day of the Lord and the Great Tribulation are one-and-the-same. This is an assumption; as is also the belief that individuals were teaching the Thessalonians they would go through the Tribulation.

> …the passage clearly *implied* that Paul had taught them that they would not enter the day of the Lord and that the Rapture would come before the final persecutions of the saints…

Where does it specifically state that saints "would not enter the day of the Lord"? Where is there *any* mention of the "final persecutions of the saints"? Lack of evidence makes this *speculation*, not fact, especially not *Scriptural* fact.

All of this sets up two questions that need to be asked: *Why* are the Thessalonian believers "shaken and… disturbed"? Paul makes it perfectly clear: because they believed "the Day of the Lord had arrived." *Why* is that important to them? Walvoord speculates it is because they fear they missed the Rapture and would have to go through the Tribulation. But, the truth is, if you look at this passage from an evidentiary perspective, Paul *does not say* why they are shaken and disturbed: *There is not one word given as a reason for their concern.* To offer a reason, then, when no evidence exists is *speculation*. And one wonders if it is not *projection*: *my* concern is *their* concern; and *I* certainly wouldn't want to miss the Rapture…

Though there is not a stated reason for the Thessalonian believers concern, there might be indicators within the letter itself. Let's look.

Paul commends the Thessalonians for their faithfulness (1:4). He affirms their reward will be glory at Christ's coming (v. 10). That reward is a result of their having believed Paul's previous testimony to them (v. 10), a belief that produced faith (v. 4), which caused a willingness to persevere in their persecutions and afflictions (v. 4).

What is Paul's previous "testimony"? That they were called through "our" gospel, i.e. Paul's gospel about Jesus (2:14); that they were chosen for sanctification (2:13); that they may gain the glory of our Lord Jesus Christ (2:15)—the same concept provided in verse 1:10 of glory going to the saints for their beliefs. The wrap-up in verse 3:15 is, "So then, brethren, stand firm and hold to the traditions ("our testimony"; v. 1:10) which you were taught [i.e. "previously"], whether by word of mouth or by letter from us." (Notice the same wording "message or letter" in 2:2.)

The Thessalonians weren't concerned about the Rapture, they were concerned about their *reward*, their *inheritance*, the inheritance they expected for undergoing their current and past suffering of persecutions and afflictions. If the Day of the Lord had come and they, obviously, had not received the promised glory (1:10; 2:15); they then were not "considered worthy of the kingdom of God" (1:5). And their suffering would have been, to them, for nothing.

This is what the Thessalonians were concerned about. The scriptural evidence so indicates. To apply these verses to the timing of the Rapture does not have the same Biblical evidence. As a result, the Pre-tribulational view is further weakened.

This leaves us with the final issue raised by Paul with the Thessalonians, that of the man of lawlessness, and his relationship to the Day of the Lord.

CHAPTER 3

THE DAY OF THE LORD

…[Do] not be quickly shaken… to the effect that the day of the Lord has come. Let no one in any way deceive you, for it will not come unless the apostasy comes first, and the man of lawlessness is revealed, the son of destruction, who opposes and exalts himself above every so-called god or object of worship, so that he takes his seat in the temple of God, displaying himself as being God. Do you not remember that while I was still with you, I was telling you these things? (2nd Thessalonians 2:2-5).

A third, *significant* primary "cornerstone" within Pre-tribulationalism is that of defining what the Day of the Lord is, and the timing of its relation to other events of the Second Coming. The importance of this is unmistakable: If that identification is flawed and its timing off, the Pre-tribulational position is severely weakened because much of it is based on these two aspects.

John F. Walvoord again encapsulates the position in clear terms when he states the position in his book *The Rapture Question.*

> The day of the Lord as presented in the Old and New Testaments includes rather than follows the tremendous events of the tribulation period. There *seems* some evidence that the day of the Lord begins at once at the time of the translation [Rapture] of the church. The same event that translates [raptures] the church begins the day of the Lord. The events of the day of the Lord begin thereafter to unfold… [culminating in] the climatic event [which] is the second coming of Christ to establish His

kingdom, and the millennial age... In a word, the day of the Lord begins *before* the Great Tribulation.[36]

Of investigative note, observe the word *seems*, "there seems some evidence," which makes this *speculation*. If there *is* direct evidence, it needs to be shown. Worse, note that the statement, "There seems some evidence that the day of the Lord begins at once at the time of the translation of the church," is followed *immediately* by "The same event that translates the church begins the day of the Lord." This second statement is the *exact* same thing as the first, but now it is presented *as a statement of fact*. At best, without support of evidence to uphold the assertion, this is weak scholarship. At the worse, it has the possibility of being *very* misleading, *especially if someone takes it as fact*, which is the way the second sentence is presented.

Tim LaHaye, in the Forward to his book *Revelation: Illustrated and Made Plain*, provides the following diagram to illustrate this position:[37]

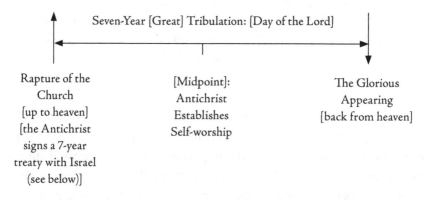

Seven-Year [Great] Tribulation: [Day of the Lord]

| Rapture of the Church [up to heaven] [the Antichrist signs a 7-year treaty with Israel (see below)] | [Midpoint]: Antichrist Establishes Self-worship | The Glorious Appearing [back from heaven] |

With this as background, let's analyze what Paul says regarding the Day of the Lord in 2nd Thessalonians.

> ...[Do] not be quickly shaken... to the effect that the day of the Lord has come. Let no one in any way deceive you, for it will not come unless the apostasy comes first, and the man of lawlessness is revealed... who opposes and exalts himself above

---

36 Walvoord, 175; emphasis added, but last emphasis in original.

37 Tim LaHaye, *Revelation: Illustrated and Made Plain*. (Grand Rapids, Michigan: Lamplighter Books, 1973, 1975), Forward.

every so-called god or object of worship, so that he takes his seat in the temple of God, displaying himself as being God (2nd Thessalonians 2:2-4).

Paul *clearly* states that the Day of the Lord can *not* occur until the man of lawlessness (the Antichrist) "*is revealed*" as he "takes his seat in the temple of God, displaying himself as being God," i.e., establishes his self-worship. It is, therefore, *impossible* for the Day of the Lord to start sooner than that event. *Impossible*—unless, of course, Paul is mistaken.

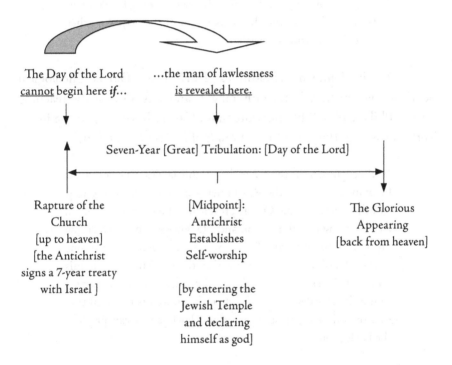

The Day of the Lord cannot begin here *if...*   ...the man of lawlessness is revealed here.

Seven-Year [Great] Tribulation: [Day of the Lord]

Rapture of the Church [up to heaven] [the Antichrist signs a 7-year treaty with Israel]

[Midpoint]: Antichrist Establishes Self-worship

[by entering the Jewish Temple and declaring himself as god]

The Glorious Appearing [back from heaven]

The Pre-tribulational perspective also believes that the Rapture of the Church is concurrent to the Antichrist signing a 7-year treaty with the nation of Israel. As Hal Lindsey states in his book *The Late Great Planet Earth,*

> According to Daniel's prophetic chronology, the minute the Israeli leader and the Roman leader [Antichrist] sign a pact, God starts His great timepiece which has seven allotted years left on it.

This event marks the beginning of the period of Biblical history previously noted as the [Great] Tribulation, [i.e. the Day of the Lord].[38]

As we've seen, LaHaye also equates this with the time of the Rapture. In fact, Pre-tribulational scholars believe 2nd Thessalonians 2:6-8 is a confirmation of this.

And you know what restrains him [the man of lawlessness, the Antichrist, (v. 3)] so that in his time he may be revealed. For the mystery of lawlessness is already at work; only he who now restrains will do so until he is taken out of the way. And then the lawless one will be revealed...

J. Dwight Pentecost, holding a Th.D. from Dallas Theological Seminary, where he subsequently taught, and was also on the teaching staff of Philadelphia Bible Institute (now, Cairn University), wrote in his world-renowned *Things to Come: A Study of Biblical Eschatology*,

Paul's argument in verse 7 is that... this lawless one could not be manifested until the Restrainer was taken out of the way. In other words, some One is preventing the purpose of Satan from coming to culmination and He will keep on performing until He is removed (vv.7-8).... The *indication* here is that as long as the Holy Spirit is resident within the church, which is His temple, this restraining work will continue and the man of sin cannot be revealed. It is only when the church is removed that this restraining ministry ceases and lawlessness can produce the lawless one.[39]

The Antichrist is revealed when he enters the Jewish Temple and declares himself as god, as we've seen 2nd Thessalonians 2:2-4 clearly (direct evidence) stated. Every Pre-tribulational scholar states this is in the *middle* of the 7-year period (again, refer back to LaHaye's chart). *If* the Holy Spirit,

---

[38]   Lindsey, with Carlson, 152.

[39]   J. Dwight Pentecost, *Things to Come: A Study in Biblical Eschatology* (Grand Rapids, Michigan: Zondervan Corporation, 1958), 205-206; emphasis added.

"resident in the Church," *is* the restrainer, the Rapture, then, cannot begin before this event either. So, as the diagram above shows, those who hold to a Pre-tribulational Rapture, and who have so strongly linked the Rapture to the Day of the Lord and its *subsequent* 7-year Tribulation, are without Scriptural basis for their timing. No other conclusion can be drawn.

One final observation regarding this. Where does it say anywhere in 2nd Thessalonians 2 the restrainer is the Holy Spirit? In truth, the restrainer is not identified. To state categorically the restrainer is the Holy Spirit is, again, *speculation*. In regards to the need for preparation, one must take notice of the continuing pattern here of presenting speculation as fact.

Before we go on to look at further Scriptural evidence concerning the Day of the Lord in relation to Pre-tribulational timing, there is one more issue that needs to be addressed: If the Thessalonians were not to experience the revelation of the Antichrist because they had been raptured 3½ years before, why would Paul tell them about the event? Why not simply say, "You know perfectly well that you will be gathered to the meet Jesus long before the arrival of the Day of the Lord."

However, if the Thessalonians, believing they would be alive when Jesus returned for them, were being given a significant event to look for *before* all that happened, it has to be because they would experience it. That Paul has to tell them this twice ("Do you not remember that while I was still with you, I was telling you these things?"), tells of its significance and that *it was something for which they should be looking*. It is a benchmark event, that of the timing of the revelation of the Antichrist, and especially its relation to the Day of the Lord.

Let's return to the timing of the Day of the Lord. J. Dwight Pentecost, previously cited, supports Walvoord and LaHaye's views that the Day of the Lord, which includes the Great Tribulation, begins with the Rapture.

> The term Day of the Lord occurs in [Pentecost cites 21 Old and New Testament] passages. These passages reveal that the idea of judgment is paramount in all of them. This is so clearly brought out in Zephaniah 1:14-18. This judgment includes not only specific judgments upon Israel and the nations at the end of the tribulation that are associated with the second advent, but, from a consideration of the passages themselves, includes judgments that extend over a period of time prior to the second

advent. Thus, *it is concluded that the Day of the Lord will include the time of the [great] tribulation...* beginning with God's dealing with Israel after the rapture at the beginning of the tribulation period and extending through the second advent...[40]

Let's look at the Zephaniah passage, quoted by Pentecost, as it is clearly representative of the other 21.

> Near is the great day of the LORD, near and coming very quickly. Listen, the day of the LORD! In it the warrior cries out bitterly. A day of wrath is that day. A day of trouble and distress. A day of destruction and desolation. A day of darkness and gloom. A day of clouds and thick darkness. A day of trumpet and battle cry against the fortified cities and the high corner towers. I will bring distress on men so that they will walk like the blind, because they have sinned against the LORD; and their blood will be poured out like dust. And their flesh like dung. Neither their silver nor their gold will be able to deliver them on the day of the LORD's wrath; and all the earth will be devoured in the fire of His jealousy, for He will make a complete end, indeed a terrifying one, of all the inhabitants of the earth (Zephaniah 1:14-18).

To be more precise, the events presented in Zephaniah are an exact description of the elements identified in the Book of Revelation as the *Wrath of God* (see Revelation 15:1ff, "in [the seven bowls]... the wrath of God is finished," etc.). No mention is made of Tribulation.

This leads to the question, which indicates one of the two greatest weaknesses in Pre-tribulationalism: Where *in Scripture* is the Great Tribulation stated to be the *exact* same thing as the Day of the Lord? These terms are used interchangeably throughout Pre-tribulational writings, as indicated by Pentecost's quote above. If there is no such verse, to conclude the Great Tribulation and the Day of the Lord are the same thing is *speculation*.

Notwithstanding, are there further indicators regarding the timing. Continuing to use the Old Testament as a source, let's see if there is some element of timing that supports the previous assertion that the Day of the Lord is subsequent to the Rapture which, allegedly, occurred seven years

---

[40] Pentecost, 230-231; emphasis added.

previously. This will provide a Second Witness. If it exists, this would further weaken the Pre-tribulational timeline, making it untenable.

> "Behold, I am going to send you Elijah the prophet *before* the coming of the great and terrible day of the Lord" (Malachi 4:5; emphasis added).

If Elijah comes *before* the great and terrible day of the Lord, and Elijah is anticipated as one of the two witnesses identified in Revelation 11:3-12,[41] the Day of the Lord can *not* occur before this event. *And*, if the Day of the Lord doesn't begin until *after* Elijah's ministry, there is a 3½ year period (see Revelation 11:3) that needs to be factored into *any* timeline.

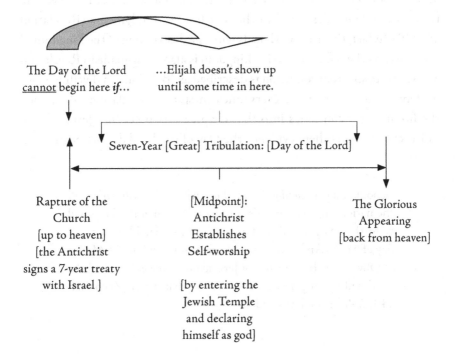

Which leads to the next investigative question: If the Day of the

---

41 As an example, see Jack Van Impe, *Revelation Revealed: Verse By Verse* (Mount Pleasant, Michigan: Enterprise Printers, Inc., 1982), pp. 121-122.

Lord cannot occur until after Revelation 11:3, how deep into the Book of Revelation do we have to go to actually reach the Day of the Lord?

> "And I will display wonders in the sky and on the earth, blood, fire, and columns of smoke; the sun will be turned into darkness, and the moon into blood, *before* the great and awesome day of the Lord comes " (Joel 2:30-31).

> For the day of the Lord *is near* in the valley of decision. The sun and moon grow dark, and the stars lose their brightness... (Joel 3:14b-15a)

Although blood, fire, columns of smoke, etc., are present in the trumpet judgments (Revelation 8:7ff), they do not include *darkness*. However, *all* these elements *are* described in the first five bowl judgments (Revelation 16:2-10). In fact, the fifth bowl deals with the destruction of the kingdom of the beast. As the reference to this kingdom is also being made in Revelation 18, where its spiritual condition is described as "Babylon... a dwelling place of demons and a prison of every unclean spirit" (Revelation 18:2), then the fire imagery continues into that chapter, just preceding Jesus' return in Revelation 19. Is there evidence the Day of the Lord doesn't begin until then?

> Behold, *a day is coming for the Lord* when... "I will gather all the nations against Jerusalem to battle..." Then the Lord will go forth and fight against those nations, as when He fights on a day of battle. And in that day His feet will stand on the Mount of Olives, which is in front of Jerusalem on the east... And the Lord will be king over all the earth in that day... (Zechariah 14:1, 2-4a,9; emphasis added).

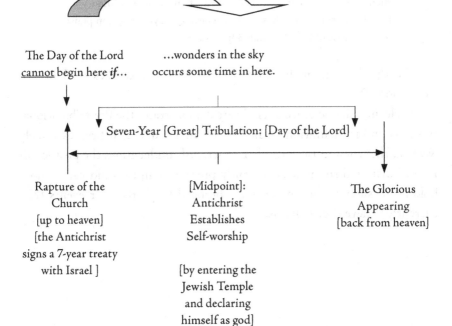

The Day of the Lord   ...wonders in the sky
cannot begin here *if*...   occurs some time in here.

Seven-Year [Great] Tribulation: [Day of the Lord]

Rapture of the   [Midpoint]:   The Glorious
Church   Antichrist   Appearing
[up to heaven]   Establishes   [back from heaven]
[the Antichrist   Self-worship
signs a 7-year treaty
with Israel]   [by entering the
                           Jewish Temple
                           and declaring
                           himself as god]

It seems very clear *by direct statement* that the Day of the Lord doesn't begin until the Lord actually goes to fight for Israel... which is Revelation 19. Is there a Second Witness?

> "I have commanded My consecrated ones, I have even called My mighty warriors, My proudly exulting ones, to execute My anger.... The LORD of host is mustering the army for battle; they are coming... from the farthest horizons... Wail for the day of the LORD *is near*! It will come as destruction from the Almighty.... Behold the day *is coming*, cruel with fury and burning anger, to make the land a desolation; and He will exterminate sinners from it. For the stars of heaven and their constellations will not flash their light; the sun will be dark when it rises, and the moon will not shed its light.... At the fury of the LORD of hosts in the day of His burning anger... it will be like that [of] a hunted gazelle... Anyone who is found will be thrust through, and anyone who is captured will fall by the sword." (Isaiah 13:3,4b,6,9-10,13b-14a,15; emphasis added).

> For the LORD's indignation is against all the nations, and His wrath against their armies; He has utterly destroyed them, He has given them over to slaughter... The sword of the LORD is filled with blood... For the LORD has a day of vengeance, a year of recompense for the cause of Zion. (Isaiah 34:2-3,6a,8).

Clearly, the Day of the Lord is when Jesus comes back to fight—in Revelation 19.

In closing, the evidence offered here demonstrates the Pre-tribulational timeline, and its definition of the Day of the Lord, are, at best, extremely weak, at the worst, unscriptural. This *seriously* undermines the position of Pre-tribulationalism as it is currently presented and should cause those holding to such a view to consider the need to prepare for events they currently believe they will miss.

CHAPTER 4

THE DOCTRINE OF IMMINENCE

Be alert for you do not know which day your Lord is coming (Matthew 24:42).

A. ANALYSIS

A fourth, *major*, primary "cornerstone," *the* cornerstone, within Pretribulationalism is that of Imminence, the "at any moment" return of Jesus Christ for His Church. Though lengthy, the most encapsulating description of this doctrine is found in the previously cited work of J. Dwight Pentecost, *Things to Come: A Study of Biblical Eschatology.*

> Many signs were given to the nation Israel, which would precede the second advent, so that the nation might be living in expectancy when the time of His coming should draw nigh. Although Israel could not know the day nor the hour when the Lord will come, yet they can know that their redemption draweth nigh through the fulfillment of these signs. To the church no such signs were ever given. The church was told to live in the light of the imminent coming of the Lord to translate them into His presence (John 14:2-3; Acts 1:11; 1 Cor. 15:51-52; Phil 3:20; Col. 3:4; 1 Thess. 1:10; 1 Tim 6:14; Jas. 5:8; 1 Pet. 3:3-4).

Such passages as 1 Thessalonians 5:6; Titus 2:13; Revelation 3:3 all warn the believer to be watching for the Lord Himself, not for signs that precede His coming. It is true that the events of the seventieth week will cast an adumbration [foreshadow] before the rapture, but the object of the believer's attention is always directed to Christ, never to these portents....

> The doctrine of imminence, or "at any moment coming"... forbids the participation of the church in any part of the seventieth week [of Daniel]. The multitude of signs given to Israel to stir them to expectancy would then also be for the church, and the church should not be looking for Christ until these signs had been fulfilled. The fact that no signs are given to the church, but she, rather, is commanded to watch for Christ, precludes her participation in the seventieth week.[42]

There are six distinct elements presented in this cited passage, and each must be addressed to fully confirm the doctrine of Imminence's veracity. The first element that "many signs were given to the nation Israel" will be better dealt with when we look at the fifth element, dealing with "the signs given to Israel [were to] stir them to expectancy."

Let's start then with the second assertion:

> To the church no such signs were ever given. The church was told to live in the light of the imminent coming of the Lord to translate them into His presence (John 14:2-3; Acts 1:11; 1 Cor. 15:51-52; Phil 3:20; Col. 3:4; 1 Thess. 1:10; 1 Tim 6:14; Jas. 5:8; 1 Pet. 3:3-4).

This immediately leads to a very basic investigative question: Where in Scripture, preferably in the New Testament, is the Church *directly* told they were not to look for signs? If there is no direct statement to this affect, then this conclusion must be based on *something*, or else it, again, is speculation.

Pentecost lists nine passages, (one might think an overkill), from Scripture in support of the statement and its follow-up, "The church was told to live in the light of the imminent coming of the Lord to translate [rapture] them into His presence." The answer to our question *should* be in those passages, which is implied by the standard scholarly principle of

---

them being listed thereafter. Because of its similarity, and in order to avoid having to re-examine the passages a second time, let's also look for element six in this review, "The fact that no signs are given to the church… she is commanded to watch for Christ…"

So, let's begin. The first passage cited is from the Gospel of John.

> Let not your heart be troubled; believe in God, believe also in Me. In My Father's house are many dwelling places; if it were not so, I would have told you, for I go to prepare a place for you (John 14:2-3).

This absolutely proves that the Lord will return for us, which is agreed upon by all Pre-, Mid-, Pre-Wrath, and Post-Tribulationalists. At some point in an unspecified, future time, Jesus will take us to His Father's house. This too is agreed upon by all views on the timing of the Rapture. This verse, however, can as easily be fulfilled at the Second Coming of Christ, i.e. *after* the Great Tribulation, as it can in a Pre-tribulational Rapture, because there is no mention of a timeframe. The Church's ultimate destiny is the New Jerusalem, a heavenly abode (see Revelation 21, which takes place well after the judgments of that book), which is a fulfillment of this passage.

This leads to a series of questions: Where is the issue of Imminence discussed or implied, much less *proven* as Pentecost asserts? It is not. Where is the church being "*commanded* to watch for Christ"? It is certainly not in this passage. Where is the church being told to *not* watch for signs, i.e., that "to the church no signs were ever given"? Again, it is not here either.

This holds true for all the remaining cited passages. Here they are listed. Again, apply these three questions to each as we go through them. The first passage confirms that Jesus will return, but in no way addresses, much less confirms, any of Pentecost's three assertions.

> Men of Galilee, why do you stand looking into the sky? This Jesus who has been taken up from you into heaven, will come in just the same way as you have watched Him go into heaven (Acts 1:11).

The next confirms there will be a Rapture and a resurrection, but nothing more:

> Behold, I tell you a mystery; we shall not all sleep, but we shall all be changed, in a moment, in the twinkling of an eye, at the last trumpet; for the trumpet will sound, and the dead will be raised imperishable, and we shall be changed (1st Corinthians 15:51-52).

This next verse proves that we are citizens of heaven and that we eagerly wait for our Savior—*whenever* that occurs (again, no timeframe is given). This is agreed upon by Pre-, Mid-, Pre-Wrath, and Post-tribulational scholars as well:

> For our citizenship is in heaven, from which also we eagerly wait for a Savior, the Lord Jesus Christ (Philippians 3:20).

Next, we see that Christ is our life and when He is revealed (at the *end* of the Revelation judgment events [Rev. 19]), we also will be revealed with Him in glory:

> When Christ, who is your life, is revealed, then you also will be revealed with Him in glory (Colossians 3:4).

The next proves that we are to wait for God's Son from heaven (without telling us *what* we should be doing while we wait), which the Church *has* done for almost 2,000 years.

> ... and to wait for His Son from heaven, whom He raised from the dead, that is Jesus, who delivers us from the wrath to come (1st Thessalonians 1:10).

This following calls us to live holy lives until the appearing of Jesus (which, again, is at the *end* of the Revelation judgment events [Rev. 19]):

> ... that you keep the commandment without stain or reproach until the appearing of our Lord Jesus Christ (1 Timothy 6:14).

This next verse requires some comment. On the surface James would seem to indicate imminency because the issue of "the coming of the Lord *is at hand*" which appears to indicate "any second now." The fact is, the book of

James is dated as being written around AD 45-50. Thus, the "soon" hasn't happened in almost 2,000 years. This would seem to place the verse as similar to "the things which must *shortly* take place" in Revelation 1:1, which also have yet to happen. As one commentary noted, "This word does not indicate that the events described will necessarily occur soon, but that when they do begin to happen they will come to pass swiftly (the same Greek word is translated 'speedily' in Luke 18:8)."[43]

> You too be patient; strengthen your hearts, for the coming of the Lord is at hand (James 5:8).

The last verse raised by Pentecost deals with the inheritance, not imminency:

> Blessed be the God and Father of our Lord Jesus Christ, who according to His great mercy caused us to be born again to a living hope through the resurrection of Jesus Christ from the dead, to obtain an inheritance which is imperishable and undefiled and will not fade away, reserved in heaven for you (1 Peter 3:3-4).

The only conclusion that can be reached here is that although on the surface there appears to be an overwhelming amount of scriptural support for imminency, once the cited verses are investigated, it is shown they do not support the allegation of an imminent return of Christ. They, in fact, address other issues.

It is important to state here His return could be at any moment, but other Biblical passages would have to be provided for proof of that. Again, the verses cited do not.

B. The "Be Alert" Verses

The second element of Pentecost's quote provides an additional three passages, but this time the observation is that they "all warn the believer to be watching for the Lord Himself, not for signs." Let's see if they, in fact, do that.

---

[43] Ryrie, *Study Bible*, 1895.

... so let us not sleep as others do, but let us be alert and sober (1st Thessalonians 5:6).

We need to define *alert* and *sober*, and we need to put this verse in its context. Here is how the full concept reads:

> You yourselves know full well that the day of the Lord will come just like a thief in the night. While [the unsaved] are saying "Peace and safety!" then destruction will come upon them suddenly... But you, brethren, are not in darkness, that the day [of the Lord] should overtake you like a thief; for you are all sons of light and sons of day. We are not of night, nor of darkness; so then let us not sleep as others do, but let us be alert and sober.... [And] since we are of the day, let us be sober, having put on the breastplate of faith and love, and as a helmet, the hope of salvation.... Therefore, encourage one another, and build up one another, just as you also are doing. (1st Thessalonians 5:2-3a,4-6,8,11).

The passage itself defines *sober* as "putting on the breastplate of faith and love, and as a helmet, the hope of salvation" (v. 8). Does this have anything to do with "watching for the Lord"? It is describing military equipment. This makes it more akin to Ephesians 6:10-18, which defines Christian spiritual warfare also in terms of military equipment, and admonishes, "Put on the full armor of God that you may be able to stand firm against the schemes of the devil" (v. 11).

Obviously, at least half of the verse in 1st Thessalonians cited by Pentecost deals with calling for a Christian to be involved in spiritual warfare. In this way we shall not be defeated by the devil, which would place us in darkness, allowing the Day of the Lord to "overtake us like a thief" (v. 4). If that is the case, being *alert*, which is combined with *sober* by the conjunction "and," deals with being alert to this warfare. Both verbs indicate what we should be involved in a Christian's responsibility of engaging in spiritual warfare to occupy us until the Day of the Lord arrives.

Let's look at other verses in Scripture that also deal with being alert. First let's define the word from its original Greek, *gregoreuo*, keep awake; BE VIGILANT; which is based from *ageiro*... to GATHER, connoting the idea of COLLECTING ONE'S FACULTIES. *Vine's Expository Dictionary of New Testament Words* states, "[it is] used… of spiritual alertness," and cites Acts 20:31, 1ˢᵗ Corinthians 16:13, Colossians 4:2, and the verse cited by Pentecost under discussion here.[44] Let's look at these passages using the verb *gregoreuo.*

> Be on guard for yourselves and for all [your] flock… [for] I know that after my departure savage wolves will come in among you, not sparing the flock… Therefore, be on the *alert*…(Acts 28,29,31; emphasis added).

> Be on the *alert*, stand firm in the faith, act like men, be strong (1ˢᵗ Corinthians 16:13; emphasis added).

> Devote yourselves to prayer [a spiritual weapon in the Ephesians passage previously cited], keeping alert in it with an attitude of thanksgiving… (Colossians 4:2; emphasis added).

Do these verses relate to Jesus' returning, or, more accurately, *what we should be doing until He does?* They not only indicate, but actually state, the latter.

Further, and even more dramatic in that these next verses are often used by Pre-tribulational scholars to confirm we should be looking for Christ's return and not for signs, are those quoting Jesus in the Gospels.

> Be *alert* for you do not know which day your Lord is coming (Matthew 24:42, see also vv. 43-51; cf. Mark 13:35, 37; emphasis added).

> Be on the *alert* then, for you do not know the day nor the hour (Matthew 25:13, see also vv. 1-12; emphasis added).

These passages relate to individuals who were responsible for certain required actions: the householder should have been on the alert for the coming thief to prevent the thief's entry (Matthew 24:43), the faithful and sensible slave should be doing his duties instead of getting drunk, etc. (Matthew 24:45-50), the virgins should have paid the price necessary for

---

[44] Vine, 1213.

the extra, needed oil as preparation for meeting the arriving bridegroom (Matthew 25:1-13).

What then are these individuals to be vigilant towards? The coming thief? The returning Lord? The coming bridegroom? *Or how they should not fail to be doing their duty at the time of the relevant event?* To ascribe these passages to the need to be looking for the coming person rather than performing the established duties is to take them completely out of context.

On the surface it might appear that the coming individual is the object of the vigilance: The head of house would be looking for the thief (Matthew 24:43); the master of that slave will come on a day when he does not expect him and at an hour which he does not know (Matt. 24:50); the bridegroom arrived and those who were ready went in with him to the wedding feast, and the door was shut. And later the other (unprepared) virgins also came saying, "Lord, lord, open for us" (Matthew 25:10-11).

However, what was it that made the *successful* individuals in each of these verses *successful* in each instance? That they were watching for the thief or their master's return or the bridegrooms arrival, *or that they were* vigilant *in performing their required duties?*

If the head of house had locked the door he need have no worry of the thief, *whenever* he attempted entry. If the slave was handling his household chores instead of getting drunk he would not have to worry at what hour his master returned; everything would be in readiness for him when he *did* return. Had the lazy virgins been prudent and done what was required of them, buying additional oil, it would not matter when the bridegroom arrived for they would be ready for him.

What then is the thrust of each of these passages? *That they were* vigilant (*gregoreuo*) *in carrying out there* required *duties.* This confirms the previous passages cited by *Vine's.* Therefore, the "be alert" (*gregoreuo*) of 1st Thessalonians 5:6 has *nothing* to do with "watching for the Lord's return." It has *everything* to do with how we conduct ourselves awaiting His arrival.

Penetcost then offers Titus 2:13,

> ... looking for the blessed hope and the appearing of the glory
> of our great God and Savior, Christ Jesus.

The reader is referred back to Chapter 1—"The Blessed Hope," where this verse was previously discussed.

The last verse offered by Pentecost for the doctrine of Imminence is that of Revelation 3:3, which states,

> Remember therefore what you have received and heard; and keep it, and repent. If therefore you will not *wake up* [*gregoreuo*], I will come like a thief, and you will not know at what hour I will come upon you (Revelation 3:3; emphasis added).

Again, let's look at the entire passage to get a context of the issue being presented:

> And to the angel of the church in Sardis write: ... I know your deeds, that you have a name that you are alive, but you are dead. *Wake up* [*gregoreuo*], and strengthen the things that remain, which are about to die; for I have not found your deeds completed in the sight of My God. Remember therefore what you have received and heard; and keep it, and repent. If therefore you will not *wake up* [*gregoreuo*], I will come like a thief, and you will not know at what hour I will come upon you (Revelation 3:1-3; emphasis added).

The issue here is that of the Sardisian church members' *deeds*: "*I know your deeds*: You have the name that you are alive, but you are dead." The first key here is "but you are dead." Is John speaking of physical life-and-death in this comparison? He can't be; dead church members would be incapable of reading the letter. John must be referring to *spiritual* life-and-death. What then is the *name* of being alive? The very same John said in his Gospel, "In Him— [Jesus]—was life" (1:4). The name of being alive then is... *Christian*.

"But you are dead," continues John. Can we adequately define this spiritual death? Paul admonished the Ephesian church, "And you were *dead* in your trespasses and sins" (2:1). That this is a reference to a spiritual condition is confirmed in verse 5: "When we were *dead* in our transgressions, [God] made us *alive* together with Christ..."

The issue of spiritual life (and death) as being Christ Himself also confirms our first assertion that the name of being alive is *Christian*. Paul goes on to say to the Ephesians what caused—*why*—they were considered spiritually dead: "You walked according to the course of this world, according to the prince of the power of the air—[Satan]—the spirit that is now working in the sons of disobedience."

What is wrong with the Sardis church? *It is living as if unsaved:* "For I have not found your *deeds* completed in the sight of My God" (3:2). The original Greek root for "completed," *plerophoreo,* literally means "to carry out fully." This further confirms that the Sardis church was not living according to Christian teachings: "I have not found your deeds being carried out fully," i.e. *as they should be.* Wasn't this the problem with the "evil slave," of Matthew 24:45-51?

"Remember therefore what you have [previously] received and heard and keep it" (3:3), continues John; yet a further confirmation we are on the right track. In fact, the original Greek for "keep," tereo, means *to watch,* and more literally, *keep an eye on.* How many times has a parent disciplined a wayward child with, "You better watch it!" That is exactly what is implied here. The final command, "Repent" (v. 3) means *to turn from; i.e. change your mind about.* The Sardis church was to turn from its evil-living ways. They should diligently *get back to* that which they had been called, i.e. godly-living, that they might live the name of life, *Christian.*

And what is the outcome if the Sardisians don't do what they should? "If therefore you will not *wake up [gregoreuo],* I will come like a thief…" (v. 3). If we were to continue the previous quote from John's Gospel about Jesus we would be told, "In Him was life, and the life was the light of men. And the light shines in the darkness, and the darkness did not comprehend it" (1:4-5). This imagery is exactly what we saw in 1st Thessalonians 5:4, also part of the context of verse 6 quoted by Pentecost: "But you brethren, are not in darkness, that the day [of the Lord] would overtake you like a thief…"

Our conclusion: If you live in darkness, you reap its reward of being unaware of Jesus coming, *and, thus, unprepared for it.* Revelation 3:3 is a Second Witness to 1st Thessalonians 5, both of which have *nothing* to do with watching for Christ's return. They are both a call to *watch* what we *do,* our deeds, until Christ does return. In essence, then, we have now come full-circle in our proof of this.

C. Not Looking For Signs

The *awareness* of Christ's Second Coming, whether a person is alert to His coming or is caught unawares, i.e. He comes as a thief, brings us back to Pentecost's other assertions. The first, fourth, and sixth elements all state in one form or another, "No signs were given to the church." Let's see if that is Scriptural:

> And as He was sitting on the Mount of Olives, the disciples came to Him privately, saying, "Tell us... what will be the *sign of Your coming*, and the end of the age?" And Jesus answered and said to them... (Matthew 24:4-3a; emphasis added).

> And He was sitting on the Mount of Olives... Peter and James and John and Andrew were questioning Him privately, "Tell us, when will these things be, and *what will be the sign* when all these things are going to be fulfilled?" And Jesus began to say to them... (Mark 13:2-5a; emphasis added).

> And they questioned Him, saying, "Teacher, when therefore will these things be? And *what will be the sign* when these things are about to take place?" And He said... (Luke 21:7-8a; emphasis added).

Let's be investigators here and ask the obvious question: Does Jesus rebuke the disciples for asking for signs? Does Jesus say, "Don't worry; *as the soon-to-be church* and no longer Jews (Galatians 3:28), you don't need signs"? No, He doesn't. He, in fact, gives them signs!

If this passage were only in Matthew, a Gospel written primarily to the Jews, one would have to take notice of that, and see an *implication* of Jesus' response being for a Jewish audience. But the passage is repeated in Mark, *universally* portraying Christ as the Suffering Servant, and in Luke, the "Son of Man" Gospel, a *universal* perspective.

Further, Luke *is a Gentile*, thus writing *in particular* to a *Gentile audience* (as Luke draws from his Greek [Gentile] cultural background). Further, Luke was not one of the twelve original disciples of Jesus and, thus, was not "a disciple who came to Him privately" to learn this. Hence, Luke *does not have this firsthand.* It is, therefore, *being passed down to him,* a *Church* member, and from him to us for whom the New Testament has been written:

> These things have been written that you may believe... and that believing you may have life in [Jesus'] name (John 20:31).

The New Testament, including Luke's Gospel, is written principally for *believers,* and, because it has been passed down, for those who will come to believe. Look at how many of the epistles are opened:

> ...to all who are beloved of God in Rome, called as saints... (Romans 1:7).

> ...to the church of God which is at Corinth, to those who have been sanctified in Christ Jesus, saints by calling (1ˢᵗ Corinthians 1:2)

> ...to the churches of Galatia... (Galatians 1:2).

Etcetera. This is all being written, and passed down, *for the Church.* Further, Luke, the *Gentile* writer, goes on to add

> And [Jesus] told them a parable, "Behold the fig tree [Israel], and all the trees [the Gentile nations]; as soon as they put forth leaves, you see it and know for yourselves that summer is now near. Even so you, too, when you see these things happening recognize that the kingdom of God is near. Truly I say to you, this generation will not pass away until all things take place (Luke 21:29-32).

Doesn't this say we are to keep watch on how the nations begin to align? That this alignment is a *sign* the Kingdom of God—Christ's return—is within a "generation"? Every Pre-Tribulational scholar lauds the birth of the nation of Israel as a most profound sign. As an example, Tim LaHaye in his book, *The Beginning of the End,* has an entire chapter on this subject entitled "The Infallible Sign."[45]

By LaHaye's own admission, then, if one were looking for the return of the Jews to Israel, an indicator (sign) of the end drawing near, he would have been

---

[45] LaHaye, *Beginning of the End,* 43-60.

"rewarded" when they did, in fact, return – and this *before* the Rapture. Along these same lines, if one were looking for the return of Jerusalem to the Jews, an indicator (sign) of the end drawing near, he would have been "rewarded" in 1967 when they did re-take Jerusalem—again *before* the Rapture.

Now, if one is currently looking for the "sign" of a re-built Jewish Temple in Jerusalem– *before* the Rapture…

Let's also notice that if one were looking for the signs given by Jesus: an increase in false Christs, in wars and rumors of wars, in famines, and in earthquakes in diverse places, he or she would be *rewarded* in actually seeing them today—especially as they continue to increase in frequency and intensity, as Jesus said, like the of pains surrounding childbirth.

In light of all this, how can we be told we are *not* to look for the signs that are happening right before our eyes *and* are so obviously Scriptural? Weren't the Pharisees condemned by Jesus because they knowingly turned a blind eye to the signs of the times of His First Coming (Matthew 16:3)? How, then, are the signs of His Second Coming *not* for the Church?

The last point on this issue is seen in the concept of the Church living "in light," as 1st Thessalonians 5 clearly states, *and*, as a result, the Day of the Lord will not come upon us as a thief, i.e. unawares. Apart from looking at the obvious signs around us, how—by what method(s) —is the Church able to discern it *is* living in the Last Days, the days preceding the Lord's return, if it is not looking for signs?

To lay a foundation that we should not be looking for signs has the huge potential to have individual Christians blindsided as they have been directed to not look for them! The potential for disaster is immense.

A final observation: A justifiable, deep respect is warranted for J. Dwight Pentecost. He is indeed a learned man of God, deeply committed to Jesus Christ. Notwithstanding, in regards to his work on a Pre-tribulational Rapture, there are indications he has missed the mark. At a quick glance, the *amount* of verses presented by him makes it appear there is *overwhelming* evidence in support of Imminence. As it turns out, however, after actually looking at the verses presented as conclusive evidence, it is discovered that they have *nothing* to actually do with that subject.

This can leave an individual Christian unprepared as he or she believes they will not undergo any aspects of the Great Tribulation. Such a perspective may not be as solid as it first appears.

CHAPTER 5

KEPT FROM THE HOUR

Because you have kept the word of My perseverance, I also will keep
you from the hour of testing, that hour which is about to come upon
the whole earth, to test those who dwell upon the earth. (Revelation
3:10).

Though not a "cornerstone" of Pre-tribulationalism, this verse in Revelation
is an internal "girder" used to build upon the four cornerstones previously
reviewed. It is one of the verses used by Pre-tribulational scholars to show
absolute proof of their perspective, and is so widespread that it cuts across
most denominational lines.

Let's begin with Tim LaHaye's quote from *Revelation: Illustrated and
Made Plain*:

> The world has never known a universal Era of tribulation. This
> passage is an obvious reference to the Tribulation Era of seven
> years... This promise to the church at Philadelphia [is that]
> she will be raptured before that Tribulation begins. It seems
> difficult to understand why some false teachers suggest that the
> Church must go through the Tribulation in view of this clear-
> cut statement of our Lord.[46]

The argument in support of this viewpoint is contained in J. Dwight
Pentecost's *Things to Come*:

---

[46] Tim LaHaye, *Revelation*, 57.

[In] Revelation 3:10... John is promising a removal from the sphere of testing, not a preservation through it. This is further substantiated by the use of the words "the hour." God is not guarding from the trials but from the very hour itself when these trials will come on those earth dwellers.[47]

This is shared by John Walvoord as well:

Because of their faithfulness the Christians in Philadelphia are promised that they will be kept from the hour of trial which will come upon the earth as a divine judgment.... In view of the context of the book of Revelation, however, as it subsequently unfolds the horrors of this very tribulation period, it is evident that the promise here to the church at Philadelphia is one of deliverance from this time of trouble.[48]

And last, Donald Grey Barnhouse:

Will the Church pass through the great tribulation? Let the risen Lord answer this question most definitely. "Because thou has kept the Word of my patience I also will keep thee from the hour of tribulation the one which is about to come on all the inhabited works. To test those dwelling on the earth." Escape was definitely promised by the Lord Jesus Himself (Luke 21:36). If the Church is to come through the tribulation, there is no blessed hope in the Bible.[49]

Notice, Barnhouse links the removal he sees in Revelation 3:10 with the Blessed Hope. If, as we've seen, the Blessed Hope deals with the inheritance, not the Rapture, this line of thinking begins to immediately unravel.

Let's look at these conclusions in depth. We are going to start with a unique issue, but one that is most often overlooked by scholars, both for or against the Pre-tribulational view. It deals with the Philadelphia Church itself and its timing in relation to the Church Age.

---

[47] Pentecost, 216.

[48] John F. Walvoord, *The Revelation of Jesus Christ* (Chicago: Moody Press, 1966), 86, 87.

[49] Donald Grey Barnhouse, *Revelation: God's Last Word* (Grand Rapids, Michigan: Zondervan Publishing House, 1971), 76-77.

Every Pre-Tribulational scholar, including those cited above, agrees that the seven churches in Revelation 2 and 3 also perfectly describe the entire Church Age with each of the seven churches fitting into specific Eras beginning in roughly AD 33. Hal Lindsey in his book *There's a New World Coming: An In-depth Analysis of the Book of Revelation*, devotes two entire chapters to this, entitled "Panorama of Church History."[50]

Although the dating for each Era varies slightly from author to author, the dates are within a few years of each other, and so anyone of them will do. Using Lindsey's, we are told the Philadelphia Church Era was from AD 1750-1925. Laodecia, the last Church Era is from AD 1900 to the Tribulation.

Here's the problem. *Philadelphia is not the last Church Era.* If the Laodecian Church, the last Era, were promised to be "kept from the hour," one could see its possibility as referring to the Rapture. But it is not. The obvious question becomes: How does the promise to the Philadelphia Church, *not* the last Church Era, apply to Laodecia, which *is* the last Church Era?

Some author's, like Lindsey in *There's A New World Coming*, try to bypass this obvious problem by stating that Philadelphia is the true Church, while Laodecia is an apostate Church. They both run concurrent up until the Great Tribulation, where Philadelphia is Raptured and Laodecia is not, thus Laodecians endure the Tribulation's horror.[51]

The problem with this is it violates the concept of Church *Era.* If all the other churches of Revelation 2 and 3 have a distinct beginning and end, where is there any justification to alter that pattern for Philadelphia? Further, Laodecia is promised a reward like the other six churches ("...he who overcomes I will grant..." [3:21]), which tells us it *is* part of the Church.

The simplest explanation, if we just let the witness, John, speak for himself, is that the Philadelphia Church, which came to an end in roughly AD 1925 as a Church Era, *has* been kept from the hour of testing... in that, except in very rare instances, they are now all dead. This is not an attempt to be comical here. The truth is that the Philadelphia Era church member has now definitely been kept from the Great Tribulation.

---

[50]   Hal Lindsey, *There's a New World Coming: An In-depth Analysis of the Book of Revelation* (Eugene, Oregon: Harvest House Publishers, 1973, 1984), 26-45.

[51]   Ibid., 48, 52.

So, if one embraces the concept that each of the churches in Revelation 2 and 3 represents a succession of ever-progressing Church Age Eras, which most Pre-tribulational scholars do, the conclusion that the promise to the Philadelphian Church applies to those in the last days before Christ's return is erroneous. Philadelphia is not the Last Days Era.

Which leads to a related observation: Laodecia, the actual Last Days Church, is told to "buy from Me [Jesus] gold refined by fire" (3:18). Scripture makes it clear that the issue of "cost" relates to suffering, i.e. trial(s).

> In this—a living hope... to obtain an inheritance—you greatly rejoice, even though now for a little while, if necessary, you have been *distressed by various trials*, that the proof of your faith, *being more precious than gold* which is perishable, even though *tested by fire*, may be found to result in praise and glory and honor at the revelation of Jesus Christ (1st Peter 1:3b, 4a,6-7).

> And I—the LORD—will bring [the Jews] through the fire, refine them as silver is refined, and test them as gold is tested. They will call on My name, and I will answer them I will say, 'They are My people,' and they will say, 'The LORD is my God" (Zechariah 13:8a,9).

Clearly, testing is related to trials and suffering, and Jesus offers such a concept in his words "buy from Me" to the Last Era Church, where the word "buy" is an issue of *cost*.

To have a possible understanding of the extent of Church members' suffering, let's look here in Revelation's seven churches, which also maintains internal integrity of our witness, John. Take special notice that the Smyrnan Church was told that some would "suffer" and "be tested" and have "tribulation" even "until death" (Revelation 2:10). And the Thyatiran Church, if they remained backslidden ("commit [spiritual] adultery"), would experience "great tribulation" (Revelation 2:22). Suffering, i.e. caused by tribulation, then, even unto martyrdom and great tribulation, has been part of the Church experience.[52] To deny this is to deny Scripture.

Notice also that the backslidden Christian is confronted by *great tribulation*. This fits in perfectly with what we've already seen in 1st

---

[52] The reader is encouraged to read *Fox's Book of Martyrs*.

Thessalonians 5:3-8, where those living in spiritual darkness will be caught unawares; also confirmed in Revelation 3:1-3, the Sardis Church, where these church members similarly living in spiritual darkness will also be caught unawares. Both groups will be totally unprepared for the coming judgment. This can only mean the tribulation for them will prove much *greater* to bear. Let the reader take notice of this need for preparation!

It is at this point that we need to define what "the hour" referred to in this verse actually means. Every Pre-tribulational scholar believes "this passage is an obvious reference to the Tribulation Era of seven years..."[53] But, is it? There is no direct statement that it is and so this again is speculation. Let's allow Scripture to interpret itself:

> And I saw another angel flying in midheaven, having an eternal gospel to preach to those who live on the earth... and her said with a loud voice, "Fear God, and give Him glory, because *the hour* of His judgment had come..." And another angel, a second one, followed saying, "Fallen, fallen is Babylon the great, she who made all the nations drink of the wine of the passion of her immorality" (Revelation 14:6-7,8).

Here within the same Book of Revelation that contains verse 3:10, we have a definition of "the hour." *And it is linked with Babylon's destruction.* Why is that so important? Because the world has placed its faith in Babylon: "She who made all the nations drink of... her immorality" (14:8). With the destruction of Babylon, that false faith is shown to be impotent and valueless. This will be a *tremendous*, (shall one say "great"?), trial (testing) and tribulation for them:

> And the kings of the earth, who committed acts of immorality and lived sensuously with her [Babylon], will weep and lament over her when they see the smoke of her burning, standing at a distance because of fear of her torment saying, "Woe, woe, the great city Babylon, the strong city! For *in one hour* your judgment has come." And the merchants of the earth weep and mourn over her, because no one buys their cargoes any more......
> The merchants... who became rich from her, will stand at a distance because of the fear of her torment, weeping and

---

53 LaHaye, *Revelation*, 57.

mourning, saying, "Woe, woe, the great city... for *in one hour* such wealth has been laid waste!" (Revelation 18:9-11,15-17a).

If, by some chance, the promise to the Philadelphia Church in 3:10, that it will miss the hour of testing coming on the whole world, applies to the whole Last Days Church, than the "hour" they are "kept from," is the hour of Babylon's judgment. This judgment is God's Wrath (Revelation 15:1), and a much more literal fulfillment of 1st Thessalonians 5:9: "God has not destined us for wrath..."

With this in mind, a better understanding of Revelation 3:10 is provided by Robert H. Gundry in his book, *The Church and the Tribulation.* Here, Gundry allows Scripture to interpret Scripture:

> Where a situation of danger is in view, *tereo* (keep) means to *guard....* Throughout the Septuagint [Greek translation of the Old Testament] and the New Testament, *tereo* always occurs for protection within the sphere of danger. In our Lord's prayer for His own we find a striking confirmation that keeping necessarily implies the presence of danger: "I am no more in the world; and yet they themselves are in the world.... keep them" (John 17:11, 12). Jesus contrasts His absence from this earthly scene with the presence of His disciples here. The keeping is required by their presence in the sphere of danger. The plain implication is that were they absent from the world with the Lord, the keeping would not be necessary. Similarly, were the Church absent from the hour of testing, keeping would also not be necessary.

> There is but one other place in Biblical Greek (Septuagint and New Testament) where *tereo* and *ek* occur together, John 17:15: "I do not ask Thee to take them out of the world, but to keep them from the evil one." The parallels between John 17:15 and Revelation 3:10 are very impressive. Both verses appear in Johannine literature [i.e., the same author]. Both come from Jesus' lips. A probability arises, therefore, of similar usage and meaning. In John 17:15 the words, "take out of" (*airo... ek*) mean to *lift up* or *raise up* and *remove.* The expression gives an exact description of what the rapture will be, a lifting up and removal. Yet, it is this expression against which Jesus throws *tereo ek* in full contrast. How then can *tereo ek* refer to the rapture or to

the result of the rapture when in its only other occurrence the phrase opposes an expression which would perfectly describe the rapture?[54]

From the above passage, allowing the Word of God to define the true meaning of Revelation 3:10, we clearly see the Church is meant to go through the Great Tribulation. Even if one rejects this as a probability, planning should be conducted considering it as a possibility. Evidence has been presented here to indicate the "kept from the hour of trial" may not refer to a Pre-tribulational Rapture. This would be a worst-case scenario for its adherents.

Plan accordingly.

---

[54] Robert H. Gundry, *The Church and the Tribulation: A Biblical Examination of Post-Tribulationaism* (Grand Rapids, Michigan: Zondervan Publishing, 1973), 58-59.

CHAPTER 6

NOT APPOINTED US TO WRATH

God has not appointed us to wrath, but to obtain salvation by our
Lord Jesus Christ. (1st Thessalonians 5:9).

This is the wrap-up verse to the 1st Thessalonians 5 passage we discussed
in the" Doctrine of Imminence" under the "Be Alert" verses. Again, it is
seen more as an internal "girder" used to build upon the four cornerstones
of Pre-tribulationalism and provide "strength" to its viewpoint structure.

On the surface, this verse appears to *strongly* contradict the viewpoint
expressed in the previous analysis, "Kept From The Hour," where evidence
was presented that the Church could possibly endure the Great Tribulation.
Before we address that, let's see what the Pre-tribulational view actually is.
Tim LaHaye states in his book *How to Study Prophecy for Yourself*:

> In 1 Thessalonians 5:9, after talking about "the times and season"
> [v. 1] and "the day of the Lord" [v. 3], Paul said, "For God has
> not appointed us to wrath, but to obtain salvation through our
> Lord Jesus Christ." This is an obvious reference to the "day of
> wrath"... This confirms the fact that the church is not appointed
> to wrath but to salvation or deliverance... [because] *Christ at His
> coming* will "deliver us from the wrath to come."[55]

There are a number of issues raised here. Let's look, however, at the

---

55   Tim LaHaye, *How To Study Bible Prophecy For Yourself* (Eugene, Oregon: Harvest
House Publishers, 1990), 82; emphasis added.

main one, that of "salvation or deliverance." If we can resolve this, the verse will be clearly understood and the other sub-issues can be ignored because they lack importance.

The word translated into English "saved" is from the original Greek *soteria*, which literally means just that, "saved." Virtually everywhere else it is used in the New Testament it deals with *Christ saving us*, ultimately from the final (Great White Throne) judgment (see Acts 16:31; Romans 1:16, 5:10; 2nd Thessalonians 2:13). Thus, this verse could mean the same thing, that we are saved from the Great White Throne judgment to come.

However, the word can, as LaHaye notes, also mean *deliverance*. Because Paul, our witness here, is speaking about the Day of the Lord in 1st Thessalonians 5:2, verse 9 *must* be related to it, as there is no evidence in verses 3-8 to show a change of that viewpoint. And, as Paul is also clearly talking about the Rapture in the preceding passage of 1st Thessalonians 4:15-17, Christians are, thus, being saved (delivered) from the destruction (5:3) concurrent with the Day of the Lord (5:2). Here, then, the clear translation is *deliverance*, as the issue is not that of faith in Christ, i.e. salvation, but actually removal from destruction. This conclusion is supported, our Second Witness, in Matthew 24:

> "Then they will deliver you to tribulation, and will kill you, and you will be hated by all nations on account of My name. And at that time many will fall away and will deliver up one another and hate one another. And many false prophets will arise, and will mislead many. And because lawlessness is increased, most people's love will grow cold. But the one who endures to the end [of these things], *he shall be saved*" [*soteria*] (vv. 9-13; emphasis added).

Please note, however, the clear chronology here. Saints will suffer tribulation and then be delivered, at least those who endure—i.e. not compromise their faith as others have done (v. 10)—through it. While we are on this subject, also note that verse 29 states, "But immediately after the tribulation of those days the sun will be darkened, and the moon will not give its light, and the stars will fall from the sky, and the powers of the heavens will be shaken." Isn't this an encapsulation of the Wrath of God judgments contained in the Book of Revelation? If it is, these verses clearly delineate tribulation (v. 9), great tribulation (v. 21), and Wrath of God (v. 29). Each is distinct and separate, with its own unique events.

This perspective also does not negate the verses so often used by Pre-tribulational scholars to support their position: Genesis 5:22-24—Enoch being taken up before the Flood (Genesis 6); Genesis 19—Lot being removed before the judgment of Sodom;, etc. Still, Enoch had to go through, endure, the wickedness of his time (Genesis 4:23, 6:5-6), as did Lot (Genesis18:20). They were not spared the Satanic influence surrounding them (see also Job 1-2). Should these be types of the Church, it is a confirmation that we will endure Satan, and whatever wrath may come our way from him, and yet be spared the Wrath of God in fulfillment of these types.

So, on the issue of "not appointing us to wrath," there is total agreement with the Pre-tribulational view that the Church will be raptured before God's Wrath. But, this does not exclude us from enduring Satan's wrath, which, being worldwide, would indeed be great tribulation.

If there is the possibility of undergoing Satan's wrath, that contingency should be considered in a worst-case scenario... and factored in to any pre-planning.

CHAPTER 7

NOT MENTIONED AFTER REVELATION 4

> After these things I looked, and behold, a door standing open in heaven, and the first voice which I had heard, like the sound of a trumpet speaking with me, said, "Come up here, and I will show you what must take place after these things." (Revelation 4:1).

This is the third internal "girder" of Pre-tribulationalism used to build upon the four cornerstones previously reviewed. It is a verse used to show absolute proof that the Rapture precedes the judgments of the Book of Revelation. The viewpoint is expressed best by Dr. Jack Van Impe, one of the staunchest advocates of the Pre-tribulational perspective, in his book *Revelation Revealed* :

> Chapter [four] begins the prophetical future. Remember chapter 1, verse 19: *Write the things which thou has seen, and the things which are, and the things which shall be hereafter.* That text presented three tenses and informed us that the Book of Revelation is written in chronological order: the past – chapter 1; the present – chapters 2 and 3 (the history of the seven churched to the present time); and the future – chapters 4 through 22.
>
> > Verse 1: *After this I looked, and, behold, a door was opened in heaven: and the first voice which I heard was as it were of a trumpet talking with me; which said, Come up hither, and I will shew these things which must be hereafter* [KJV]. John states, *After this.* After what? After the completion of the history of the seven

churches.... After this John sees a door opened in heaven and hears a trumpet-like voice loudly and victoriously crying, *Come up hither*. This is the Rapture of the church of Jesus Christ...

The Bible clearly teaches that there is a difference between the Rapture and the Revelation of Christ.... The first phase we have already designated as the Rapture. The second phase is called the Revelation. Chapter 4 described phase one, while phase two is described in Chapter 19. The intervening chapters – 6 through 18 – basically cover a seven-year period called the Tribulation. The Rapture (chapter 4) precedes the Tribulation, and the Revelation (chapter 19) follows the seven-year period of judgment. Chapter 4 is a meeting in the air, whereas chapter 19 is a return to the earth.....

The question arises, "Will the church of Jesus Christ be on earth during the Tribulation hour?" The answer is an emphatic, "NO!" *The church is mentioned 16 times in the first three chapters of the Book of Revelation, but is not found in chapters 6 through 18 – the Tribulation period.*[56]

Tim LaHaye supports this view in his *Revelation: Illustrated and Made Plain* (1975):

The absence of any mention of the Church indicates that it is not on earth during the Tribulation. There are sixteen references to the Church in the first three chapters of Revelation, whereas chapters 6 through 18, which cover the Tribulation, do not mention the Church once. The natural conclusion drawn from this is that the Church will be absent during the events of the Tribulation.[57]

Note from both of these quotes that Pre-tribulational scholars use Revelation 4:1 to show *absolute proof* that the Rapture precedes the judgments of the Book of Revelation; that because the Church is not mentioned, it is not present. Is this conclusion valid, i.e., based on Scripture?

Here is the weakness of such a conclusion: Find the name "Satan" in

---

[56] Jack Van Impe, *Revelation Revealed*, 47,49,50; last emphasis added.

[57] LaHaye, *Revelation*, 76.

the book of Genesis; find it in the first five books of the Pentateuch; find it in Joshua; in Judges; in 1ˢᵗ or 2ⁿᵈ Samuel; in 1ˢᵗ or 2ⁿᵈ Kings. Is Satan not there? Are his activities not there? The first mention of Satan is in 1ˢᵗ Chronicles 21:1, and it is a passing reference, not identifying who he is or what he is about.

The first real exposure, *by name*, of Satan is in the book of Job. Apart from that he is only mentioned once in both Psalm 109 (v.6), and in Zechariah 3 (vv. 1, 2). Does this exclude him from all the rest of the Old Testament because he is not mentioned by name? Lack of mention does *not* provide solid evidence of "non-existence." To draw that conclusion is speculation.

Let's take a moment to look at the principle of "First Activity": In Genesis 1 God provides information on His act of creation. In Genesis 2, He provides *additional information* regarding what was provided in Chapter 1. Hence, events in Chapters 1 and 2 are *not linear in time*; they are concurrent. Chapter 1 and 2 should be placed parallel to each other rather than in one continuous line, as if the activities of Chapter 2 were all subsequent to those of Chapter 1.

By aligning those aspects of creation which expand the information of Chapter 2 directly under its counterpart in Chapter 1, we get a more extended view of creation.[58] As this parallel structure exists within the very first two chapters of the first book of the Bible, it would not be unusual, then, if such presentation occurs in the last book.

Additionally, Chapter 3 is an abrupt shift from the information presented in the first two chapters of Genesis in that, without preamble, we go from creation events to those events of the Fall of Man. What is the timeframe between 2:25 and 3:1? A second? An hour? A thousand years? How often had Eve dealt with a talking snake before Genesis 3 that she showed no reservations in interacting with *this* snake?

Because of the change in perspective, does this mean the events of Chapters 1 and 2, not mentioned in Chapter 3, no longer are in effect? Does the sun and moon still shine and orbit? Do the seas still swell, separating the dry land? Is there no longer day or night? The lack of mention of these

---

[58] The reader is encouraged to turn to Genesis to see that Genesis 2:5 is additional information regarding 1:11-13, and that 1:26 and its following verses is expanded by 2:15 and its following verses.

things, yet the certainty they still exist into Chapter 3, as well as the abrupt perspective change, again, an "activity" within the first three chapters of the first book of the Bible, lays a foundation for understanding the last book.

Further, Pre-tribulational authors acknowledge that the Book of Revelation contains a number of "parentheses" passages in which the activities presented in the "parenthesis" are happening concurrent to other events presented in Revelation. This confirms the Parallel View first offered by God in Genesis 1 and 2, a confirmation of how closely the first and last books of Scripture conform to each other.

As an example of the Pre-tribulational perspective, Tim LaHaye in the previously cited *Revelation: Illustrated and Made Plain* stated,

> The first nine chapters of the book of Revelation have brought us almost to the middle of the Tribulation.... [N]ow chapters 10 and 11:1-14 comprise a parenthetical section given to John just before the prophecy concerning the last half of the Tribulation [occurs]: *a description of conditions that existed during the particular period of time covered by the preceding judgments.*"[59]

By LaHaye's own writing, it is the Pre-tribulational scholar's view that previous events continue to occur during the parenthetical material— exactly like Genesis 3, no doubt, has many continuing activities of Genesis 1 and 2, though all the aspects are not so named.

In fact, *every* break in the book of Revelation from the apparent chronological "time line" is referred to as a parenthesis by Pre-tribulational writers, and they acknowledge preceding events *as continuing....* Except for Chapters 3 and 4, where they say there is a complete break. Ponder that for a moment.

A second issue is that which is brought up, again, by LaHaye:

> Chapters 2 and 3 of Revelation give the message of Christ to the seven churches of Asia *and go beyond them to the churches which "shall b e hereafter."* ... A study of history reveals the Church has gone through seven basic periods or stages.[60]

---

59   LaHaye, *Revelation*, 144; emphasis added.

60   Ibid., 16, 22; emphasis added.

We've already discussed the seven churches of Revelation as representing seven separate and distinct Eras of the Church Age in "Kept From The Hour Of Testing." The point here, beginning in Revelation 4:1, is that Pre-tribulational scholars see a further timeline breakdown.

Dr. Van Impe is representative of them. In his quote regarding Revelation 1:19: "Write the things which you have seen, the things which are, and the things which shall take place after these things," he delineates the "breaks" as following: Revelation 1 ("have seen": past tense), Revelation 2 and 3, the "Church Age" ("which are": present tense), and Revelation 4, and thereafter, ("which shall take place": future).[61] Hence, the reasoning goes, because the Church Age overview ends with Chapter 3, everything thereafter is past the Church Age chronologically.

The drawback to this delineation is that John is still living in the first century Church, i.e. the Ephesus Era. The "things which shall be" still include the Smyrna through Laodicea Eras, *which are future*. To re-quote LaHaye: "Chapters 2 and 3 of Revelation give the message of Christ to the seven churches of Asia *and go beyond them to the churches which 'shall be hereafter.' "* By their own writings they agree that the Church Age still extends into the future, hence, *which shall take place after John's experience of seeing the events of Revelation.*

Additionally, we've previously seen, Jesus recommended to the Laodicean lukewarm (notice, not *cold*; hence, those "saved" but no longer *vigilant*) Church (Era) that they "Buy from Me gold refined by fire..." We've also seen that this involves "cost" and, from 1ˢᵗ Peter 1, that it refers to "trial or testing." Again, *how* might that testing occur?

What if what follows, beginning in Chapter 4, is an explanation, making it a "large parenthesis," to identify, at least in part, the trials faced by the Last Era Church—the era when these events will occur? This would, like the other parentheses in the book of Revelation, run concurrent.

To return to the issue at hand, to say that Revelation 4:1 is the beginning of "that which shall be," a period beyond the Church Age, is *speculation.* Pre-tribulational writings demonstrate that almost all of Chapters 2 and 3, dealing with the Church Eras of the Church Age, *are future* relative to the timeframe of John's writing, i.e., the Ephesus Era.

The next issue, one of the most intensely valued by Pre-tribulational

61   Van Impe, *Revelation Revealed*, 47.

scholars, is that of Revelation 4:1, "Come up here," where they offer this as a type of the Rapture. Thus, it occurs before the judgments which begin in Chapter 6.

There are two responses to this. First, although John *does* get to go to heaven, note that he *does not get to stay there*. For the Book of Revelation to be made available to the Church, *John returns in his natural body to Patmos* (confirmed by historians such as Eusebius), from which he is later released (giving him the opportunity to disseminate the book).

How is this, then, a type of the Rapture? Pre-tribulational scholars—across the board—agree that once the Rapture occurs we can only come back with Jesus in Revelation 19, i.e., in our resurrected bodies. That makes John's trip to heaven, in which he returns to earth in his natural body after completing the Book of Revelation, *not* really a true type of the Rapture.

Is not a better "type" found in Revelation 11:12, a point that is well into the judgments of Revelation (Trumpet 6 has sounded, and the First Woe [v. 14] is, at least, underway)? In Revelation 11:12 the two witnesses, after having been dead over three days, are told to "Come up here"—the *exact* same wording as Revelation 4:1—and they, like John, go up into heaven.

However, it appears, this is a *permanent* departure as there is no mention of a return anywhere in Scripture. Further, 1st Thessalonians 4:15-17 clearly states, "The dead in Christ shall rise first." Isn't Revelation 11:12, then, a more Biblical view of the events surrounding the Rapture, where the *dead* witnesses are raised?

An acceptable Pre-tribulational proponent's response is: "How can Jesus come 'as a thief' (1st Thessalonians 5:2) if all these obvious judgment events occur before His return, events *no one* should miss?" A legitimate question. Notwithstanding, in Revelation 16:15, *just before the last bowl judgment occurs*, i.e., after *all* the other judgments of Revelation *have occurred* (v. 17), the reader is admonished: " 'Behold, I am coming like a thief.' " For those living in darkness, that is exactly how His return will be.

So, the issue of Jesus' "unexpected" return has nothing to do with "no signs" occurring beforehand. Notice, in 1st Thessalonians 5:4 the unsaved are still going to misinterpret the events, hence they *still* are taken by surprise. In essence, in Revelation 16:15, Jesus is, in His mercy, giving everyone *one final notice*. Also, refer back to the analysis of Imminence where we saw those living in spiritual darkness—those oblivious the obvious signs—as going to be unprepared… just like one who is robbed by a thief in the night.

In closing, Revelation 4:1 does not specifically state it is a type of the Rapture. To conclude that is speculation. Additionally, there is credible evidence, Scriptural evidence, that Revelation 11:12 is a much better example of the elements of the Rapture than verse 4:1. This, then, would indicate the Rapture does not occur before the events presented further into the book of Revelation. In developing a worst-case scenario, this must be taken into consideration.

CHAPTER 8

A FIRM COVENANT

And he will make a firm covenant with the many for one week, but in the middle of the week he will put a stop to sacrifice and grain offering; and on the wing of abominations will come one who makes desolate, even until a complete destruction, on that is decreed, is poured out on the one who makes desolate (Daniel 9:27).

Any study of the events preceding the return of the Lord Jesus Christ requires an analysis of the "Seventy Weeks" prophecy contained in Daniel 9:24-27. This very important prophecy, considered by most evangelical scholars to be the "backbone of all prophecy,"[62] is a major key to understanding the chronology of events dealing with the Jewish people, their Messiah, and, of equal significance, the end of this, the Church age. In attempting to correctly interpret this passage, twentieth century Bible-believing scholars feel certain that most of the chronology occurred prior to, and including, Jesus' First Advent. For most evangelical Christians, then, especially those who believe that Christ will come to rapture the Church before the events of the Book of Revelation, there remains only a seven year period for the completion of Daniel's Seventy Weeks.

In analyzing this passage, a period of time is obviously implied as Daniel records "seventy *shebu'ah* have been determined for your people" (Daniel 9:24); he then describes events taking place during that period. The original

---

[62] Sir Edward Dewey, writing as early as the 1800s described it as just that; quoted in Jack Van Impe, *Israel's Final Holocaust* (Nashville, TN: Thomas Nelson Publishers, 1979), 33.

Hebrew word used here, *shebu'ah*, is translated "week(s)" by both Christian and Jewish linguistic scholars alike because it signifies a grouping of seven (thus "week"), much like the English word "dozen" signifies a grouping of twelve. These scholars have also concluded that the correct standard for the implied period of time should be *years*. Thus, seventy *shebu'ah*, or 490 years (70 times 7) are involved to fully complete the prophecy.

Accepted interpretation of Daniel's prophecy by Christian theologians provides that the last *shebu'ah* is separated from the first sixty-nine. In this interpretation, the first sixty-nine *shebu'ah* have already occurred in history, with one period of seven years, the 70th *shebu'ah*, remaining for the prophecy's fulfillment.

Among those holding to this view are Dwight Pentecost, Hal Lindsey, Jack Van Impe, Grant Jeffrey, and Tim LaHaye. All of these noteworthy, latter-twentieth century giants of Pre-tribulational eschatology base their conclusion largely on the work of Sir Robert Anderson, a nineteenth century assistant commissioner of Scotland Yard and a very committed lay apologist of the Christian faith.[63]

Writing in his classic book *The Coming Prince*, Anderson concluded that the first sixty-nine weeks of Daniel's prophecy had been completed in a continuous string of years beginning with the "decree" of Artaxerxes recorded in Nehemiah 2:1-8, and ending with the triumphal entry of Jesus into Jerusalem (Matthew 21:6-9). This conclusion was the result of his extensive calculations based, in part, on dating determined by the Astronomer Royal, the director of the Royal Observatory, Greenwich, England.[64]

Anderson's calculations are seen consistently by most scholars, Pre-tribulational or otherwise, as an undeniable proof there exists a 7-year period which remains on God's timeclock regarding not only the Jews, by also the Church... for many of them, especially the Church.[65]

---

[63] Pentecost, no doubt reflecting the view of them all, stated in his book *Things To Come*, "No more careful study has been made of the problem of the seventy weeks of Daniel than that of Sir Robert Anderson," 245.

[64] Sir Robert Anderson. *The Coming Prince* (Grand Rapids, Michigan: Kregel Publications, 1984), 117-129.

[65] Ibid. Anderson arrives at his figures in this manner:
Believing that Daniel was referring to a "prophetic year" of 360 days, not a Sothic (annual rising of the star Sothis) year of 365 1/4 days, Anderson determined that 69 weeks would thus be 173,880 days (or 69 x 7 x 360).

The remaining 70th week, Pentecost and the others believe, will begin with Israel signing a peace pact with what Hal Lindsey describes in his world-acclaimed best-seller, *The Late Great Planet Earth*, as "the future fuehrer," the Antichrist. Interpreting Daniel 9:27 to be this incarnate Satan, Lindsey goes on to say, "He (the Antichrist posing as the Jewish Messiah) will make 'a strong covenant' with the Israelis, guaranteeing their safety and protection.... According to Daniel's prophetic chronology, the minute the Israeli leader and the [Antichrist] sign this pact, God starts His great timepiece which has seven allotted years left on it,"[66] i.e. the last *shebu'ah*. "'This event marks the beginning of the period of Biblical history (known as) the (Great) Tribulation."[67]

It is this last statement that makes the correct interpretation of Daniel 9:24-27, and more importantly, correct *timing* of Daniel's 70th Week prophecy, so significant: The horrific events of the Book of Revelation will be unleashed, events described by Jesus Himself as being "a great tribulation, such as has not been from the beginning of the world until now, no, and never will be, that if those days had not been shortened, no human being would be saved" (Matthew 24:21-22a). True preparation for those events, then, rely, in part, on a correct interpretation of Daniel 9:24-27. Let us, therefore, "revisit" those verses.

History identifies the twentieth year of Artaxerxes reign (the year the "edict" to rebuild Jerusalem was given by Artaxerxes in Nehemiah 2:1) as 445 B.C., while Nehemiah identifies the month as "Nisan," our March. Although no day is given, Anderson concludes it is the first day of Nisan (as this fits perfectly with the calculations that are to follow), which can be identified as our 14th. Thus, the beginning date is March 14, 445 B.C.

Determining that the triumphal entry was on the 10th of Nisan, our April 6, he calculated the year to be A.D. 32. ("The statement of St. Luke is explicit and unequivocal, that our Lord's public ministry began in the fifteenth year of Tiberius Caesar... shortly before Passover; the date can thus be fixed as between August A.D. 28 and April A.D. 29. The Passover of the crucifixion therefore was in A.D. 32," pp. 121-122.)

The intervening period was 476 years and 24 days (the days being reckoned inclusively, as required by the language of the prophecy, and in accordance with the Jewish practice)

But 476 x 365 =	173,740 days
Add 14 March to 6 April, both inclusive	24 days
Add for leap years	116 days
	173,880 days

For Anderson, and his followers, this corresponding exactness of the days in both calculations is conclusive proof that all of his dating is correct.

---

[66] Hal Lindsey, with C.C. Carlson, 152.

[67] Ibid.

"Seventy *shebu'ah* have been determined for *your people* and *your holy city*..." (v. 24). The angel delivering this prophecy to Daniel, a Jew, is, thus, obviously referring to *the Jews* and the Jewish holy city of *Jerusalem* (see verse 25 which confirms this).

This same Jewish perspective is maintained in verse 25 with reference to *their Messiah*: "from the issuing of a decree to restore and build Jerusalem until *Messiah* (there will be) seven weeks and sixty-two weeks; it will be built again, with plaza and moat, even in times of distress." This Jewish perspective continues into verse 26: "Then after sixty-two weeks the *Messiah* will be cut off and have nothing."

With so much evidence that these verses deal with the Jews, and more specifically, their Messiah, why is it that most evangelical expositors now shift and make the "he," opening verse 27, as a reference to the Antichrist, the "prince who is to come" referred to in verse 26b? A more natural interpretation is that the Messiah, the central person in these verses, is still in view.

Let's look at verses 26 and 27 schematically. In so doing, we clearly see that there is a perfect parallelism to these two verses that cannot be ignored. Yet, for many scholars this evidence is overlooked.

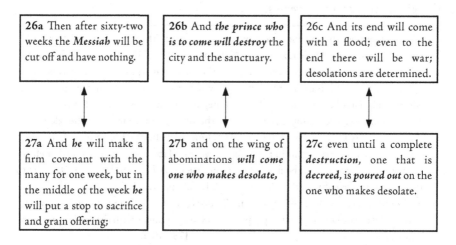

If this structure, and interpretation, is correct, then the "he" spoken of in verse 27a, is *not* the Antichrist, but the Jewish Messiah. And, as we shall soon see, there are only 3 1/2 years left on God's prophetic timepiece!

As previously stated, the consensus among evangelical scholars studying eschatology is that the "decree" of verse 25 is that of Artaxerxes found in

Nehemiah 2 which, through the study of history, can be identified as being given on 1st Nisan, 445 B.C. Pentecost argues that "in the Scriptures are contained several (other) decrees that have to do with the restoration of the Jews from the Babylonian captivity.[68] However, in all these (but the one given by Artaxerxes in Nehemiah 2), permission was granted (only) for the rebuilding of the temple and nothing was said about the rebuilding of the city; (therefore), none of the (other) decrees met the condition of Daniel 9:25."[69]

Accepting, for the moment, a *re*-building is implied, Jerusalem *begins* to be rebuilt when the Temple is rebuilt. Any authorization for the Temple applies, in part, to the city itself where the Temple is located. Though Pentecost argues otherwise, discounting the rebuilding of the Temple as, in part, a rebuilding of the city, the Word of God is emphatic: In Isaiah 44:28 it is declared that Cyrus' decree to rebuild the Temple *is* a declaration of the rebuilding of the city! And, by logical extension, the other "decrees" must also.

Further, nothing in the sentence's original Hebrew requires that the authorizing decree be for a full and complete rebuilding. On the contrary, the wording indicates that the process will be staggered between two separate periods of time: an initial period of "restoring," followed by a more lengthy period of "building" (*banah*, new construction)---which is *exactly* how the Revised Standard Version translates this passage.[70]

restore	and	*rebuild*
↕		↕
seven weeks	and	*sixty-two weeks*

---

[68] The other decrees are those of Cyrus (Ezra 1:1-3), Darius (Ezra 6:3-8), and Artaxerxes' initial decree which allowed the Jews to return to Jerusalem and restore the Temple ("house of your God" [v. 16]), but which said nothing about the city's (re)building (Ezra 7:7-27).

[69] Penecost, 244. But the Hebrew word used here is *banah*, build---not *re*-build. To say *re*-build is a hermeneutical error; a better interpretation is that Jerusalem is to be *built-up* (i.e. *new* construction).

[70] "from the going forth of the word to restore and build Jerusalem... there shall be seven weeks. *Then* for sixty-two weeks it shall be built again..."

Added to Pentecost's erroneous conclusion that the decree referred to here is that given in Nehemiah 2, he and *every* current-day End Time scholar have overlooked the word "restore" in their exposition of this verse. They immediately go to the word "build" (a typical example is the previous Pentecost quote [footnoted as 68]). Yet, the verse clearly indicates that a "restor(ing)" is of equal importance in the process. More significant, if there is a time difference between the two actions, the re-storing begins first (as it is given first) and then the (re)-building.

Additionally, the Hebrew verb *shawb*, constantly translated "restore," indicates that the Jewish Temple, to be fully operational, would have to have been *re-stored*, that is, *re-provisioned* with the grains and animals necessary for enforcement of the full sacrificial system ordained by God in the Old Testament (Pentateuch). The "decree" of Nehemiah 2 did not fulfill this, for there was no mention of re-provisioning there.

Finally, and probably most glaring, is the word "decree" itself. In Daniel 9:25 it is the Hebrew word *dabar*, "to speak," implying a spoken matter, and by extension, relating to a (verbal) command. In the Nehemiah passage (2:7,8) the word translated "decree" is the Hebrew *'iggereth*, which actually means "letter." Nehemiah, then, is *not* referring to a decree, that is, a command, but to letters of transit ("...let letters be given me to the governors... that they may let me pass through until I come to Judah") and a letter of acquisition ("and a letter to Asaph... that he may give me timber"). Nowhere in the passage does King Artaxerxes give a command of any type for the (re)building of Jerusalem; he merely gives his *assent* to Nehemiah's request to rebuild. In a literal interpretation of the Bible, the principal of hermeneutics requires a specific word to be matched with a similar specific word where Scriptural concepts and passages are being compared. Nehemiah 2, therefore, does not fulfill Daniel 9:25: An *'iggereth*, a letter, is not a *dabar*, a (spoken) command. We must look elsewhere for this condition of a "decree" to be actually met.

Interestingly, in Ezra chapter 7 both the condition of "re-provisioning" (re-storing) and of a command, a *dabar*-like decree, exists. Beginning in Ezra 7:12, and on into verse 13, we find: "(king) Artaxerxes to Ezra the priest: now I make a *decree* that any one of the people of Israel... who freely offers to go to Jerusalem may go with you." Because the sons of Israel had been raised in Babylon for nearly a generation, Ezra, and for that matter Daniel too, used some Chaldean (Babylonian) words in their writings. The word for decree here is *te'em*, which means an edict or decree, as in a spoken command. It is the Chaldean word for "decree," and is an *exact* equivalent of the Hebrew word *dabar*. Thus, it is in Ezra 7 that Daniel 9:25 is *exactly* fulfilled!

Further, in conjunction with that decree, Ezra 7:17-22 establishes a literal fulfillment of the "re-storing" of the Temple and, by extension, Jerusalem, (because the one [the Temple] is a part of the other [the city of Jerusalem]). This restoration will continue during the first period given by Daniel in 9:25, the "seven weeks" (49 years), which will include the *restoring* of the wall by Nehemiah around the city to its previous raised, fortified condition instead of torn down rubble first encountered by Nehemiah. Thereafter, during the "sixty-two weeks" (434 years) period, Jerusalem will be in a constant state of "*building*" (new construction) as one generation passes on the city to the next, up until the time of Jesus, the Messiah.

Again, this view is not only historical, but is also a literal fulfillment of Daniel 9:25. And the timing of the Ezra 7 decree (457 B.C.) fits perfectly into a more accurate timeline of *all* the periods spoken of in Daniel's Seventy Weeks passage, especially those relating to the Messiah.[71]

Let's view that timeline:

---

[71] Additionally, the Messiah is here referred to as "Prince" (v. 25), not as the "King" as He is referred to everywhere else in Scripture, beginning with the Davidic Covenant ("will establish his **king**dom") [II Samuel 7:12-16], and culminating in "King of Kings" [Revelation 19:16]; (see also Zechariah 14:9). A Prince is a King *in the making*. Thus, when the Messiah arrives, whatever the timing, He will *have* to come fulfilling some *Princely* role—which was *exactly* fulfilled in Jesus' First Advent (where, during those 3 1/2 years, He was not yet "King" [John 12:13]). When does the Messiah *actually* become "King" to the Jewish people, (i.e. ascend the promised throne of David)? Zechariah 14:16 indicates *after* His triumphal return battling the Jews' enemies (Zechariah 12:12) at the conclusion of Daniel's 70th week. The "King" takes His throne at His Second Advent, the beginning of the Millennial Kingdom.

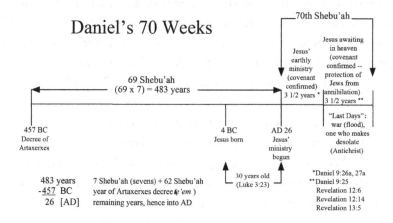

It should be noted that this view is significantly different from that accepted by Sir Robert Anderson, who receives the full support of Dwight Pentecost and the other twentieth century eschatological scholars.[72] Yet, in Daniel 9:26a, we are told that *after* the second period, the sixty-two weeks, when the full sixty-nine week period is completed, the Messiah will be "cut-off and have nothing." It is important to note here that it does not state at the "immediate" end of the sixty-nine weeks, only that this occurs "after" that period of time is completed. Most commentators assume that the "cutting off" *begins* the 70th week. But this is not what is stated: The "after" merely signifies that this sixty-nine week period must be fully completed before the Messiah is cut off. The only safe conclusion is that this occurs sometime *during* the 70th week (which could be as fulfilled, literally, in the middle of the seven-year period, as on its first day).

---

[72] Pentecost, 244. Speaking for them all, he states that "in Ezra 4:1-4 the rebuilding of the Temple was stopped because the Jews were rebuilding the city without authorization" and, therefore, he implies this is not *the* decree spoken of by Daniel because—at this point—there is no decree. For Pentecost, "the condition of Daniel 9:25 is (not) met." But, as has already been shown, the "decree" (*te'em*) in Ezra chapter 7 (*not* chapter 4) *is* a rightful authorization. Pentecost continues to argue that "in (the Ezra 7 decree) permission was granted for the rebuilding of the Temple (*only*, with) nothing being said about the rebuilding of the city." However, and to state the obvious, it is an absolute fact that the Ezra 7 decree to rebuild the Temple causes Jerusalem to also begin to be (re)built/built(-up)—thus literally fulfilling Daniel 9:25. Further, Daniel's prophecy does not state the decree will say to restore and build *all* of Jerusalem *immediately*, only that a decree will be given for restoring and building.

And, in reference to the "cutting off" itself, virtually every Christian scholar agrees that this is referring to the crucifixion.[73] As the Hebrew word *karath* means "to cut" and by implication "to destroy," the indication is that this is the Messiah's death (an event confirmed in Isaiah 53). Further, the Messiah will "have nothing." The Hebrew *'ayin* means "to be nothing" and is followed by a preposition which indicates "to (Him)." Literally, then, this implies "not for Himself," which is how the King James Version translates this passage: The Messiah would die (be cut off), but *not for Himself* — He would die for others. If, as we shall show below, verse 27a provides information about the Messiah, (not the Antichrist, the "one who makes desolate"), then the point at which this cutting off takes place is "in the middle of Daniel's 70th week."

In analyzing verse 27a we find someone (a "he") who "will confirm a covenant." The Hebrew verb here, *gabar*, means "to be strong," and implies that the covenant in question is "made strong," thus "confirmed." Pentecost and the other Pre-tribulational scholars state emphatically that it is the Antichrist who confirms this covenant.[74] For them, this "confirming" is really an "initiating" or "originating" of a new covenant that is to last seven years.

But the clear meaning in the original Hebrew is that a *prior existing* covenant is "made strong," thus *confirmed*. As Marvin Byers in his book *The Final Victory* observes:

> The original says: "And he shall confirm a covenant one week."
> Therefore, regardless of who this phrase is speaking of, the person who confirms a covenant does so for "one week" or seven years, not 3½! He does not confirm a covenant that is *suppose* to last

---

73 Yet this causes a great interpretation dilemma. Though most Pre-tribulation scholars accept that this speaks of the death of the Messiah, thus Good Friday, Sir Robert Anderson (with whom they all also agree) identifies this as Jesus' rejection by the Jewish religious leaders at His public advent, i.e. Jesus' triumphal entry into Jerusalem, hence Palm Sunday. The problem? It can only be one. Yet Anderson's entire system of chronological dating, as he states: "to the day" (and upon which all Pre-tribulationists rely) depends on the "cutting off" of the Messiah to be the Palm Sunday rejection— which is *not* what the original Hebrew implies! The Hebrew clearly indicates the Messiah's death, not His rejection. For this reason (though not the only reason), Anderson's calculations must be viewed as faulty.

74 Pentecost, 249.

seven years, and then break it in the middle. Rather, he "confirms it seven years." He cannot "confirm it seven years" and at the same time break it after 3½ years! This interpretation contradicts itself.[75]

Certainly, then, there is a better interpretation for this verse: If the first sixty-nine weeks identified in Daniel 9:24-27 specifically concern the Jewish Messiah, and the opening of the prophecy clearly states that "seventy weeks are determined for your people" (v. 24), the Jews, then it stands to reason the events of the last week, the 70th week, should also deal with the Messiah—*unless they specifically state otherwise* (as in "the one who will... destroy; one who makes desolate").

What covenant then is being spoken of here? It *cannot* be that of the Antichrist who has *never* made a prior existing covenant with the Jewish people that can now be "made strong." It must, therefore, be related to the Messiah. And what covenant concerning the Messiah is waiting to be confirmed? The Davidic Covenant recorded in II Samuel 7:12-16. Here God promised the Jews that one day He would establish a kingdom whose King, the Messiah, would have a throne that would be established forever.

The New Testament gives voice that this is exactly what is being confirmed. In Luke 16:16 it is written: "the Law and the Prophets (a Jewish euphemism for the Old Testament) were proclaimed until John (the Baptist); *since then the gospel of the kingdom is preached...(!)*"

This is an astounding verse. The Holy Spirit, through the third Gospel writer, Luke, is clearly stating that, in God's view, "gears have been shifted." The Law and the Prophets were being superseded by "the good news of the kingdom," that is, the Davidic Covenant was about to be fulfilled. As J. Sidlow Baxter observes in his book *The Strategic Grasp of the Bible*,

> When John the Baptist and our Lord (Jesus) came announcing that the Kingdom was at hand, they meant—and the (Jewish) people so understood—the Kingdom promised in the Old Testament scripture of Israel under the reign of the coming Messiah.[76]

---

[75] Marvin Byers, *The Final Victory* (Shippensburg, PA: Companion Press, 1991), 276; emphasis in original.

[76] J. Sidlow Baxter, *Strategic Grasp of the Bible*, 245. Baxter goes on to state: "When John and our Lord came preaching, 'Repent ye; for the kingdom of heaven is at hand,' they were referring to something publicly understood, namely, the long-promised Messianic kingdom which was the grand subject of the Old Testament prophecy"; 234.

The soundest interpretation here, then, is that the Davidic Covenant was being confirmed *by the very presence of the Messiah*—a literal fulfillment of Daniel's verse!

There is additional New Testament confirmation that Daniel 9:27a refers to the Messiah not the Antichrist: The covenant expressed by Daniel would be confirmed "with *the many*." In Mark 14:24, when inaugurating the New Covenant,[77] Jesus uses this exact same wording to identify its recipients, "This is My blood of the covenant, which is to be shed on behalf of *the many*."

And this issue of sacrifice related to the covenant does not stop there. Verse 27a goes on to state that "he will put a stop to sacrifice and grain offering" (also referred to as "oblation"). Again, Dwight Pentecost and the others believe this refers to the Antichrist as he puts a stop to the sacrificial system he initially allowed the Jews to re-institute at the beginning of his "confirmed"-covenant, seven year "week."

But why would he only put a stop to two portions of the sacrificial offering system? In the book of Leviticus the Jews are required to fulfill *five* types of offerings.[78] Most twentieth century commentators ignore this and merely point out that the "sacrifice" is taken away, as if the word "sacrifice" is all-inclusive for the "grain offering" (oblation), which is mentioned, and the other three unmentioned offerings required of the Jewish nation. Yet the Word of God, so specific everywhere else, must have reason to be specific here. Though the word "sacrifice" *may* be all-inclusive, a review of the two offerings specifically stated shows why only *they*, and not all of the offerings, are identified.

The verse says that "he" will put a stop to the "sacrifice" and "grain offering." The Hebrew word for "sacrifice" is *zebeck*, a word meaning "slaughter" and implies the slaughter of an animal. The very essence of the burnt and sin offerings, this was a *blood* sacrifice. The Hebrew word used for "grain offering" is *minchah*, a word that implies a "bloodless cereal offering."[79] In Leviticus 2, where the grain offering is specifically cited, it is

---

[77] cf. Matthew 26:28.

[78] Some form of burnt offerings, cereal offerings, peace offerings, sin offerings, and trespass offerings are used to fulfill the numerous regulations for sacrifice contained in the Old Testament.

[79] Strong, Hebrew #4503.

identified as "dough from wheat flour to make (unleavened) *bread.*"[80] (When this bread is made by roasting the dough it is specifically "used for the offering of first fruits."[81]) Thus, this verse indicates that the sacrificial rites conducted in the Jewish Temple are to be stopped by an individual ("he") in the middle of the last seven years (i.e. 3 1/2 years) of Daniel's 70th week, that are specifically identified with *bread* and *blood* of the Jewish offering system.

Do these two specific elements, the bread and blood, have any application to the Antichrist? No, for nowhere in Scripture is this counterfeit-Christ identified with them. But they *are* identified with Jesus, the Messiah, who, we are told, also put an end to the Temple's sacrificial system. In Hebrews 7:27 it states that when the Lord Jesus was crucified for our sins ("cut off, but not for himself" [Daniel 9:26a]), He also "put a stop to daily sacrifice (and oblation)" by that very death ("once for all when He offered up Himself"). Knowing this, Jesus at the Last Supper indicated His coming death by changing the centuries-honored Passover ritual sequence: Jesus "took some *bread* and said, 'this is My body.' And took a cup with wine and said, 'this is my *blood*'" (Matthew 26: 26, 28).[82] It is *He* who is specifically identified with the bread and blood in Scripture! And so this is a further confirmation that it is to the Messiah that this verse (27a) is referring, not the Antichrist.

The impact of this conclusion is astounding. There no longer exists seven years on God's clock concerning the return of Jesus, there are only 3½![83] And

---

[80] James I. Packer, Merrill C. Tenney, and William White, Jr., ed., *The Bible Almanac* (Lynchburg, VA: The Old-Time Gospel Hour, 1980), 402.

[81] Ibid.; cf. also Leviticus 23:13 and I Corinthians 15:22-24.

[82] It is also interesting to note that Jesus' death was further confirmation *He* was the Messiah and thus additional "confirm"-ation that the Messiah had come—*the* core element of the Davidic Covenant. (See Luke 24:13-35, especially verse 26 when He rebukes the two disciples: "Was it not necessary *for the Messiah to suffer* (and die)?" Jesus then goes on to demonstrate from Old Testament Scriptures (the only "Bible" available to the two disciples) "the things concerning Himself," the Jewish Messiah.

[83] Nowhere in Scripture is there a period of seven years mentioned in regards to the Last Days. *Every* reference is specific as to the remaining timeframe: 3½ years. Cf. Daniel 7:25—"time, times, and half a time"; Revelation 12:6— "one thousand two hundred and sixty (1,260) days"; Revelation 12:14—"a time and times and half a time"; and Revelation 13:5—"forty-two months." Further, any interpretation of Daniel's 70 Weeks *must* give explanation as to Jesus' 3½-year earthly ministry already accomplished. Yet, none do! Absolutely no mention is made concerning the rather awkward period of time Jesus spent on earth at His First Advent. In contrast, the

those looking for a seven year "peace" treaty between Israel and the Antichrist (then parading as a man of benevolence towards the Jewish nation) look in vain because verse 27a deals with the Jewish Messiah, not the Antichrist. Yes, a treaty will exist,[84] but it is of *unspecified duration*. As a result, the desecration of the Temple, the "abomination of desolation,"[85] cannot be specifically identified as to the time of its occurrence—but it is *not* dependent on a seven-year treaty between the Antichrist and Israel, because, on God's time clock, Israel—and the world—no longer have a full "week."

This understanding of Daniel 9:24-27 is possibly the most critical in impacting a Pre-tribulational view. Not just that it shows the weaknesses of that belief, but, more importantly, that those who hold to it *are looking for the wrong series of events.* If the perspective presented herein of this Daniel passage proves true, Pre-tribulationalists will be placed in the dire position of being potentially, completely blindsided. Should that occur they will be seriously unprepared for the events that will follow.

One final reflection on this chapter: The belief that there is a seven-year timeline remaining on God's prophetic clock is not only embraced by Pre-tribulationalists. It is the standard Evangelical view, including those who hold to the other perspectives on the timing of the Rapture. For that reason, it is believed that they too will be blindsided when events do not occur as they thought they would.

This chapter, then, is for them too... thus making its content an element of the *worst* worst-case scenario.

---

conclusion arrived at in this writing finally addresses this subject—and makes perfect sense of it—it is half of a *shebu'ah*, the first half of the last "week."

[84] In fulfillment of Isaiah 28:15, "because you (the Jewish nation) have made a covenant with Sheol (hell)..." An interesting note is that the word "covenant" here is the Hebrew *beriyth*, better translated a "compact," an agreement which initiates a confederation (an alliance between two separate countries, in contrast to a "federation," an alliance where both political entities surrender their individual sovereignty to a central power.) It causes one to wonder what type of agreement this "compact" will actually turn out to be. But the implication is that it is between two countries, *not* between an individual and a country.

[85] Matthew 24:15; cf. Daniel 12:11, which also identifies the action closing the first 3½ year period ("sacrifice is abolished" [Hebrew: *suwr*, "to turn off," so, literally, "the sacrifice is shut down"] --- "once for all" at Jesus' death [Hebrews 7:27], and the beginning of the last half of the 70th "week" ("setting up of the abomination of desolation").

CHAPTER 9

THE GREAT TRIBULATION

Therefore when you see the abomination of desolation which was
spoken of through Daniel the prophet, standing in the holy place (let
the reader understand)… then there shall be a great tribulation such
as has not occurred since the beginning of the world until now, nor
ever shall (Matthew 24:15,21).

This leads us to the issue of the Great Tribulation being an all-inclusive term
for Day of the Lord, Wrath of God, 7-year peace treaty, etc. Let's begin by
acknowledging that Scripture makes it perfectly clear, by direct evidence,
that Christians *will* encounter tribulation in our walk with Jesus Christ:

> "In this world you will have tribulation," [Jesus said] (John
> 16:33).

> Do not be surprised at the fiery ordeal among you, which comes
> upon you for your testing, as though some strange thing were
> happenings to you (1st Peter 4:12).

> Consider it all joy, my brethren, when you encounter various
> trials… (James 1:2).

> "Through many tribulations we must enter the kingdom of
> God," [quoted Luke of Paul] (Acts 14:22).

The Greek word translated "tribulation" is *thlipsis*, and means, literally, *pressure.* That mankind has experienced tribulation, *pressure,* is the general condition since The Fall in Genesis 3. It is the result of that Fall, and can be directly attributed to Satan who caused it.[86] As we will soon see, tribulation is different from God's Wrath.

Returning to "tribulation," Jesus warned in Matthew 24:21 that at some point in the future there would be *great* tribulation. The Greek word here is *mega,* meaning *big* or *exceeding.* He went on to say, "...such as has not occurred since the beginning of the world until now, nor ever shall [be]." As we now know *what* will occur—a *mega* tribulation—it seems fair to inquire *when* and *where* this will occur.

Jesus gave us signs to look for regarding this. He proclaimed there will be false Christs (v. 5), and wars, rumors of wars, famines, and earthquakes (v. 6). He then said that these "are merely the beginning."

When have there not been false Christs, wars and rumors of wars, famines, and earthquakes? John said the spirit of the antichrist was prevalent even in the first century AD (1st John 4:3). There is historic proof that wars and rumors of wars, as well as famines and earthquakes have been going even longer than that. Yet, these past occurrences can hardly qualify as *mega* tribulations, except maybe in isolated or local instances. The question is: How are these different from what has been experienced by the world for roughly, at least, the last 2,000 years encompassing the Church Age?

One *could* say that in the past 100 years these tribulations have increased in their frequency and intensity. And Jesus addresses that very observation in verse 8: "...beginning of birth pangs." Bible scholars have noted that as birth pangs increase the closer a woman comes to an actual birth, that these occurrences would also increase in number and intensity. But there is still nothing *mega* here.

In verse 9 Jesus begins to become more specific—and He actually uses the word "tribulation," a key piece of evidence—by departing from "general tribulations" to something distinct:

> "Then they will deliver you to tribulation, and will kill you, and you will be hated by all nations on account of My name."

---

86   See Genesis 3:14-19; note especially the "Because you have done this," which continues into verse 15, where God is speaking to the spiritual force behind the serpent, Satan.

This *might* be great tribulation, especially for those experiencing martyrdom, but the church at Smyrna in the first century AD was told the exact same thing:

> I know your tribulation... and the blasphemy by those who... are a synagogue of Satan. Do not fear what you are about to suffer. Behold, the devil is about to cast some of you into prison, that you may be tested, and you will have tribulation... Be faithful until death and I will give you the crown of life (Revelation 2:9-10).

Note that this suffering, even "until death," is *not* characterized as *mega* tribulation. (This is in contrast to Revelation 2:22 where the church at Thyatira is told they *will* experience *mega* tribulation.) Note also that the tribulation *is the result of Satan*, not God. This is in support of our previous view from Genesis 3 that Satan is the cause of tribulation.

So when does this *mega* tribulation start?

> "Therefore, when you see the abomination of desolation which was spoken of through Daniel the prophet, standing in the holy place... then there will be a great tribulation..." (Matthew 24:15,21a).

The abomination of desolation standing in the holy place is considered by scholars to be when the Antichrist enters the Holy of Holies in the rebuilt Jewish Temple and proclaims himself God.[87] This is confirmed in the passage we saw in the letter to the Thessalonians:

> The man of lawlessness is revealed, the son of destruction, who oppose and exalts himself above every so-called god or object of worship, so that he takes his seat in the temple of God, displaying himself as being God (2nd Thessalonians 2:3b-4).

And, as we saw in the analysis of the 2nd Thessalonian 2 passage, this

---

[87] For example, see Arthur E. Bloomfield, *The End of the Days: The Prophecies of Daniel Explained* (Minneapolis, Minnesota, 1961), 218; cf. Benware, 259, where he elaborates "the Antichrist... will then set up an idol of himself in the temple."

happens *before* "our gathering together with [Jesus]" (v.1), *before* the Day of the Lord (v. 2). Matthew 24 confirms this chronology.

> "Immediately *after* the tribulation of those days the sun will be darkened, and the moon will not give its light, and the stars will fall from the sky, and the powers of the heavens will be shaken..." (Matthew 24:29; emphasis added).

First, notice that these celestial events occur *following* the "tribulation of those days," i.e. the great tribulation spoken of in the previous verse 21, which is followed with additional information about it in verses 22-28. Notice also that verse 29 is a synopsis description of the trumpet and bowl judgments of Revelation, described in a wrap-up verse (15:1) as "the wrath of God."

What we have here, then, is that there are three distinct events, each with its own distinct elements: (1) tribulation, (2) great tribulation, and (3) wrath of God. To describe them *all* as The Great Tribulation *is unscriptural*; there is not one verse or passage in the Bible that says they are one-and-the-same. Nor, for that matter, is there anything that even implies this. Yet, as we began to discuss in the last chapter, virtually every Evangelical scholar, Pre-tribulational or otherwise, states that these events (and terms) are interchangeable when they set up their Daniel 9:24-27 seven-year timeline.[88]

Further, prophetic scholars—regardless of their view on the timing of the Rapture, but particularly those who are Pre-tribulational—have consistently remarked on how the events described in Matthew 24 are perfectly matched with those of Revelation 6, the Seal Judgments. The first seal releases a false Christ (with a bow instead of the sword held by the real Christ [cf. Revelation 19:15]); the second releases war; the third, famine; the fourth, a *mega* war ("over a fourth of the earth," v. 8); the fifth, persecution; the sixth, "the sun became black as sackcloth... the whole moon became like blood; and the stars of the sky fell to the earth... and the sky was split apart like a scroll"—similar wording to Matthew 24:29. How do the "kings of the earth and the great men and commanders and the rich and the strong

---

[88]   For example, see Allen Beechick, *The PreTribulational Rapture* (Denver, Colorado: Accent Books, 1980), 8ff; John F. Walvoord, *Rapture Question*, 42-44; and LaHaye, *Revelation*, front-matter; amongst others.

and every slave and free man" (6:15) describe these celestial events? "...for the great day of [God's] wrath has come; and who is able to stand?" (v. 17).

Using this chronology, what happens *after* that?

> "Then... they will see the Son of Man coming on the clouds of the sky with power and great glory." (Matthew 24:30).

This is the revelation of Jesus to the entire world, and, as we've seen from the analysis of 2nd Thessalonians 2, it is the Day of the Lord event. Thus, the Day of the Lord is also a separate occurrence, a fourth event, if you will, with its own distinct element. For this reason its term should also not be used interchangeably with the other three.

What can we conclude from this? First of all, the church can expect to see the Antichrist violate the Jewish Temple, as Paul made explicitly clear in 2nd Thessalonians 2. This will ignite the *mega* tribulation, an event linked to Satan through the Antichrist, *not God*. In no way does this violate the promise in 1st Thessalonians 5:9 that we are "not destined for [God's] wrath." We are not. But that wrath occurs after the *mega* tribulation, *Satan's* wrath, as we've see here.

What separates this wrath from all previous ones of Satan, i.e., What makes the *mega* tribulation "great"? What separates a "regular" tribulation from this "great" one? To answer that will provide insight not only in to what the *mega* tribulation is, but when it might occur, and answer the last key question *why*.

At first one would think that martyrdom would be considered great tribulation. Human beings have been tortured and murdered in a variety of horrendous ways. But, as we've already seen, if the church at Smyrna in Revelation 2 is the standard, God considers martyrdom part of "regular" tribulation. And Jesus confirms that martyrdom of the past was not *mega* tribulation:

> "...*then* there will be a *mega* tribulation, such as has not occurred since the beginning of the world until now..." (Matthew 24:21; emphasis added).

If everything that has gone before is not *mega* tribulation, what, then, is? What *is* the condition of *mega* tribulation? Jesus gives that in Matthew 24:

"Therefore, when you see the abomination of desolation... then let those who are in Judea flee to the mountains; let him who is on the housetop not go down to get the things out that are in his house; and let him who is in the field not turn back to get his cloak. But woe to those who are with child and to those who nurse babe in those days. But pray that your flight may not be in winter, or on a Sabbath.... And unless those days had been cut short, no life would have been saved... (Matthew 24:15-20,22).

There are two conditions described here: (1) the *mega* tribulation catches people, especially those "in Judea," unaware (though one would also think worldwide as they too are caught off guard; hence, those unprepared have no time for *any* preparation); and (2) the destruction that follows, for which they are not prepared, becomes *worldwide*: "unless those days had been cut short, *no life* would have been saved..."

It is critical at this point to note who is involved in this destruction: the Antichrist (v. 15), who we know is being acted upon by Satan:

The great dragon was thrown down, the serpent of old who is called the devil and Satan... Woe to the earth and the sea, because the devil has come down to you, having great (*mega*) wrath... And when the dragon saw that he was thrown down to the earth, he persecuted the woman [Israel] who gave birth to the male child [Jesus]... And the woman fl[ed] into the wilderness... And the dragon was enraged with the woman, and went off to make war with the rest of her offspring, who keep the commandments of God and hold to the testimony of Jesus. And the dragon gave him [the Antichrist] his power and his throne and great authority... And it was given to him to make war with the saints and to overcome them; and authority over every tribe and people and tongue and nation was given to him... If anyone is destined for captivity, to captivity he goes; if anyone kills with the sword, with the sword he must be killed. Here is the perseverance and faith of the saints (Revelation 12:9, 12, 13, 14, 17; 13:2, 7, 9).

Notice the elements here: (1) the Antichrist is given the power of Satan; (2) who has *mega* wrath (creating *mega* tribulation for those to whom he is opposed) and thus; (3) Satan, through the Antichrist, attacks Israel (the woman)—which proves unsuccessful: "let those in Judea flee"; then (4) the Antichrist turns on believers ("who hold to the testimony of Jesus"), and as there are Christians throughout the world this would be "worldwide" ("authority over every... nation"); which leads to (5) captivity and murder, adverse actions through which the saints are encouraged to persevere.

It is *extremely* important to notice this is not *God's* wrath, but Satan's. This fits exactly with our previous observation that the mega tribulation is caused by Satan, making it separate and distinct from God's Wrath which is to follow.

Returning to the first condition, that of people being unprepared, we saw from our analysis of 1ˢᵗ Thessalonians 5 that the unsaved would be taken unawares:

> While they are saying "Peace and safety!" then sudden destruction will come upon them (v. 3).

But those Christians living apart from their faith, i.e. "in darkness" (vv.4-5) just like the unsaved, will also be blindsided:

> "I know your deeds, that you [church at Sardis] have a name that you are alive ["Christian"], but you are dead.... If you do not wake up [*gregoreuo*], be vigilant (as to how you should be living out your faith)], I [Jesus] will come like a thief, and you will not know at what hour I will come upon you." (Revelation 3:1,3).

> "I have this against you [Thyatira church], that you tolerate the woman Jezebel [a false prophetess], who... teaches and leads My bond-servants [Christians] astray, so that they commit acts of [spiritual] immorality... Behold, I will cast her upon a bed of sickness, and those who commit [spiritual] adultery with her into great [*mega*] tribulation..." (Revelation 2:20,22).

By contrast, believers living in their faith are not taken by surprise:

> But you brethren, are not in darkness, that the day should overtake you like a their; for you are sons of light and sons of day. We are not of night, nor of darkness; so then let us... be

alert [*gregoreuo*, vigilant (as to how we live out our faith)] (1st Thessalonians5:4-6).

"But you have a few people in Sardis who have not soiled their garments; and they will walk with Me in white; for they are worthy" (Revelation 2:4).

"But I say to you, the rest who are in Thyatira, who do not hold this teaching [of the false prophetess Jezebel], who have not known the deep things of Satan—I place no other burden on you" (Revelation 2:24).

This provides these believers, who have discerned the times (Matthew 16:3) because they are living "in the light" (exercising their faith), with the opportunity to prepare beforehand for the events they know are coming.

Yes, believers will still face captivity and martyrdom. What generation of believers hasn't? This is, as we saw above, the "normal" condition for those who believe in Jesus Christ throughout the Church Age. But the discerning believers spoken of here are clearly *not* blindsided. In fact, the *vigilant* were already preparing for that very eventuality... or, if they were wise, should have been.

Not surprisingly, all of what we have just described is linked to the issue of Imminence. The previous analysis of that subject had addressed all of the necessary issues except for two, both heavily related to the Great Tribulation. Let's look at the first, the restriction that God has Self-imposed on the return of Christ for His Church:

For I do not want you, brethren, to be uninformed of this mystery [a previously undisclosed Scriptural fact], lest you be wise in your own estimation, that a partial hardening has happened to Israel until the fullness of the Gentiles has come in; and thus all Israel will be saved (Romans 11:25-26a).

Notice that God has set a restriction that has prevented imminence these past two millennia. For His own purpose (hence, a *mystery*), He has set aside Israel, allowing a select number of Gentiles to be in their place. At some point in the future Israel will be placed back into God's plan, but not until the correct number of Gentiles have been saved. And, until that exact number is reached, *Jesus can't come back.*

Although we won't know when that number is reached, which could happen at any moment in our lifetime, it is still a factor that has limited an imminent return. Any discussion of imminency must take this Scriptural fact into account: *Imminent* may not necessarily be *immediate.* So far it hasn't been for almost 2,000 years.

The other issue of Imminence is that of the teaching of the signs. If the Church is *not* suppose to be looking for signs, how can they possibly discern the times? To ignore the signs given in Scripture, some by Jesus Himself, helps create the strong possibility that one knowingly ignores the indicators of Christ's return. This has the strong possibility to leave one unprepared for the events of the Great Tribulation as we have indicated above. On the other hand, if the signs have importance to the Church, we *need* to be so informed of them. It will keep us "in the light" so that we are not caught "unawares."

The last issue, which deals with preparation for the coming Great Tribulation, is that of Christian suffering. Let's look at the Biblical witnesses to that:

> Since Christ has suffered in the flesh, arm yourselves also with the same purpose (1st Peter 4:14).

> Have this attitude in yourselves which was also in Christ Jesus, who... emptied Himself... [and] humbled Himself by being obedient to the point of death (Philippians 2:5,8).

> Although He was a Son, He learned obedience from things He suffered, and [thus] was made perfect (Hebrews 5:8-9a).

> For to you it has been granted for Christ's sake, not only to believe in Him, but also to suffer for His sake (1st Peter 4:19).

> The Spirit testifies with our spirit that we are children of God, and if children, heirs also... with Christ, *if* indeed we suffer with Him in order that we may also be glorified with Him (Romans 8:16-17; emphasis added).

Suffer hardship with me, as a good soldier of Christ Jesus (2nd Timothy 2:3).

What do these verses say should be the mindset of a Christian in regards to suffering, especially the possible suffering of *mega* tribulation? Does the need for that mindset require advanced preparation? What is *your* mindset, currently? Do you have a need for preparation?

The American church, which has been blessed beyond measure, has not *suffered*, as say those in *Fox's Book of Martyrs*. The American Christian has become soft as a result, more wanting to dodge suffering than to embrace it, especially embrace it "as a joy."

If the Church here in the U.S. is to face the *mega* tribulation, there is every indication it is unprepared. Many deeply committed Christians are going to be significantly blindsided. They will be unprepared for suffering.

How many are prepared to be imprisoned for their faith? die for their faith? Christian leaders and pastors, regardless of their perspective of the timing of the Rapture, should be preparing their flocks for this, though most are not. *When* the tribulation hits, it will be devastating to those unprepared—making it, indeed, a *mega* tribulation for them in ways not experienced by those who *are* prepared.

CHAPTER 10

CONCLUSIONS

The prudent man sees the evil and hides himself, but the naïve go on,
and are punished for it (Proverbs 22:3).

So, what can we conclude from all that we've looked at regarding the cornerstones and girders of Pre-Tribulationism? It can be seen that this view of the timing of the Rapture is not as solid as it first appears to be. There are definite weaknesses that obviously might not be easily seen at first glance. That is not to say a Pre-tribulational Rapture is not possible; God is sovereign and can time it as He pleases. As it is currently being portrayed, however, that view has definite shortcomings.

On that note, we have presented here Pre-tribulationalism from the writings of its mainstream scholars. Three have been especially chosen because of their acknowledged stature as proponents of that view. J. Dwight Pentecost's *Things To Come* is the quintessential writing on the Pre-tribulational position. It is an excellent, scholarly look at all aspects of Endtime prophecy. Further, that work is quoted, paraphrased or acknowledged by almost every Pre-tribulational scholar since it first appeared in the late 1950s. Hal Lindsey's *The Late Great Planet Earth* was, next to the Bible itself, the greatest selling book of the 1970s decade. For many Americans it was their first glimpse into what appeared to them previously to be the complicated area of prophecy. Lastly, Tim LaHaye became known worldwide, and especially here in the United States, for his *Left Behind* series.

For name recognition alone, these three authors have been cited herein. But, that is not the only reason: each of them presents a clear, understandable grasp of Pre-tribulationalism. Their avoidance of "heavy theology," both in wording and subject content, makes it more easily understood by the reader. In this way, the weaknesses presented throughout this section should be just as easily understood by the lay reader. And that understanding is critical because the consequences are, indeed, life-or-death.

We've seen, beginning with a look at the Blessed Hope and continuing throughout, the possibility of those who espouse a Pre-tribulational viewpoint to, in many ways, be looking in the wrong direction relative to Endtime events. As a result, the searing question raised is: What will happen to the faiths of Pre-tribulationalists if they encounter tribulation, even great tribulation (note, lower case) before the Rapture when they are expecting to be taken away, avoiding it completely? Because, in relation to the Blessed Hope, there is the possibility their minds are "completely fixed" on the wrong hope, the potential catastrophic impact on the faith of *millions* of Pre-tribulational American Christians is tremendously haunting. A wrong understanding of the other elements presented just compound this problem.

By demonstrating the weaknesses in the Pre-tribulational view, it is hoped that those holding to it will see there is, at the least, the *possibility* it may not occur as they expect. For that reason, it seems wise to plan accordingly.

Having said that, one must consider who would want the Church unprepared? Would Jesus? Why then would He tell us "Behold, I have told you in advance" (Matthew 24:25)? The question is: If the best case does not materialize, who will be the most satisfied? Jesus? One would think not.

With that in mind, the age-old adage of "hope for the best, but prepare for the worst" is as true today as ever, especially with the ever-darkening of the world around us. How can one present the best-case scenario, and only the best-case scenario, and then walk away from the discussion? *What if the worst does, in fact, happen?*

It is hoped Pre-tribulationalists will ponder this... and act accordingly. Each of us should be preparing for the *mega* tribulation; spiritual, mental, and physical preparation. Just in case. Those that are not preparing might one day find themselves in definite peril.

PART II:

PRE-DETERMINARIANISM

INTRODUCTION

For we shall all stand before the judgment seat of God... so then each one of us shall give account of himself to God... (Romans 14:10, 12).

Pre-determinarianism is the belief that one is foreordained beforehand, i.e. pre-destined, to an outcome or, often in literature, a fate.[89] As the term will be explored in Part II, there are two primary applications.

The first is more easily addressed. There is the widely held view amongst many Christians that because now they are saved they are foreordained to avoid any future judgment. This is most often demonstrated by them as they live a worldly life. Paul addresses those who hold such a view in 1st Corinthians 3:

> I could not speak to you as spiritual men, but as to men of flesh [i.e., like the unsaved]... for you are still fleshly.... [A]re you not walking like mere [unsaved] men? (vv. 1, 3).

Jude adds:

---

[89]   Woolf, 905. Pre-destinarianism has been chosen over the more common "pre-destiny" to avoid solely linking this presentation with Calvinism, often called Reformed Theology. There are those who hold to part of Calvin's teachings who would not identify themselves as strictly "Calvinists." Pre-destinarianism, then, is a better fit because it is broader in scope, which is the purpose here. Further, adherents of Reformed Theology are not all in agreement to the entire five points of Calvin's teachings; there are 2-point, 3-point, etc. "Calvinists." This makes the concept of "pre-destiny" all the more confining, and so it has been avoided here in order to present the broader concept being discussed. Along those same lines, a secular definition has been chosen over a theological source to further broaden the concept of foreordination.

Ungodly persons who turn the grace of our God into licentiousness [loose living] (v. 4).

Paul then concludes the issue:

[W]here sin increased, grace abounded all the more.... What shall we say then? Are we to continue in sin that grace might increase? May it never be! (Romans 5:20; 6:1-2a).

We will explore this issue in more detail, especially as we get into Part II. But, suffice it to say here, though those who have accepted Christ as Savior are now foreordained to an eternal relationship with God, it does not exclude them from future discipline for their ungodly living. This may come as a complete shock to them when it occurs, especially because they are blindsided and, thus, unprepared.

———— ✦✦✦✦✦ ————

[I]n the later times some will fall away from the faith... (1ˢᵗ Timothy 4:1).

The second aspect of Pre-determinarianism is that those who have been saved through their belief in Christ as Savior believe they are absolutely foreordained to persevering in that faith until either their death or Jesus returns to rapture them out of this world.

This second aspect is definitely more complicated and will be looked at in-depth in Part I. Because in their belief the issue of perseverance is so closely linked to other aspects related to it, all of these will be considered in our analysis. If a saved person can fall away from the faith, and they believe this an impossibility, they might be caught unawares, and thus unprepared, for what is coming.

With that possibility, that each of these two groups might be caught unaware—thus unprepared—this would prove the worst-case scenario for them. The intent, then, is for them to see the weaknesses in their beliefs, which should cause them to consider preparing... just in case.

Thus, we will explore the basic tenets of Pre-determinarianism, in the chapters of Section 1, with special attention to the issue of Perseverance. If this belief proves faulty, the consequences could prove dire. In the chapters of Section 2, we will explore those consequences in detail.

Throughout, the reader will be given the opportunity to decide for him- or herself whether they fit the *worst* worst-case scenario.

SECTION 1

SANCTIFICATION, NOT JUSTIFICATION...

Chapter 11

OVERVIEW: FREEWILL

"This is My Son, My Chosen One" (Luke 9:35).

First impressions, as they say, are lasting. In Scripture, the First Mention of something is usually a trend setter. Special note should be taken of things first mentioned as they usually give insight into what is to follow.

So, let's begin by looking at the very first thing mentioned once the creation narrative is complete.

The creation narrative begins in Genesis 1:1 and concludes in 2:15. The very next act of God is to command Adam to refrain from eating of the tree of the knowledge of good and evil (2:16-17). Whatever period of time occurs until Chapter 3, be it a second, minute, hour, or eon of time, from verses 2:16-17 on, man willingly is obedient; he chooses to refrain from eating of that tree.

In chapter 3, however, Adam becomes disobedient. One of the main points of that disobedience is that he is not directly influenced by God in his choice. Because God directly communed with Adam from 2:15: "Then the Lord God took the man and put him into the garden... saying to him..." God had every right to intervene during the moment of testing in chapter 3, but did not. Adam knew what was expected of him and was given the opportunity to choose to obey. God did not attempt to influence Adam at his moment of decision.

As an aside, in Christ's own temptation (Matthew 4:1-11), which occurred *three* times, not once as in Adam's case, God did not intervene either.

This allowed Jesus, like the opportunity given to the first Adam, to choose to be obedient. Unlike Adam, Jesus *was* obedient: "He [Jesus]... becam[e] obedient to the point of death, even death on a cross" (Philippians 2:8).

So, in God's dealing with man, He has given man the gift of free will, allowing him to choose to be obedient. Or, as in Adam's case, reject to do so. This is seen throughout Scripture, culminating in Revelation 9:20-21, where men still reject God even after the horrendous events of His judgment. In that passage it states that "the rest of mankind... did not repent..." The word "did" indicates they chose not to do so. If there was an outside force preventing them it would have been more honest to say "they *could* not repent."

It is important to repeat here: Voluntary choice to obey is a core value in the relationship between God and man; a value initiated by God at the outset of man's creation.

In contrast, however, we also see throughout Scripture that *God chooses*. He personally selects individuals, but always with the view of them being chosen for a specific task. Beginning as early as Genesis 5, God chooses Enoch (vv. 22-24) and brings him to heaven without Enoch having to undergo death.[90] In the very next chapter He chooses Noah who, with his family, will survive the Great Flood. This choosing continues also into the Book of Revelation for we see in chapter 7 God's choice of the 144,000 from the Jewish tribes... except that of Dan. Another choice, if you will; a choice of rejection (vv. 3-8).

But, of course, the most important choice occurred before the foundation of the world—before God even began to create. We are told that Jesus Himself was chosen by God (the Father): "This is My Son, My Chosen One" (Luke 9:35; see also Isaiah 53 and John 1).

Scripture obviously teaches free will, and yet, at the same time, God's sovereignty in His, God's, own selections. To teach only one and exclude the other is to fail to present the full purpose of God (Acts 20:27). But, how can this conundrum be resolved: man's freewill, yet God's choice?

Let's start by looking to Jesus.

---

[90] Notice Enoch's name means "discipline"—an indication of his character.

CHAPTER 12

CHOSEN

Jesus said… "He who has seen Me has seen the Father…" (John 14:9).

If there is any evidence in Scripture regarding resolution of the apparent conflict between free will and election, it will be with Jesus. He stated clearly that He cannot act on His own, but only what the Father does:

> Jesus… was saying to them, "Truly, truly, I say to you, the Son can do nothing of Himself, unless it is something He sees the Father doing; for whatever the Father does, these things the Son also does in like manner" (John 5:19).

Whatever Jesus does will be an insight into the character and mind of God Himself, especially regarding this issue.

And the resolution is apparent… and immediate.

Jesus again and again during His ministry presented Himself to the crowds of Israel (e.g., Mark 3:7; Luke 7:11). We are told over-and-over that "many believed" (John 2:23, 7:31, 8:30, 10:42, 11:45, 12:42). Here we have *the* Gospel—living right in front of them—who is "proclaiming the gospel of the kingdom" (Matthew 4:23), of which He is King (John 18:37). What is apparent is that not once are we told that those who "believed" *were chosen.*

Let's confirm this with two prominent examples.

In John chapter 3, Nicodemus goes to Jesus, not the other way around (vv. 1-2). Jesus talks to Nicodemus, and it appears through this action alone that Nicodemus eventually believes in Christ (John 7:50; 19:39). There is absolutely no mention in Scripture that God chose Nicodemus as the cause to bring him to his faith. Having been presented with, literally, the Living Word, Nicodemus, of his own free will, eventually believed.

Similarly, in the very next chapter, Jesus talks to the woman at the well (4:7-42). Scripture states clearly, "...many more believed *because of His word*; and they were saying... 'We have heard for ourselves and know that this One is indeed the Savior of the world' " (vv. 41-42; emphasis added). There is no mention of these "many" being chosen. Like Nicodemus, they freely chose to believe based on hearing The Word.

Both of these examples confirm Scripture: "Faith comes from hearing, and hearing by the Word of Christ" (Romans 10:17; in these cases, literally)... There is no mention that faith comes from being "chosen."

We must conclude that those who believe, then, are part of a General Invitation (*kaleo*, to call, bid, invite) to salvation: "Jesus sa[id], "If any man is thirsty, let him come to Me and drink" (John 7:37); "Come...Let the one who wishes take the water of life without cost" (Revelation 22:17); "Ho! Everyone who thirsts, come to the waters... Come, buy... without cost" (Isaiah 55:1); "*Whoever will*... (Romans 10:13).

Further, many of those who believed began to willingly follow him, and be discipled (became "learners" of Him and His ways). These people were called His "followers" (Mark 4:10, 9:41) and "disciples" (Luke 6:17, John 6:66). But, again, nowhere in Scripture does it say they were chosen. These Biblical passages make it clear they, in fact, did the choosing.

In contrast to the General Call, there was a Specific Call: "And walking by the Sea of Galilee, He [Jesus] saw two brothers, Simon, who was called Peter, and Andrew his brother... And He said to them, "Follow Me, and I will make you fishers of men" Matthew 4:18-19.

Notice, Jesus specifically makes a personal, one-on-one request that He does not make when addressing the crowds. Further, in the Specific Call, Jesus calls the person for a specific purpose. In this case, to be "fishers of men." Again, not something provided to those of a General Call.

And though not all are given this Specific Call, The Twelve who are, are cited as being told they too will be fishers of men. All eventually do—even Judas: "He [Jesus] summoned The Twelve and began to send them out in pairs... And they went out and preached that men should repent" (Mark 6:7, 12). Hence, The Twelve given the Specific Call *are called for a* specific *purpose.* That purpose not only entails ministry in the here-and-now, but looks beyond and into the future of Christ's Kingdom. We are told that The Twelve were destined to rule the twelve tribes of Israel in Jesus' Millennial Kingdom (Matthew 19:28).

There is another aspect of the Specific Call not rendered to the General: "Jesus spoke many things to… the great multitudes… in parables… as they were able to hear it [some understood, most did not]…. And as soon as He was alone, his followers [i.e., those followers who were present], along with The Twelve, came and said to Him, 'Why do You speak to them in parables?' And He answered and said to them, *'To you it has been granted to know the mysteries of the kingdom of heaven, but to them it has not been granted'* " (Matthew 13:1,3,10-11; Mark 4:10, 33; emphasis added).

To those receiving the Specific Call, "inside" information is provided. And note, not all of Jesus' "followers" are given an understanding of the parable's meaning for, obviously, not all are present at this specific preaching. *But definitely The Twelve are.* This occurs again in verses 36-52.

To reinforce this, two additional instances must be cited. In Matthew 16:16-19, Peter declares that Jesus is "the Christ, the Son of the living God." Jesus responds to this by saying, "Blessed are you Simon… because flesh and blood [i.e., the thought process] did not reveal this to you, but My Father who is in heaven." There are two things of importance here. First, Peter, *one of The Twelve,* is given this knowledge. Who else is identified in the four gospels as ever proclaiming this "inside information"? No one. (John's declaration of it in 20:31 occurs about AD 90, roughly 60 years after this event.) Which leads to the second observation: Of The Twelve, how many of them are partial to this inside information while Jesus walked the earth? Scripture identifies, only Peter! (Also see below.)

The second instance needed to be cited is John, chapters 13-17, events and discussions during the Last Supper. Bible reading Christians take these chapters for granted because of their easy availability. But to the first century Christian, especially those who lived during the time of Jesus, what person knew—or even had access to—this information? John makes it clear that only The Twelve who were present were given this information, *information vital to Christian growth!* Yet, apart from John's Gospel completed in approximately AD 90 and taking years to disseminate, this information is unavailable to the masses of "followers" of the General-Call Assembly during, at the least, the first century AD.

The point made here in these examples is that the "General Assembly" is not privy to information that The Twelve are given... *by divine design*: "*... to them it has not been granted...*"

In conjunction with this, although The Twelve are given "inside" instruction and insights, there is even a divine division amongst *them*. In Mark 13 Jesus related, in what is often-called the Olivet Discourse, the future events preceding His return to earth to set up His kingdom. Mark tells us only Peter, James, John, and Andrew "were [there] questioning Him privately" (v.3). Thus, this vital information is not given to the other Twelve.

Further, at the Transfiguration, only Peter, James, and John are present (Matthew 17:1). The Lord's glory is withheld from even Andrew of the apparent "inner circle."

All of this leads to an inescapable fact: Certain members of The Twelve will sit in positions of greater authority than the others in Christ's Kingdom. As Jesus confirmed, "To sit on My right or on My left... is for those whom it has been prepared" (Mark 10:40). At least two will sit in those honored positions. Notice too, this is according to God's foreknowledge and foreordination because already, at Jesus' First Advent, it: "...has been prepared."

This leads to the inevitable question: Prepared exactly *when?* We will see shortly: "before the foundation of the world" (Ephesians 1:4).

But we digress. There are clear conclusions that can be drawn from those who receive a Specific Call, i.e., being "chosen." First of all, they are called to be sanctified—in the fullest sense of that word. They have been "set apart" for a specific purpose, one that deals with the here-and-now and one that will be used later in Christ's Millennial Kingdom. Additionally, they are being given the opportunity to be more "holy," living a life better, "more righteous," according to God's will—*for which that will is more fully revealed to them than others.*

Herein lays the issue of being chosen—i.e., election. Jesus clearly demonstrated that those He has chosen have been done so that (1) they may be sanctified, in the sense of being set apart for ministry, but also (2) that they have been sanctified, in the sense of being progressively made more holy. This is done so that they are better equipped for the special ministry to which they *have* been chosen.

Scripture itself clearly confirms the latter as: "God has chosen you," Paul writes believers in Thessalonica, "for salvation through sanctification" (2nd Thessalonians 2:13). This "salvation" is, as James writes, "of the soul" (1:21) i.e. the removal of "all filthiness and all that remains of wickedness" as a result of "the Word implanted." This is in harmony with Paul who, writing to the Ephesians, alerts them to a being "sanctified"—"cleansed by the washing of the water of the Word" (5:26).

And *when* were they chosen for this sanctification, in both senses of that word? To paraphrase Ephesians 1:4, "From the beginning."

The apostle Peter confirms this very fact. In his first epistle he writes to those who "were chosen according to the foreknowledge of God the Father, by the sanctifying work of the Spirit that [they] may obey Jesus" (v. 1:1). Those who are chosen have been done so by God as a result of His foreknowledge—from the beginning—that they may be sanctified—made holy—and thus be guided to more fully obey Jesus.

Election, then, is not an issue of justification, but of *sanctification*. To view it otherwise is to be in error.

Again, let's look to Jesus. As a result of His preaching about the kingdom of heaven: "…the kingdom of heaven is at hand" (Matthew 4:17), many believed in His name (John 2:23, et al). That name they believe in was "Jesus," which means *Jehovah saves*: "You shall call His name Jesus, for it is He who will save His people from their sins" (Matthew 1:21). When the jailer asked, "What must I do to be saved [justified before God without sin]?" he is told, "Believe in the Lord Jesus and you shall be saved…" (Acts 16:30-31). We need do nothing more than *believe* for justification.

However, sanctification, what Peter in his first epistle (1:9), and James in his epistle, (1:21) called the "salvation of the soul," *requires work on our part*: Jesus said to his disciples, "If anyone wishes to come after Me, let him deny himself, and take up his cross [be willing to sacrifice], and *follow Me*…" (Matthew 16:24; emphasis added). To follow Jesus, *obedience*—willing to forsake what one would like to do [deny oneself] in order to do what Jesus wants of him or her, is *sanctification*, not justification.

In justification Jesus has done all the work that is needed to be done. In sanctification *we must work*, relying upon the strength of the Holy Spirit.

As committed Reformed theologian R.C. Sproul noted, "Sanctification... demands the cooperation of the regenerate believer. We are called *to work* to grow in grace. *We are to work hard*, resisting sin unto blood if necessary..."[91]

Though those of the General Call can and should be sanctified—made holy through their obedience—by their choosing to do so, The Twelve, being chosen by Jesus—"I know the ones I have chosen" (John 13:18)—will be *most* sanctified because of the "inside" information provided to them. This is for a specific purpose, as has been previously shown, ultimately that they rule the twelve tribes of Israel.

Once this principle is understood, enigmatic passages of Scripture come into sharper view. Take for example Romans 9:18-23:

> He has mercy on whom He desires, and He hardens whom He desires. You will say to me then, "Why does He still find fault? For who resists His will?" On the contrary, who are you, O man, who answers back to God? The thing molded will not say to the molder, "Why did you make me like this," will it? Or does not the potter have a right over the clay, to make from the same lump one vessel for honorable use and another for common use? What if God, although willing to demonstrate His wrath and to make His power known, endured with much patience vessels of wrath prepared for destruction? And He did so to make known the riches of His glory upon vessels of mercy, which He prepared beforehand for glory.

Most expositors see only two distinct peoples represented here: The "honorable" and those of "common use."[92] Hence, their line of reasoning goes, the "dishonorable" are then spoken of as the "vessels of wrath."

However, knowing that the chosen are for sanctification, we then see *three* distinctions here. The "honorable," the "common use," and the "vessels of wrath." Notice that the Greek word *attimia* literally means "not honorable." It can also be translated "less honorable." Thus, the New American Standard Version translates it as "common use."

There are those who are chosen for high honor, such as The

---

91   R. C. Sproul, *Chosen By God* (Wheaton, Illinois: Tyndal House Publishers, Inc., 1986), 158; emphasis added.

92   translated "dishonorable" in the King James Version.

Twelve—including very high honor, the two who will sit directly beside Jesus—and those of "less honor"—the General Assembly. Lastly, there are those "prepared for destruction," whom God has "endured with much patience"—He has given them every opportunity to not be vessels of wrath (see The Universal Call).

A second conclusion is that those known by God who will accept His son—those *foreknown* (Ephesians 1:4)—are the ones from which He will choose, *the chosen.* This is contained in the very word *church.* In the original Greek, the word church is *ekklesia.* The word literally means out (*ek*) called (*kletos*), and can thus be translated "called-out ones." Called out from what? The simple answer, demonstrated by Jesus, is called-out of the "called."

God's foreknowledge of every human being is indeed a demonstration of His omniscience—His ability to "know all." But an even greater demonstration of that omniscience is that He not only knows all human beings, but knows what their choice will be concerning His Son.

Thus, the omniscient God who knows all, including knowing those who will embrace His Son, who respond to the Call (*kletos*), are Called-out (*ekklesia*) for a specific purpose. The foreknowledge demonstrated by God is seen in The Twelve's response to being called-out. Notice they respond "immediately" (Matthew 4:20, 22; 8:3). God knew they would! (Though it can be said for some others who are Specifically Called, they respond *eventually*, but they *do* respond, showing God's foreknowledge that they would; see Jeremiah 1:6-9.)

And because God foreknows they will accept His Son, on the surface it appears that His grace is, in John Calvin's words, "irresistible." Whether immediately accepted, or in the case of Jeremiah (and Paul, for that matter), eventually accepted, the person receiving the grace of the Call seems ultimately unwilling to reject it. In the words of the American culture: An offer one can't refuse.

The concept of irresistibility is correct, but the view is wrong. The grace is not so much irresistible—which connotes coercion—but, because of the person themself, is more like Wonderfully, Openly, *Willing*—the WOW Factor—a fact an all-knowing God would know beforehand would be the response.

And, again, this being called-out is to sanctification, set apart for a specific purpose, not justification. As Paul writes

> Paul, an apostle of Christ Jesus by the will of God... when He
> set me apart even from my mother's womb... (Ephesians 1:1;
> Galatians 1:15).

The third conclusion is that, like the division amongst The Twelve, there is even a division amongst the church, the out-called. In Revelation 2 and 3, where the seven letters are addressed to seven "churches" (*ekklessia*), only those who overcome are granted to rule and reign with Jesus in His Kingdom (2:26-27; 3:21; see The Overcomers). Note that the person who rules and reigns with a king is his queen. She has all of his power and authority and can only be over-ruled by the king himself. Thus, and contrary to popular teaching, only overcomers will be The Bride (see The Bride).

All of this can be seen in one of the few passages in the New Testament that deals with the Eternal State, Hebrews 12:22-24:

> You have come to Mount Zion and to the city of the living God,
> the heavenly Jerusalem, and to myriads of angels, to the general
> assembly and church of the firstborn who are enrolled in heaven,
> and to God, the Judge of all, and to the spirits of the righteous
> made perfect, and to Jesus, the mediator of a new covenant...

We know that this deals with the Eternal State because it states clearly it deals with "the heavenly Jerusalem." This city only occurs in the last two chapters of the Book of Revelation (21-22) and describes what will occur when the 1,000-year kingdom of Christ has come to an end.

From this passage in Hebrews we learn the inhabitants of that city. There are six individuals or groups who are so described. They include (1) the "myriads of the [faithful] angels"; (2) the "general assembly"; (3) the "church of the firstborn"; (4) "God, Judge of all"; (5) the "spirits of the righteous made perfect; and lastly, (6) "Jesus, the mediator of a new covenant."

Let's rearrange them for discussion simplicity.

(1) God, the Father and the Spirit, because...

(2) Jesus, the Second Person of the Trinity, is named specifically;

(3) angels, the full "myriad" of those that remained faithful when Lucifer rebelled;

(4) spirits of the righteous made perfect is generally accepted as "believers of the Old Testament times";[93]

(5) church of the firstborn (discussed below); and

(6) general assembly (also below)

One of the interesting things here is that those present in the Eternal State are described as not just "the church," which would be all-encompassing of those saved in the "Church Age," but rather the "church of the firstborn."

In the Old Testament we are told that the firstborn received a double portion of the inheritance (Deuteronomy 21:16-17). Other siblings receive their portion of the inheritance, but the firstborn was to receive twice as much, and usually the choicest.[94]

The implication of the "church—the called-out ones—of the first born" is that there is a group of individuals who will be preeminent in the Eternal State, set above others with more—and better—inheritance. Again, a careful reading of Revelation 2 and 3 indicates this is so of only the overcomers. Notice also in Revelation 17:14 the description of those accompanying Jesus at His return as "the called and chosen and faithful." Here is the Golden Description of those receiving a double portion; those not only chosen, but who were faithful thereafter.

This leads to the final group of people in the Eternal State, the "general assembly." This group, separately described from "the church," *has* to be all the saved of the New Testament (and those who die "in Christ" during the Millennium) who have accepted Jesus, thus receiving their portion of inheritance, eternal life, but were not chosen by God for a specific role in Christ's kingdom. The term General Assembly is a confirmation that there are those who receive (only) a General Call, in contrast to those of the church of the firstborn, who attain their higher position as a result of divine sovereignty... and their being faithful. (No doubt, the "overcomers.")

To sum up, then, election, being chosen, is for the purpose of sanctification. Those who are not thus chosen from the General Assembly, are saved, but not chosen for leadership in Christ's Millennial Kingdom.

---

[93] as stated in the *Ryrie Study Bible*, note on v. 23.

[94] see for example Jacob's final blessings upon his twelve sons, Genesis 48-49.

The Chosen Twelve, who will rule over the twelve tribes of Israel, are an example.[95]

Notice again, these Twelve were God's choice, based on His sovereignty. He chose from disciples *who numbered more than the Twelve* (Luke 6:13), disciples *who were already following Jesus* and, hence, those who would be saved. It is offered that, based on His omniscience, God knew who would make such a choice to follow Jesus and so His, God's choice of their *sanctification*, was done before He even began to create.

Jesus' ministry here on earth during His First Advent, demonstrated in His activities involving choice, clearly establishes this, thus confirming it.

---

[95] It is not germane to the issue here to determine who will fill Judas' vacancy, but it *will* be filled as there is every implication twelve apostles will judge the twelve tribes in Christ's Millennial Kingdom (Matthew 19:28). Having said that, however, this writer believes it will be Paul, who was chosen by God (Ephesians 1:1), hence Jesus, as were the other eleven remaining disciples (Mark 3:13); Matthius, on the other hand, was chosen by men tossing lots (Acts 1:26).

Chapter 13

OVERCOMERS

He who has an ear, let him hear what the Spirit says to the churches. To him who overcomes... (Revelation 2:7, 11, 17, 26, 29; 3:5, 6, 12,13,21,22).

The issue of overcoming, and who are the overcomers, is straight-forward... and usually very misrepresented.

In the letters to the seven churches of Revelation 2 and 3, each church, save for Philadelphia which is cited as being exemplary, is told how they have failed to overcome; how they have become, in a word, faithless in their walk with Christ. They are also informed—all of them—that overcoming will bring rewards, and implies those who don't overcome will forfeit those rewards.

It is important to state here that the issue is not about salvation—justification. It is about *sanctification*: As we have seen, a person cannot be a "called-out one" (*ekklesia*) unless they have responded to the call (to salvation). And each letter *is* addressed to the *ekklesia*.

But, most expositors misunderstand, and thus misrepresent, who the overcomers are:

> Who is an overcomer? 1st John 5:4,5 gives us the answer. "For whatever is born of God overcometh the world; and this is the victory that overcometh the world, even our faith. Who is he that overcometh the world, but he that believeth that Jesus is the Son of God?"

> Overcoming the world is the experience that takes place in
> the life of the individual who puts his faith in Jesus Christ.
> There is no other way by which a man or woman can become
> an overcomer.[96]

The problem here is that if a person becomes an overcomer at the
moment of belief, and, thus, they can't lose that "overcomer status" (i.e.
their salvation), why admonish those of each church in Revelation 2 and 3
to be overcomers? To LaHaye, and many others, "overcomer" is an already
completed status. To admonish them is an after-the-fact of their overcoming
(being saved, i.e., justified). This makes encouraging them to be overcomers a
moot, and, thus, worthless point. Further, the issue about their overcoming
is in *what they do*. Justification, again as we have seen, is an issue of belief in
what Christ has already done.

Notwithstanding, to counter this, the argument has been offered that
each letter is addressed to "the church at," which would include both saved
and unsaved; in the unsaved case, those "merely sitting in the pews" of that
church.

> The word "church' is used to refer to a group of people who meet
> in one specific location for worship and fellowship. In any one of
> these local congregations there are usually some true believers
> and some who are not.[97]

But, to be specific, each letter is addressed to "the church," *ekklesia*—
most often translated as the "chosen" in the New Testament, and *always*
used as referring to the saved. To change that solely for these two chapters
in Revelation is weak hermaneutics.

Further, four of the seven letters to the churches specifically state who
is the cause of the problem—Smyrna: the devil (2:10); Pergamum: Satan
(2:13); Thyatira: Satan (2:24); Philadelphia: Satan (3:9). Ephesus, Sardis,
and Laodicea do not specifically have the cause of their failures identified.
But each has drifted from Christ by their actions.

Ephesus: You have left your first love (2:4).

---

96 LaHaye, *Revelation*, 28.

97 Lindsey, *Revelation*, 29.

Sardis: You have the name that you are alive [Christian], but you are dead... your deeds have not been found completed [*pleroo*-accomplished, fulfilled] (3:1,2).

Laodicea: I know your deeds, that you are neither cold nor hot (3:15).

What is the unspoken cause of these wrongful deeds? Scripture itself gives us insight:

> For there are many rebellious men... men who turn away from the truth.... They profess to know God, but by their deeds they deny Him, being detestable and disobedient, *and worthless for any good deed* (Titus 1:10,14,16 emphasis added).

> For certain persons have crept in unnoticed... ungodly persons who turn the grace of our God into licentiousness [loose living] and deny our only Master and Lord, Jesus Christ (Jude 4).

These persons don't deny Christ as Savior, they deny him as Master and Lord... *by their actions*, exactly what is described happening in these three churches.

Is there another way Christ can be denied? The most obvious answer, the one to which most Christians will turn, is Peter.

> Jesus said to him [Peter], "Truly I say to you... you will deny Me three times. (Matthew 26:34).

But again, what is the cause of that denial?

> Jesus said, "Simon [Peter], Simon, behold, Satan has demanded permission to sift you like wheat; but I have prayed for you that your faith may not fail..." (Luke 22:31).

So, it is not really *What*, but *Who*. And, like the four churches where Satan is specifically identified, we see that he is also behind the misdeeds of the remaining three. So, it is not *the world* which must be overcome, as indicated in 1st John 5:4-5, and championed by Tim LaHaye, Hal Lindsey, and others... it is Satan.

And how is Satan overcome?

> The serpent of old who is called the devil and Satan, who
> deceives the whole world... [The] brethren... overcame him
> because of the blood of the Lamb and because of the word of
> their testimony, and they did not love their life [*psuche*–soul]
> even to death (Revelation 12:9-11).

There are three elements spoken of here. First, "the blood of the Lamb";
Satan cannot be overcome unless one first accepts Jesus, "the Lamb"
sacrificed for him or her, as Savior. Second, the "word of their testimony";
a person must be willing to publicly acknowledge Jesus as Savior. *Not* to
be saved (justified), but as part of the overcoming process, i.e., to being
sanctified. They must *overcome any fear* that would prevent this from such
public declaration (see chapter 23). Third, a life of obedience to Jesus as
Lord: "They did not love their life, (*psuche*-soul), even to death."

Because this last concept is also so often misrepresented, we need to
look at it in depth. For starters, it is not talking about martyrdom.

The New Testament identifies *psuche* as "...the seat of personality (Luke
9:24) [where it is] explained as equaling [one's] "own self"; ...the seat of
the sentient (of the senses) element in man that by which he perceives,
reflects, feels, desires..."[98] In other writings the soul is often described as
each individual's ability to experience *life*,[99] and is made up of (1) the mind,
ability to think; (2) the emotions, ability to feel; and (3) the will, ability to
decide, to commit.

The New Testament portrays the death of the soul as a person being
willing to forego the passions of sinfulness, thus allowing them to die "to
self," while being obedient to the will of God through Christ, thus increasing
in spiritual life.

> Therefore, since Christ has suffered in the flesh, arm yourselves
> also with the same purpose, because he who has suffered in the
> flesh has ceased from sin, so as to live the rest of the time in the
> flesh no longer for the lusts of men, but for the will of God (1st
> Peter 4:1-2).

And Jesus proclaims that, unlike justification, which requires nothing

---

[98]   Vine, 1067.

[99]   As it is so translated in the Revelation 12:9-11 passage cited above.

of the person except to believe, salvation of the soul,[100] *sanctification*, requires the active, willing participation of the believer:

> Then Jesus said to His disciples, "If anyone wishes to come after Me, he must deny himself, and take up his cross and follow Me. For whoever wishes to save his life [*psuche*, soul] will lose it; but whoever loses his life [*psuche*] for My sake will find it. For what will it profit a man if he gains the whole world and forfeits his soul? Or what will a man give in exchange for his soul? (Matthew 16:24-26).

> And He was saying to them all, "If anyone wishes to come after Me, he must deny himself, and take up his cross daily and follow Me" (Luke 9:23).

> [Jesus said], "And he who does not take up his cross and follow after Me is not worthy of Me. He who has found his life [*psuche*] will lose it, and he who has lost his life for My sake will find it" (Matthew 10:38-39).

Hence, the issue is one of discipleship—*sanctification*—not an issue of being saved, justification:

> "Whoever does not carry his own cross and come after Me cannot be My disciple" (Luke 14:27).

Jesus is not saying the person can't be saved (justified) if he or she does not take up his cross; He is saying that person can't be a *disciple*, a learner, if he or she is not willing to do that. Only a saved person can become a "learner," because for the unsaved all of this is "foolishness" (1st Corinthians 1:18), thus they have no desire, much less ability, to "learn."

Further, notice what taking up our cross often requires of us:

> The Spirit Himself testifies with our spirit that we are children of God, and if children, heirs also, heirs of God and fellow heirs

---

[100] The term used by James (1:21; 5:20), Peter in his first epistle (1:9); and implied by the writer of Hebrews (10:39).

with Christ, *if indeed we suffer with Him...* (Romans 8:16-17; emphasis added).

Peter further confirms this requirement to suffer is part of the sanctification process as we proceed:

> ...greatly rejoice, even though now... you have been distressed by various trials, so that the proof of your faith... may be found to result in praise and glory and honor at the revelation of Jesus Christ; ...obtaining as the outcome of your faith the salvation of your souls (1st Peter 1:6,7,9).

To better clarify, this chart provides the difference between justification and sanctification, that is, between salvation of the spirit (John 3:6b) and salvation of the soul (James 1:21, et al):

SALVATION	
SPIRIT	SOUL
♦ Christ's Cross	♦ My cross
♦ Christ's Life... given for me	♦ My life... given to Christ ○ making Him Lord of my life ○ surrender of self to Him (doing things *His* way)
♦ by Faith	♦ demonstrated through Good Works (godly, i.e. based on faith) – commitment; faithfulness

In closing, one cannot overcome if he or she doesn't know how. God, in His Word describes how; and that process has been clearly presented here in this chapter. Yet, many *Christians* are ignorant of it. Thus, it seems the only true conclusion that can be drawn is that a true understanding of what it means to overcome is revealed only to those whom God has *chosen* to reveal it. This is an issue of His sovereign choice.

In conjunction with this, one does not need to know anything about the issue of overcoming to be justified. Belief in the Lord Jesus as one's

Savior is the requirement for that. Hence, overcoming must be part of the sanctification process.

With an acknowledgement of that, the reader should now begin to see a trend in all that has been presented so far.

CHAPTER 14

THE BRIDE

Then one of the seven angels... came and spoke with me, saying, "Come here, I will show you the bride, the wife of the Lamb" (Revelation 21:9).

One of the keys to grasping that being chosen, election, is an issue of sanctification, not justification, is to identify who the Bride of Christ is. Unfortunately, this too is often misrepresented.

The place to begin is that of its First Mention. In Genesis 2, as part of the creation narrative, we are told that after the creation of man, Adam, that

> ...the Lord God said, "It is not good for the man to be alone; I will make him a helper suitable for him...." So the Lord God caused a deep sleep to fall upon the man, and he slept; then He took one of his ribs and closed up the flesh at that place. The Lord God fashioned into a woman the rib which He had taken from the man, and brought her to the man. The man said, "This is now bone of my bones, and flesh of my flesh; she shall be called Woman, because she was taken out of Man." For this reason a man shall leave his father and his mother, and be joined to his wife; and they shall become one flesh" (vv. 18-24).

A series of questions must now be asked. (1) How many *people* were there? The answer is two; Adam and Eve. (2) But how many *persons* were there? The answer is *one* (v.24). "They—the two—became one flesh." God recognizes them as a single whole. This is more easily understood when one sees that Eve was taken from, and thus a part of, Adam—thus still one person. The fullness of God in whose image Adam was made is now reflected in the both of them combined together. Hence, *one* fullness. (3) Who caused all of this? The answer is God (v. 21). This did not result from the will of any other being. (4) Further, who chose the body part, that *portion* of Adam, to be used; not only what part, but what amount of that part to be used? Again, the answer is God (vv. 21-22).

The last question, but the key to true understanding is (5) did God use *all* of Adam's body to create his bride, Eve? The answer is a resounding *No* (v. 21).

With this as background, let's look at Paul's first letter to the Corinthians. Notice in verse 1:2 that Paul is writing "to the church—*ekklesia*—of God which is at Corinth, to *those who have been sanctified* in Christ Jesus..." (emphasis added).

This letter is not to the General Assembly whom, like many Christians today who do not read their Bible, would not be interested in the letter though it were available to them. Paul is providing "inside" information to those who are lead to avail themselves of it. Notice that these Corinthians "have been sanctified," past tense. This indicates that they are *mature* in the Lord, not a new convert or one "maturing," present tense.

In his letter, Paul advises that those of the *ekklesia* are "Christ's body, and individually members of it" (12:27). He makes a similar statement to "the saints [holy ones] who are at Ephesus and *who are faithful* in Christ Jesus" (Ephesians 1:1; emphasis added). In verse 5:30 he writes, "We—the church (v.29)—are members of His body." "But now God has placed the members, each one of them, in the body, just as He desired" (1st Corinthians 12:18). Again, it is God who does this; no one else.

Paul goes on to write to the Ephesians about the relationships between husbands and wives (5:22-33). In that discourse, in verse 31, he quotes Genesis 2:24—"For this cause a man shall leave his father and mother, and shall cleave to his wife; and the two shall become one flesh."

And then he provides a remarkable insight: "This mystery is great; but I am speaking with reference to Christ and the church (*ekklesia*)." We are clearly told that the church is the Bride of Christ!

Why is all of this important? Because in the letter to the Romans we are told that "Adam… is a type of Him [Jesus] who was to come." Things concerning Adam are a foreshadow of what will be fulfilled in Jesus! With that truth, let's go back and look at Adam's bride in relation to Jesus' Bride.

If Adam's bride was taken from his entire body, we can expect that Jesus' Bride will be created that way. If, on the other hand, only a portion of Adam's body is chosen for creation of his bride, we can expect that *only a portion of Jesus' body will fulfill* His Bride's creation.

The question now becomes: If God chose the exact body part(s), and amount of it, that would be used for Adam's bride, Eve, can we expect God to do the same *choosing* for His Son's Bride, the Church?

Ponder that question for a moment.

Those who are called-out (ekklesia) to sanctification are, literally, in a spiritual race to be eligible for The Bride. But, as we've seen, only the overcomers—the faithful—will attain that position; hence, a "race" to be won. Paul clearly states in 1st Corinthians 9:24-27 that we *are* in a race:

> Do you not know that those who run in a race all run, but only one receives the prize? Run in such a way that you may win. Everyone who competes in the games exercises self-control in all things. They then do it to receive a perishable wreath, but we an imperishable. Therefore I run in such a way, as not without aim; I box in such a way, as not beating the air; but I discipline my body and make it my slave, so that, after I have preached to others, I myself will not be disqualified.

Paul *disqualified!* How could that possibly be?!? Because, like the churches in Revelation 2 and 3, a member of the *ekklesia* could become faith*less* in his or her walk, and Paul knows he is not excluded. That is why he further advises,

> Let us lay aside every encumbrance, and the sin which so easily entangles us, and let us run with endurance the race that is set before us, fixing our eyes on Jesus, the author *and perfecter* of faith… (Hebrews 12:1-2; emphasis added).

"The sin which so easily entangles *us*"; Paul identifies that this can happen to anybody within the church—even him, as he includes himself by using the personal pronoun "us." If it could possibly happen to Paul, we must be constantly mindful that it can happen to "us." So many Christians remain oblivious of that very fact.

Being saved, followed by being chosen, is not a guarantee of attaining to The Bride! (We will look at this in detail in the next chapter.)

The "Golden Chain" that we have now identified is (1) being called and responding to that call (to salvation), (2) being chosen and (3) responding to being chosen by being *faithful*—continuing to be obedient and, thus, sanctified (Revelation 17:14).

Like The Twelve, those who are chosen for sanctification have become eligible. But, as we are about to see, to attain to the reward of being part of The Bride, a person must remain faithful.

CHAPTER 15

PERSEVERANCE: THE FAITHFUL

And I saw heaven opened; and behold, a white horse, and He who sat
upon it is called The Word of God... and those who are with Him
are the called and chosen and faithful (Revelation 19:11, 13; 17:14).

So far, we have looked at some of the elements of belief of the Pre-
determinarian and found there may be some misunderstandings which
weaken their position. All of this has led to this, for our purposes, *the
primary cornerstone of their belief, perseverance.* This is centered on the
concept that Christians who are saved—justified because of their belief in
Jesus as Savior—are therefore also *guaranteed* to walk with Him *throughout
their entire lives.* For them, this "perseverance of the saints" is a doctrine
"engraved in stone."

At the outset, let us state there are a number of passages in Scripture
which show this belief is in error. As we've already seen in our analysis of the
churches of Revelation 2 and 3, falling away is something that *can* happen
to churches and church members. And the statements in those chapters
that only the overcomers will inherit is a clear indication that not all will
maintain (or return should they fall away) to fully walking with Christ,
especially those who have been so compromised.

"Falling away" is also particularly indicated in a number of other
Biblical passages dealing with the Last Days. Jesus Himself clearly stated
"many will fall away" (Matthew 24:10) in the time directly preceding His
return. A number of expositors have attempted to relate those falling away

as individuals who have not really accepted Jesus as Savior, but have only made a false showing of having done so.

The response to this is twofold. First, to fall away indicates a person is at the place they are leaving. To say a false Christian, someone not really saved, falls away from that status is hard to accept. How can they fall away from a position they never really were at? It would be more accurate to say they were *exposed as being false*, then to say they left.

But, apart from that logic, there is the Scriptural evidence. Jesus further defines this falling away in Matthew 24 by stating, "most people's love will grow cold" (v. 12). The word here for love in the original Greek is *agape*. God says of Himself that He "is *agape*" (1st John 4:8). Hence, only those who "have God" would have *agape*. Since only a Christian receives the Holy Spirit—God—at the moment he or she believes (Romans 5:5, et al), those falling away must be *Christians*. The unsaved, who have never accepted Jesus and, therefore, are without the Holy Spirit, cannot lose *agape* as they never had it!

And there is no Scriptural evidence that those who fall away during these Last Days ever return. In fact, the tone of this Olivet Discourse is they would not return because of this passage's warning nature: "Behold," Jesus states, "I have told you in advance" (24:25). Clearly, "falling away" is something we need to guard against.

In addition, Paul in his first letter to Timothy writes, "The Spirit explicitly says that in the later times some will fall away from the faith..." (4:1). And in his second letter to the Thessalonians he writes, "The day of the Lord... will not come unless the apostasy—the falling away—comes first..." (2:2,3). Further, most Christians by their own observations can name—*by name*—Christians they personally know who have departed from the faith... never to return. Such evidence that Christians can fall away, Scriptural and empirical, if ignored can only lead to ministry error.

One of these more serious errors is the belief that those who fall away weren't really saved to begin with. As we've noted above in Jesus' Olivet Discourse, this is simply not true. But, to hold that view will seriously impair any ministry that would support and encourage their return because the Gospel will be presented—again—instead of (correctly) getting them to re-commit to Christ (1st John 1:9).

Further, this error will cause unnecessary fear:

> This doctrine of the perseverance of the saints... should cause genuine worry, and even fear, in the hearts of any who are 'backslidden' or straying away from Christ. Such persons must clearly be warned that only those who persevere to the end have been truly born again. If they fall away from their profession of faith in Christ and life of obedience to him, they may not really be saved—in fact, the *evidence* that they are giving *is that they are not saved*, and they never really were saved.[101]

Scriptural evidence, as we've seen, says otherwise. It is, in fact, the *saved* who fall away.

Another serious ministry error has been observed by Joseph C. Dillow in his book *Reign of the Servant Kings: A Study of Eternal Security and the Significance of Man*. It builds off of the perspective we've just seen offered by Grudem.

> One of the great errors [of the holder of the perspective one is not saved if one does not persevere to the end] is that he seems to think he has either the responsibility or the right to pronounce upon another man's eternal destiny. Better is the attitude of the apostle Paul, "Do not go on passing judgment before the time" (1st Corinthians 4:5).[102]

It is important to point out here that those who fall away do not lose their salvation: "If we are faithless, He remains faithful" (2nd Timothy 2:13). Salvation is a free gift (Ephesians 2:8). Once accepted, a person is eternally justified—the gift cannot be given back no matter how hard we try! This is confirmed by Jesus' prayer for us, "Holy Father, keep through Your name those whom You have given Me... I... pray... for those who will believe in Me..." (John 17:11, 20).

But, though one is eternally saved, the reader should note that falling away has serious consequences. Though it is rarely preached, there *is* a judgment of Christians and it still remains "a terrifying thing to fall into the

---

[101] Wayne Grudem, *Systematic Theology* (Grand Rapids, Michigan: Zondervan, 1994), p. 806; emphases in original.

[102] Joseph C. Dillow, *Reign of the Servant Kings: A Study of Eternal Security and the Significance of Man* (Hayesville, North Carolina: Schoettle Publishing Company, 2006), 248.

hands of the living God" (10:31). For many Christians this will be a *painful* experience—that could have been avoided!

Scripture is clear the *saved* will stand before Jesus to give an account.

> We shall all stand before the judgment seat of God... So then each one of us shall give account of himself to God (Romans 14:10, 12).

> For we must all appear before the judgment seat of Christ, that each one may be recompensed—get what we deserve—for his deeds in the body according to what he has done, whether good or bad (2nd Corinthians 5:10).

Notice Paul says "we." He is referring to *Christians*. (He refers to the unsaved as "they.")[103] The judgment seat in the Greek is *bema*. This was not a judicial seat dealing with violation of law; it was the place where athletes participating in (Olympic) games would go to receive their prize for winning... or be reckoned to receive nothing for losing.

Thus, this is not judgment for our sins—Christ has paid that penalty (1st John 2:2); it is a judgment regarding our discipline: How well did we run the race (as we saw in 1st Corinthians 9:24 and Hebrews 12:1). Remember, the Great Commission is "to make disciples" (Matthew 28:19)... and a disciple lives by discipline.

Paul makes it clear we are to "discipline [our]self for the purpose of godliness" (1st Timothy 4:7). Why? Because God Himself has stated: "Those whom I love, I discipline" (Hebrews 12:6). The reality, so ignored by Christians (and pastors) today, is that if we have lived undisciplined *here*, He will discipline us *there*, at the Bema Seat.

Paul provides further details in his first letter to the Corinthians regarding this event:

> According to the grace of God which was given to me, like a wise master builder I laid a foundation, and another is building on it. But each man must be careful how he builds on it. For no man can lay a foundation other than the one which is laid, which is Jesus Christ. Now if any man builds on the foundation with

---

103   As an example, see Romans 1:20ff.

gold, silver, precious stones, wood, hay, straw, each man's work will become evident; for the day will show it because it is to be revealed with fire, and the fire itself will test the quality of each man's work. If any man's work which he has built on it remains, he will receive a reward. If any man's work is burned up, he will suffer loss; but he himself will be saved, yet so as through fire (vv.10-15).

A number of things from this passage: First, this has to relate to the *saved* as the people being judged have a "foundation... which is Jesus Christ." Second, this is an issue of *works*, thus not judgment of sin. Third, the judgment instrument is that of *fire*.

There are two types of natural cleaning agents, water and fire. We are told that the Word of God cleanses a person—sanctifies them—by the "washing of water" (Ephesians 5:26). Obviously, those that reject less painful cleansing *here* by water will be purified *there* by fire. Again, note also, the issue is one of sanctification, not justification. Fourth, the experience will be painful. The verb in the phrase "suffer loss" in the Greek is *zemioo*, to experience injury. It is from the Greek root *zemia*, meaning "damage," and is akin to *damazo*, to tame through violence. You get the picture: An act of discipline... to tame the unruly, those who have lived godlessly.

The last thing to be noted is that "if any man's work is burned up... he himself will be saved, yet so as through fire." The implication is that if anyone's *total* amount of works is burned up, that still cannot take away from his or her "foundation in Christ." The person will be saved, but that is all. There will be absolutely no rewards, nothing beyond the basic gift of eternal life.

It is important at this point that the other group of Pre-determinarians, those who believe they are *guaranteed* all the blessings of heaven, even if they do not live for Christ in the here-and-now, should take note. The concept that God will persevere with putting up with them in spite of what they do because in Christ all their sins are forgiven is unfounded. This passage makes it perfectly clear, *there is a judgment of Christians.* (More on this in Section 2.)

This is not an attempt, in any way, to denigrate the free gift of God in Christ's sacrifice. But God has *so* much more beyond just living eternally for those who are faithful: for some, as we have begun to see, the opportunity to be The Bride, which will qualify us to rule and reign with Him. This authority will not only be for His Millennial Kingdom, but also on in to eternity (Revelation 21:8ff).

Also note this Corinthian passage has two keys dealing with perseverance. First, and this seriously weakens the Pre-determinarian position, *not all persevere*. The implication that some survive this trial by fire with nothing but their foundation in Christ alone, is inescapable. In life they did *nothing* for Him.

This leads to the second key, our *destiny of eternal life—justification—is not dependent upon us*. We don't need to persevere in it to have it, maintain it, or *even to demonstrate we have that life*, especially to others. We *know* we have it because God's Spirit testifies to our spirit it is so (Romans 8:16). That is the proof. Any other demand for proof, especially so that others may "see," is false. Thus, perseverance is an issue of *sanctification*. And for *that* we will be judged, not our sins. This passage clearly states that.

To provide a better understanding of all this, let's look at some of Jesus' parables.

> And while they [The Twelve] were listening to [Him, Jesus], He went on to tell a parable, because... they supposed that the kingdom of God was going to appear immediately. He said, therefore, "A certain nobleman went to a distant country to receive a kingdom for himself, and then return. And he called ten of his slaves [*doulos*—one who is bound to another person], and gave them ten minas and said to them, 'Do business with this until I come back....'
>
> "And it came about that when he returned, after receiving the kingdom, he ordered that these slaves, to whom he had given the money, be called to him in order that he might know what business they had done.
>
> "And the first appeared, saying, 'Master, your mina has made ten minas more.' And he said to him, 'Well done, *good* slave, because you have been *faithful* in a very little thing, be in authority over ten cities.' And the second came, saying, 'Your mina, master, has made five minas.' And he said to him also, 'And you are to be over five cities.'

"And another came, saying, 'Master, behold your mina, which I kept put away in a handkerchief; for *I was afraid* of you, because you are an exacting [*austeros*–severe] man; you take up what you did not lay down, and reap what you did not sow.' He said to him, 'By your own words I will judge you, you worthless [*poneros*–one who does evil] slave. Did you know that I am an exacting man, taking up what I did not lay down, and reaping what I did not sow? Then why did you not put the money in the bank, and having come, I would have collected it with interest [i.e., if unwilling to invest in others, at least to have invested in yourself]?'

"And he said to the bystanders, 'Take the mina away from him, and give it to the one who has the ten minas.' And they said to him, 'Master, he has ten minas already.'

"I tell you, that to everyone who has shall more be given, but from the one who does not have, even what he does have shall be taken away. (Luke 19:12-27; emphasis added).

First of all, the nobleman represents Jesus. We are told these are ten slaves *of the nobleman*. Take note, the unsaved are slaves to sin (John 8:34), duty-bound to Satan (John 8:44), and enemies of God (James 4:4). They are *not* Jesus.' Hence, although many attempt to make the last mentioned slave someone who is unsaved, that cannot be.

As to the first two slaves who produce for their master—*through their works*—they are described by Him as "good" and "faithful." Faithful is self-explanatory, they are obedient, fulfilling their masters command to "do business." "Good," however, needs additional insight.

In Mark 10:18 Jesus declares that, "No one is good except God." Thus, the "good" slaves have conducted themselves in a *godly* manner. So states the nobleman (Jesus). This godly manner has to be their willingness to be led by the Holy Spirit given them at the moment they believed. For their efforts they are *rewarded*.

The worthless slave is *disciplined* by the master. He, literally, "suffers loss" for not having attempted—persevered—through the required task. Notice, however, the nobleman does not disown the slave. This is critical to understanding: Justification cannot be lost. The issue here then relates to sanctification—what is *done for the master*. And the message here is clear: There are some who are saved who will not persevere." To know this fact, or reject it, will impact a Christian's ministry, especially those who are shepherds.

Lastly, notice that the reward for these faithful servants is that they are given *authority over cities*. They get to rule with (and for) their master. We'll see why this is important shortly.

In a parallel passage, this time in the Gospel of Matthew, we see the same situation, but additional facts are presented by Jesus:

> "Now after a long time the master of those slaves came and settled accounts with them. And the one who had received five talents came up and brought five more talents... His master said to him, 'Well done, *good* and *faithful* slave; you were faithful with a few things, I will put you in charge of many things, enter into the joy of your master.'

> "And the one who had received two talents came up and said, '...I have gained two more talents.' His master said to him, 'Well done, good faithful slave; you were faithful with a few things, I will put you in charge of many things, enter into the joy of your master.'

> "And the one who had received one talent came up and said, 'Master... I was afraid, and *went away* and hid your talent in the ground; see, you have what is yours.' But the master answered and said to him, 'You wicked [*poneros*—one who does evil], lazy [*okneros*—hesitant, slothful] slave... you ought to have put my money in the bank, and on my arrival I would have received my money back with interest [*tokos*—interest; from *teko*: to produce]. Therefore, take away the talent from him, and give it to the one who has the ten talents.' For to everyone who has shall more be given, and he shall have an abundance; but from the one who does not have, even what he does have shall be taken away (Matthew 25:14-29; emphasis added).

The first additional information is that the worthless slave "went away." By his own admission he declares that he departed—*fell away from*—doing what he knew was required of him. The implication that slaves of the master can fall away is unmistakable. But, again, he is not "disowned" by the master. He is only disciplined; his penalty is to suffer loss. That he fell away does *not* indicate he never was a slave of this master. Jesus clearly states he was. It *does* indicate he failed to be obedient to Him.

Which leads us to this second parable's reward. The faithful here are being put in charge of *many things* (v. 23).

There is one last parable we'll consider:

> Who then is the *faithful* and *sensible* [*phronimos*—thoughtful, wise] slave whom his master put in charge of his household *to give them their food at the proper time?* Blessed is that slave whom his master finds so doing when he comes. Truly I say to you, that he will put him in charge of all his possessions. (Matthew 24:45-47).

Notice that the reward for those being faithful here is that they are put in charge of *all* of the master's possessions. What becomes apparent in comparing each group of faithful slaves in these parables is that they all receive a reward, but there is an increasing responsibility in the second and third group—and thus increased *honor* in the reward they can receive.

It is interesting to note this corresponds to Jesus' relationship to The Twelve. Observe that there appears to exist *three* circles within The Twelve. We have already looked at the inner circle, but Scripture implies a mid-level as well.

> Now there were some Greeks among those who were going up to worship at the feast; these then came to Philip, who was from Bethsaida of Galilee, and began to ask him, saying, "Sir, we wish to see Jesus." Philip came and told Andrew; Andrew and Philip came and told Jesus (John 12:20-22).

The Greeks identified here go to Philip, who does not immediately take them to Jesus. He goes first to Andrew, a member of the inner circle, who, now with Philip in-tow, informs Jesus. Based on the degree to which each of The Twelve is recognized in the Gospels, keeping in mind some are only identified by name as belonging to The Twelve, one can see an inner, middle, and outer circle of authority, influence, and recognition in relation to Jesus. This is exactly like what we see in regards to the rewards of these three parables.

As a final note, loss at the Bema Seat includes some severe penalties not discussed here because they are not germane to the issue of perseverance. However, the reader is strongly recommended to see chapter 23.

In closing, we have seen, especially from the parables presented herein: Perseverance of a Christian is not required for salvation—justification, *nor is it a measure as to whether one is saved or not*. Perseverance is directly related to sanctification, that is, obedience, which can lead to rewards, or, with disobedience, suffering loss of them.

A lack of awareness of this is particularly worst-case for those who believe perseverance is optional. When they stand before Christ at the Bema Seat to be judged for their disobedience, it will come as a total (disciplinary) surprise.

Equally worst-case is the misunderstanding that perseverance is a measure of one's *justification*; to not persevere is an indication one is not saved. This perspective leads to one more easily being blindsided when they, or those with whom they are associated, are confronted by a situation in which they do, in fact, fall away. Fearing they are, thus, unsaved can cause improper reaction, wasting precious time, energy, effort, and resources in crucial life-or-death moments. Worse, if they are shepherding and provide the wrong solution, they will be misguiding others which can lead to disastrous results.

This would make it the *worst* worst-case scenario for such shepherds should, in these cases, Matthew 23:16 be the standard: "Woe to you, blind guides..."

CHAPTER 16

THE INHERITANCE

Through Jesus Christ our Savior... we might be made heirs according
to the hope of eternal life (Titus 3:6-7).

The first thing we note about the topic of The Inheritance is that it is a subject rarely, if ever, discussed. For example in Wayne Grudem's 1291-page *Systematic Theology*, a book that looks at every other aspect of the Christian faith, a quick glance at the Table of Contents or the Subject Index will reveal it is not a listed topic!

The second thing to know is that it is not guaranteed, which most Christians would argue otherwise. In fact, that is why it is so rarely discussed: Christians believe The Inheritance is "automatic" immediately when one believes in Christ. As we shall see, it is not.

As it should be, the answer begins in the definition of faith.

> Faith is the assurance of things hoped for, the conviction of things not seen (Hebrews 11:1).

"Faith is the assurance," hence, faith says *it is so*; it is a complete *guarantee* of that which is hoped. Thus, hope itself is not a guarantee. It may be a "confident expectation," but not a guaranteed one. This is confirmed in Titus.

> Through Jesus Christ our Savior... we *might* be made heirs according to the hope of eternal life (3: 6-7; emphasis added).

"We might" clearly indicates that there are those who "might not"; it does not say we all *will*.

What separates the haves from the have-nots?

> ...we are children of God, and if children, heirs also... with Christ, *if* indeed *we suffer with Him* in order that we may also be glorified with Him (Romans 8:16-17; emphasis added).

We become heirs—those who receive The Inheritance—*if* we suffer with Jesus. Scripture makes it perfectly clear that The Inheritance *is* *conditional*. In fact, Paul goes on to write that he welcomes such suffering:

> ...that I might know Him [Jesus]... and the fellowship of His sufferings... (Philippians 3:10).

This, while most Christians avoid suffering for Christ's sake! Peter expands on the issue of suffering:

> Blessed be the God and Father of our Lord Jesus Christ, who according to His great mercy has caused us to be born again to *a living hope* through the resurrection of Jesus Christ from the dead, to *obtain an inheritance* which is imperishable and undefiled and will not fade away, reserved in heaven for you.... In this you greatly rejoice, even though now for a little while, if necessary, you have been distressed by various trials, that the proof of your faith, being more precious than gold which is perishable, even though tested by fire, *may be found to result in praise and glory and honor* at the revelation of Jesus Christ (1st Peter 1:3-4, 6-7; emphasis added).

There are a number of issues raised here. First, the "living hope" occurs at the moment we are "born again." This hope is *never* available for unbelievers (but, see below). Thus, anyone who is unsaved has a false hope in what he or she believes awaits them after death, the erroneous belief *"but He is a loving God"* notwithstanding.

Second, hope is again linked with The Inheritance, a second confirmation it is not a guarantee and thus is conditional. Notice also that we are told that it *"may* be found" to result in reward. The passage does not say it *will* be found. Again, indication of it being conditional.

Third, the various trials we "suffer" for our faith in Christ, i.e. as we enter into "the fellowship of His sufferings" is for our benefit. They not only purify us ("more precious than gold... tested by fire"), but they are a confirmation of the coming "praise and glory and honor" which potentially awaits us at the Bema Seat. No wonder Paul exalted in his sufferings!

And what is The Inheritance? Peter writes clearly that it is "praise and glory and honor." We've seen in Revelation 2 and 3 that only the overcomers attain this. It will not be granted to all who are chosen! Though it is often preached that way.

Another important fact of Peter's writing, which confirms not all receive the reward of The Inheritance, is seen in to whom his letter is addressed:

> "Peter, an apostle of Jesus Christ, to those... who are chosen... by the sanctifying work of the Spirit, that you may obey Jesus Christ" (1st Peter 1:1-2).

The opportunity for receiving The Inheritance is, by divine sovereignty, *only for The Chosen.* And for what are they chosen? *To be sanctified!* That they *may* obey Jesus. A clear indication that not all The Chosen *will.*

Further, it becomes clear that not all The Chosen are aware of this. Paul writing to the Ephesians makes this clear:

> I pray that the eyes of your heart *may be* enlightened, so that you may know what is the hope of His calling [of you], what are the riches of the glory of His inheritance... (1:18; emphasis added).

Again, that they *may* know. Obviously, they don't know yet, or Paul would not be praying for them about this.

The clear indication is that some (many?) may never be so enlightened. Why? Peter made that clear: Obedience. There are some, even though they are chosen, who will not obey (see chapter 21)—and like Esau, lose out on the Inheritance!

One additional comment on Paul's writing here. Notice to whom he is writing:

Paul, an apostle of Jesus Christ... to the saints (holy ones) at Ephesus, *who are faithful* in Christ Jesus... (1:1; emphasis added).

This letter isn't going out to just "the saved"—the General Assembly—at Ephesus, nor even to "The Chosen." It is going out to *the faithful.* To be The Faithful, they had to be Called, and then Chosen. As we've seen, Revelation 17:14 makes that perfectly clear; *the* Golden Chain. To be faithful, they must be obedient. So, the Faithful are receiving "inside" information that The Called and the disobedient Chosen are not.

This is just like those Christians whose Bible is collecting dust on the mantlepiece. The letter to the Ephesians is available to them as well, just as it was to any Ephesian who was willing to avail him- or herself of that letter. But, through slothfulness, thus disobedience, they are left "in the dark."

Also note that because this letter is to The Faithful, the verse "He [God] chose us in Him [Jesus] before the foundation of the world" (v. 4) *does not apply to all Christians*, as is so often presented by expositors. God chose The Faithful only (otherwise the Holy Spirit would have addressed the letter to the Ephesians differently).

This brings better understanding of "those whom He foreknew He predestined..." (Romans 8:29). Those He foreknew *to be The Faithful* is the inescapable conclusion. These are the people chosen to be The Bride for His Son.

God's foreknowledge of every human being to be born is tremendous, but a further indication of His omniscience is that He also knew who should be in the running to be The Bride (see concerning Isaac and Rebekah, below). Hence, He *chose* them. Of those chosen, the Faithful are those who obey. Jesus made it clear that "If you love Me you will obey My commandments" (John 14:15).

What father does not want a bride for his son except one who loves that son? Thus, the heavenly Father has chosen—before the foundation of the world—those He knew would love His Son; those who would obey, The Faithful, and predestined them to be The Bride.

In His mercy, He has chosen a number of individuals to give them an opportunity. But, like Jesus who, as an example to us, earned *His* position as King because of His obedience (Philippians 2:8; Revelation 19:16), those chosen "for the race" (Hebrews 12:1) to be The Bride, must also be obedient.

Thus, again, the Father has made Jesus our standard as we are called to "follow in His steps" (1st Peter 2:21) of obedience.

Let's look at Isaac and Rebehah, who are a type of this.

> Abraham buried Sarah his wife.... Now Abraham was old, advanced in age. Abraham said to his servant... who had charge of all that he owned, "Please... swear by the Lord, the God of heaven and the God of earth... you will go to my country and to my relatives, and take a wife for my son Isaac." The servant said to him, "Suppose the woman is not willing to follow me to this land." "But if the woman is not willing to follow you, then you will be free from this my oath...." So the servant... set out... and went to Mesopotamia, to the city of Nahor [i.e., Abraham's kin] and [stops] outside the city by the well of water.... [And] behold, Rebekah, who was born to... Abraham's brother Nahor, came out with her jar on her shoulder. The girl was very beautiful, a virgin. [The servant makes known to the family Abraham's desire for a wife for his son, Isaac, to be taken from Abraham's family.] And they [Rebekah's family] said, "We will call the girl and consult her wishes." Then they called Rebekah and said to her, "Will you go with this man?" And she said, "I will go."
>
> [As Rebekah's journey ended], Isaac went out to meditate in the field toward evening; and he lifted up his eyes and looked, and behold, camels were coming. Rebekah lifted up her eyes, and when she saw Isaac she dismounted from the camel. She said to the servant, "Who is that man walking in the field to meet us?" And the servant said, "He is my master." Then she took her veil and covered herself. The servant told Isaac all the things that he had done. Then Isaac brought her into his mother Sarah's tent, and he took Rebekah, and she became his wife, and he loved her... (Genesis 23:19; 24: 1-5, 9-11, 15-16, 57-59).

We have a picture in type of God choosing a bride for His Son, Jesus. Abraham typifies God the Father; Isaac, God the Son; Eliezer, the Holy Spirit; and Rebekah, the Bride of Christ. In the *Selected Writing of A. Edwin Wilson*, editor Arlen L. Chitwood includes Wilson's observations on this passage:

(1) Abraham was very old when he became interested in a bride for his son. This old age typifies... the eternity of God... [and] that the church was chosen in Christ before the foundation of the world.

(2) Eliezer typifies the Holy Spirit. Abraham [advised] Eliezer [to] not take a bride for Isaac from the Canaanites (the lost), but from his own kindred (Christians). The Bride of Christ is to be *chosen from the family of God* [called-out of the called; note, not all of daughters are chosen—Eliezer selects from among many (v. 13)].

(3) Abraham sent Eliezer into a far country to get Isaac's bride and return with her. Likewise, God the Father sent the Holy Spirit into the world to call out a Bride for Christ. At the appointed time the Holy Spirit will bring her to meet Christ in the air.

(4) Abraham did not seek a bride for Isaac until after Isaac had been placed on the altar as an offering and had returned (Genesis 22:1-19). Neither did God the Father call out the church for a Bride of Christ until after Christ's death, resurrection, and ascension.

(5) Eliezer... was supernaturally brought in touch with Abraham's family. Likewise, members of the Bride of Christ are supernaturally chosen by God and sought by the Holy Spirit.

(6) Eliezer met Rebekah by a well of water... Water typifies salvation [and] the Word (Isaiah 12:3; 55:1,2). [Thus] the Bride are saved people who through the study of the Word become [sanctified]... leading them into a life that qualifies to be a member of the Bride of Christ. (Not all the family of God constitute the Bride of Christ.)

(7) After, Eliezer... invited her to go with him to be the bride of his master. There is no force, no coercion... Rebekah had to make the choice herself. Likewise, individual Christians are invited to so live and obey the Lord that they will become a part of the Bride. The Holy Spirit does not force a Christian; saved

by grace the Christian then must decide whether he wants to
rule and reign with Christ or just be content to be a subject in
the coming kingdom.

(8) As Rebekah and Isaac approached each other, Rebekah puts
a veil over her face. This typifies the truth that the identity of the
bride is not revealed until the marriage of the Lamb [i.e., after
the Bema Seat judgment]. As there were others in Rebekah's
party, so there will be others... beside the bride [the *prepared*
wedding attendants (Matthew 25:1-13); see chapter 21].[104]

Wilson's exposit is very self-explanatory. What needs to be stressed,
however, it that not all will receive The Inheritance. As we saw previously,
only overcomers—The Faithful—get to be The Bride (the "I have this
against you..." of those who are not overcomers is hardly praise even though
they are "chosen").

It is overcomers, like Rebekah, who say "yes" by their obedience that
are accepted. They are from The Chosen and go on to be The Bride. Many
of others from The Chosen who fail to be The Bride, but have remained
"partially faithful," will be Bridal Attendants (Matthew 9:15). However,
some will be excluded altogether; (see chapter 21). The faithful of the
General Assembly, along with the righteous of the Old Testament will
be The Guests (Matthew 22:10). It is important to note these different
participants at the Bridal Feast, which are usually overlooked by most
expositors.

Let's look at a parable to further clarify this.

Jesus spoke to them again in parables, saying, "The kingdom of
heaven may be compared to a king who gave a wedding feast for
his son. And he sent out his slaves... [and] said to [them], 'The
wedding is ready... Go therefore to the main highways, and as
many as you find there, invite to the wedding feast.' Those slaves
went out into the streets and gathered together all they found,
both evil and good; and the wedding hall was filled with dinner
guests (Matthew 22:1-3, 8-10).

104   Arlen L. Chitwood, *Selected Writings of A. Edwin Wilson* (Hayesville, North Carolina:
Schoettle Publishing Co, Inc., n.d.), 106-110.

Does it say anything about these individuals being "chosen"? No. They are merely "invited" (*kaleo*—called)... but they *willingly* respond to that invitation.

Does it say they are in any relation to the Bride—the Bride herself or her Attendants? No. Again, the wedding hall is filled with *dinner guests*. Spiritually, these are the individuals who respond to the call of God to salvation, but are not chosen by Him for the opportunity to be The Bride.

Is this unfair? Paul says not at all: The potter has "a right over the clay to make from the same lump one vessel to honorable use, and another for common use" (Romans 9:21).

So be it! As we've seen, only "He who overcomes shall inherit..." (Revelation 21:7). And no one else. It couldn't be clearer.

And so,

> "we desire that each one of you show the same diligence so as to realize the *fullness* of hope until the end, that you may not be sluggish, but imitators of those who through faith and patience inherit the promises" (Hebrews 6:11-12 R.V.; emphasis added).

It must be said again, *some won't...* which provides them with a *worst* worst-case scenario because it is of their own making.

CHAPTER 17

TOTAL DEPRAVITY

*The Helper... when He comes will convict the world concerning sin,
and righteousness, and judgment (John 16:8).*

There is an issue within Christian circles of the Total Depravity of fallen man. The term does not mean that unbelievers are incapable of doing any good, but that sin which entered mankind as a result of Adam's fall has corrupted *all* aspects of a human being.

This concept is best expressed by Wayne Grudem in his *Systematic Theology*:

> In our natures we totally lack spiritual good before God. [E]very part of our being is affected by sin—our intellects, our emotions and desires, our hearts (the center of our desires and decision-making process), our goals and motives... Paul says, "I know that nothing good dwells within me, that is, in my flesh" (Romans 7:18).... Scripture is not denying that unbelievers can do good in human society *in some senses*. But it is denying that they can do any *spiritual* good or be good *in terms of a relationship with God....*
>
> We also lack the ability to do anything that will in itself please God and the ability to come to God in our own strength. Paul says that "those who are in the flesh cannot please God" (Romans 8:8). Moreover, in terms of bearing fruit for God's kingdom and doing what pleases Him, Jesus says, "Apart from Me you can do

nothing" (John 15:5). When Paul's readers were unbeliever's, he tells them, "You were dead through the trespasses and sins in which you once walked" (Ephesians 2:1-2). Unbelievers are in a state of bondage or enslavement to sin, because "everyone who commits sin is a slave to sin" (John 8:34). Though from a human standpoint people might be able to do much good, Isaiah affirms that "all our righteous deeds are like a polluted garment" [literally, a menstrual rag] (64:6). Unbelievers are not even able to understand the things of God correctly, for the "natural man does not receive the things of the Spirit of God, for they are folly to him, and he is not able to understand them because they are spiritually discerned (1ˢᵗ Corinthians 2:14). Nor can we come to God in our own power, for Jesus says, "No one can come to Me unless the Father who sent Me draws him" (John 6:44).[105]

There are a number of issues raised here. Let's begin to address them with the ones in which we *agree*.

First, no one comes to Christ apart from God initiating the process. We are told "There is no one who seeks for God" (Romans 3:11). To remedy that, as Gudem points out, "No one can come to Me unless the Father who sent Me draws him." God has to initiate because, Scripture is clear, unbelievers wouldn't do it on their own.

Second, unbelievers indeed are slaves to sin and in that state of sinfulness are spiritually dead—unable to be with, fellowship with, God. Worse, and Grudem overlooks this, they are His *enemies* (James 4:4).

Third, unbelievers, in-and-of themselves, are *completely* unable to understand the things of God.

Fourth, unbelievers can *never* please God. They are *totally* incapable of doing *any* spiritual good or to be good in terms of a relationship with God *ever*. As we've seen, they are His *enemies*. Indeed, their deeds are filth before Him.

In light of all this, fifth, they could *in no way* bear fruit for the kingdom.

Have any of the issues raised here been disagreed with? It appears none have. On the surface all appears normal. Let's investigate.

As Grudem notes, we are told that the Father draws an individual to Christ. The Greek word here is *helko*, which means literally *drag*. (Because,

---

[105] Grudem, 497-498; emphasis in original.

as we've seen, we won't come on our own!) For what purpose is this initial dragging being done? The clue is in His name: Jesus, which means *Jehovah saves*. We are being dragged to the *Savior*.

Saved from what? Again, Grudem is correct: From our sins.

Why is this necessary? Because we are separated from God and will be for eternity if we are not saved. Thus, the unbeliever *needs* Jesus.

Does the reader see the Gospel message here? This is the reason we are dragged to Christ.

The key question now becomes: How does Scripture say this dragging is done? Scripture tells us clearly the Holy Spirit "will convict the world concerning sin, and righteousness, and judgment" (John 16:8).

Unbelievers could not in-and-of-themselves do this at all, much less do it effectively. But God—through the Holy Spirit does: "Who can be saved?" [the disciples asked]... Jesus said to them, "*With people this is impossible*, but with God all things are possible" (Matthew 19:25-26; emphasis added).

Further, the stark reality is that *men do not choose Jesus to please God*. As Grudem has so perfectly pointed out, at the point of decision they have no real concept of that. But through the conviction of the Holy Spirit they *do* become convinced they are sinners, that they deserve to be separated for eternity from God, and, ultimately, that Jesus will save them from that punishment.

Every sinner chooses because of his or her own self-interest. Yet, in doing so, they become—for the first time in their lives—in agreement with God and thus *new life begins in them*.

Is God honored? Yes. Was the motivation of the sinner-now-saved to honor God? Absolutely not! A challenge is put out to every saved person reading this: Was your motivation to honor God when you chose Christ? I would offer, NO! You were convinced (convicted) of the truth of the Gospel and willingly chose Christ as a result. It is so for *every* saved person!

For the unsaved, they refuse to accept the truth and so *willingly reject Christ*. As Reformed theologian Alva J. McClain points out in his book *Romans: The Gospel of God's Grace*, "If any man goes to hell... it will be his own fault because he rejected the mercy and longsuffering of God."[106]

---

[106] Alva J. McClain, *Romans: The Gospel of God's Grace* (Chicago, Illinois: Moody Press, 1973), 183; see also Chapter 16 – The Inheritance.

What, then, can we conclude?

It does not matter that we do not seek after God: He seeks after us; that is more than enough.

It does not matter we are slaves to sin: The Holy Spirit uses this very issue to convict us... which turns us towards the Savior.

It does not matter we don't understand the things of God: The Holy Spirit does and He is *fully* capable of convicting us of—making known to us—sin and righteousness and judgment leading us to believe in Christ.

It does not matter that we are incapable of doing any good: We do not need to please God to be saved; we need to *believe the Gospel*. Pleasing God comes as a *result of salvation*, that is, through the sanctification process (see below).

Lastly, at the moment of being saved we are not bearing fruit, *we are being "born from above"* (John 3:7). Fruit-bearing comes afterward *through sanctification*. Ephesians 2:8-10 makes the chronology of God's plan for each saved individual perfectly clear:

> For by grace you have been saved through faith; and that not of yourselves, it is the gift of God; *not as a result of works*, so that no one may boast. For we are His workmanship, created in Christ Jesus for good *works* [here is the fruit-bearing], which God prepared beforehand so that we would walk in them [emphasis added].

In conclusion, Scripture makes it clear that every individual who is convicted by the Holy Spirit has the opportunity to decide for Christ, the barriers raised by Grudem notwithstanding. The concept of Total Depravity is in error because it focuses on the limitations of man, not on the power and plan of God.

Thus, those who hold to this belief might be misguided. And if they are misguiding others, we will see in Section 2, both these conditions have dire consequences.

CHAPTER 18

THE UNIVERSAL CALL

"Behold the Lamb of God who takes away the sin of the world" (John 1:29).

There is a question within Christianity as to what extent did Jesus' death on the cross apply to mankind. Some hold that it applied to all, but that the pardon being offered had to be personally accepted—a freewill choice by the individual. Pre-determinarians hold that in God's foreknowledge of who would accept His Son's sacrifice, the atonement only applied to those accepting; a Limited Atonement.

For theologians, this seems to be an important topic. From a layperson's perspective it seems more theory than practical application. The practical viewpoint is that Christ did die to pay the penalty of sin. Those who accept this are saved; those who reject it are not.

However, to satisfy theologians, the topic should be explored.

We've seen that the Holy Spirit "will convict *the world* concerning sin, and righteousness, and judgment" (John16:8; emphasis added). But there is more:

> "Behold, the Lamb of God who takes away *the sin of the world!*" (John 1:29).

> God was *reconciling the world* to Himself" (2nd Corinthians 5:19).

He [Jesus] Himself is the propitiation—satisfaction—for our sins; and not for ours only, but also for those *of the whole world* (1st John 2:2).

Wayne Grudem has insightfully stated that "a free offer of the gospel can rightly be made to every person ever born.... This free offer of the gospel is extended in good faith to every person."[107] Alva J. McClain agrees. In his previously cited book *Romans: The Gospel of Grace* he states,

> Paul... talks about human responsibility in chapter 10 [of Romans].... Verse 8 [states]... "The Word is nigh thee." It is right near you, in your mouth and in your heart. The first fact the apostle insists upon is that *the gospel is within reach of all....* Verse 11 declares, "For the Scripture saith, whosoever." Again in verse 13, "whosoever." That word occurs twice. In the twelfth verse the word all also occurs twice. "Whosoever" and "all." The second fact is simply this: *the gospel is offered to all....* These... facts for the outline of the chapter: (1) the gospel is within the reach of all; and (2) the gospel has been offered to all..."[108]

If the offer is universal, but it would not apply universally, that offer would be false. Put another way, to make such an offer of salvation to all, if God is true, the offer *must* be legitimate to all to whom it is offered, otherwise it is a false offer and God has lied. As Scripture says "it is impossible for God to lie" (Hebrews 6:18); then for the offer to be true, Christ had to die for all.

Let's use an example which looks at this from a legal view point: In a court of law if a person is found guilty of a crime they will face the prescribed penalty. God says the penalty for sin is death (Romans 6:23). If, however, a person in legal authority offers a pardon, as the governor can in his or her state, the penalty need not be paid. There is one caveat: The convicted criminal needs to accept the pardon. If the pardon is refused, *legally* the penalty for the crime must then be carried out, because the sentence for that penalty remains in force. Again, *because the pardon has been rejected the original penalty remains in effect.*

---

[107] Grudem, 597.

[108] McClain, 185-186; emphasis in original.

This is why Alva J. McClain definitively states regarding the unsaved in Romans 9:22 who are "fitted for destruction..."

> The middle voice of the Greek verb ["fitted"] means that *man fits himself* for destruction. God never does that.... If any man ever goes to hell... it will be his own fault. It will be because he rejected the mercy and longsuffering of God. He will fit himself for destruction.[109]

Thus it is with the person who rejects the Gospel offer. The sentence of death—"the wages of sin is death" (Romans 6:23)—must then be enforced.

But this in no way negates that "Christ has died for all." It is just that not all will accept that pardon. The atonement is not limited in its availability, only in its application. And this as a result of the sinner's own choice.

If this is a correct understanding, then Limited Atonement does not hold true, further weakening Pre-determinarianism.

---

109 Ibid., 183.

CHAPTER 19

ROMANS NINE

He has mercy on whom He desires, and He hardens whom He desires...." (Romans 9:18).

As part of the Pre-determinarian argument against freewill, critical to their beliefs, Romans 9:9-18 is often quoted. In fact, R.C. Sproul in his book *Chosen by God* states it is a "most significant passage."[110]

> For this is the word of promise: "At this time I will come, and Sarah shall have a son." And not only this, but there was Rebekah also, when she had conceived twins by one man, our father Isaac; for though the twins were not yet born and had not done anything good or bad, so that God's purpose according to His choice would stand, not because of works but because of Him who calls, it was said to her, "The older will serve the younger." Just as it is written, "Jacob I loved, but Esau I hated."

> What shall we say then? There is no injustice with God, is there? May it never be! For He says to Moses, "I will have mercy on whom I have mercy, and I will have compassion on whom I have compassion." So then it does not depend on the man who wills or the man who runs, but on God who has mercy. For the Scripture says to Pharaoh, "For this very purpose I raised you up, to demonstrate My power in you, and that My name might be proclaimed throughout the whole earth." So then He has

---

[110] Sproul, 148.

mercy on whom He desires, and He hardens whom He desires (Romans 9:9-18).

Sproul goes on to say,

> "'So then, it is not him who wills, nor of him who runs, but of God who shows mercy.' This is the *coup de grace* to [those who believe in freewill]. This is the Word of God that requires all Christians to cease and desist from views... that make the ultimate decision for salvation rest in the will of man. [Thus], this one verse is absolutely fatal to those [who believe in freewill]."[111]

On the surface he appears to be correct: It does look like God has made the decision in each case. And verse 18 makes it clear He is sovereign in His choices. However, let's investigate.

We'll start with Pharaoh because the circumstances dealing with him are more straight-forward. First of all, the issue with Pharaoh does not deal with salvation. "Moses and Aaron came and said to Pharaoh, 'Thus says the LORD, "Let My people go that they may celebrate a feast to Me in the wilderness"'" (Exodus 5:1). The issue, as it is first raised, is that of *worship*.

Already the chosen people (over 400 years earlier; cf. Genesis 12:1-3), the Israelites knew of, and had an on-going relationship with, the Lord (for example, see Genesis 45:5, 7). Because God requires to be worshiped "in spirit and in truth" (John 4:24), and, as we've seen multiple times, the unsaved can do neither for they remain "enemies of God," this is an underlying issue of *sanctification*. God is removing the Israelites from the pagan Egyptians that they may worship in purity. The Lord may ultimately make this a permanent removal, but that is not how Pharaoh is first addressed.

Further, notice that Pharaoh—of his own freewill—chooses to not let the Israelites go: "But Pharaoh said, "Who is the LORD that I should obey His voice to let Israel go? I do not know the LORD, and besides, I will not let Israel go (v. 2)." Had God hardened Pharaoh's heart? No. In fact, God states clearly, "Pharaoh's heart is stubborn" (7:14). It is the condition of Pharaoh's heart *before* God influences it.

Pharaoh then goes on to refuse to let the Israelites go *six more times!* (Exodus 7:13, 22; 8:15, 19, 32; 9:7). And we are clearly told during each

---

111   Ibid., 151.

of these instances that *"Pharaoh hardened his heart* and did not listen..."
(Exodus 8:15; emphasis added). Throughout, *Pharaoh hardened his own
heart.*

It is at this point that God steps in. After seven previous attempts by
Moses, it is during the sixth plague that "the LORD hardened Pharaoh's
heart" (9:12). God merely ratifies what Pharaoh has done.

But what takes place next is a true demonstration of God's character...
and why He should be glorified: That His name *should* be proclaimed
throughout the earth. During the seventh plague we are told, "Pharaoh...
sinned again and *hardened his heart....* And Pharaoh's heart was hardened"
(9:34-35; emphasis added).

God, in His abundant mercy, *allows Pharaoh one last chance to obey.* "I
will have mercy on whom I have mercy... It does not depend on the man
who wills or the man who runs, but on God who has mercy... " God gave
mercy to Pharaoh *obviously* not because Pharaoh willed it... or deserved it.
God did it because it is His character alone to do so.

However, once Pharaoh rejected that mercy, God then accepted
Pharaoh's decision as final and thereafter God hardened Pharaoh's heart.
The Lord hardens whom He desires... *and when.* But, if Pharaoh is the
example that Paul is so demonstrating in Romans 9, God does not harden
without allowing an individual to express what is the desire of his or her
heart to begin with. Thus, as we saw in the last chapter (and we see with
Pharaoh), *man fits himself for destruction.* To state otherwise violates Romans
9.[112]

Further, God's dealing with Pharaoh is an example of every unbeliever
in their final judgment. They *choose* to reject the testimony of the Holy
Spirit—the unpardonable sin (Matthew 12:31)—and so God ratifies their
decision... *for eternity.* In the Lake of Fire without the leading and power of
the Holy Spirit, the unbeliever will be unable to choose Christ even if, like
Esau, they might attempt to do so "with tears" (Hebrews 12:17).

This brings us to the first part of the Romans passage which deals with
Esau.

There can be no doubt that God, in His sovereignty, chose Jacob over

---

[112] From a more practical sense, one can see why it is critical, then, to heed the admonition
in Hebrews 3:15: "Today if you hear His voice, do not harden your hearts."

Esau. But *not in regards to salvation*. Let's look at the circumstances of Jacob and Esau.

In Genesis 25:29-34 we are told that the firstborn, Esau, sold his birthright to Jacob, his younger twin.

> When Jacob had cooked stew, Esau came in from the field and
> he was famished; and Esau said to Jacob, "Please let me have a
> swallow of that red stuff there, for I am famished." ...But Jacob
> said, "First sell me your birthright." Esau said, "Behold, I am
> about to die; so of what use then is the birthright to me?" And
> Jacob said, "First swear to me"; so he swore to him, and sold his
> birthright to Jacob. Then Jacob gave Esau bread and lentil stew;
> and he ate and drank, and rose and went on his way. Thus Esau
> despised his birthright.

There are two significant issues here. First, Esau, *of his own freewill*, sold his birthright. This fact is irrefutable. Second, Esau, of his own freewill, sold his *birthright*. This fact is equally irrefutable. He did not sell his *salvation*.

The birthright deals with the *inheritance*.[113] The inheritance, for Christians, *is the reward* (see The Inheritance). It does not deal with salvation. As we've previously seen, the reward *is a result of sanctification*.

Why did God hate Esau?

> See to it that no one comes short of the grace of God... that
> there be no immoral or godless person like Esau, who sold his
> own birthright for a single meal" (Hebrews 12:15-16).

Esau lived godlessly. He deserved what he got. God, in his foreknowledge ("though the twins were not yet born and had not done anything good or bad"), simply ratified Esau's choice... and demonstrated that ratification in His choice of Jacob.

And how was that demonstrated? "The older will serve the younger." It is demonstrated in who would rule, who would have primacy—*not of one being saved and the other not*.

---

[113] Ryrie, *Study Bible*, 47: "The birthright of the eldest son gave him precedence over
his brothers (cf. 43:33) and assured him a double share of his father's inheritance (cf.
Deut. 21:17)."

Because of his freewill choice to sell his birthright, we are not saved through the God of Abraham, Isaac, and *Esau*. Why? *Esau lost that reward!*

And because Esau treated his *God-given* birthright (Deuteronomy 21:17) so cheaply, God rejected him ("Esau I hated") and chose Jacob ("Jacob I loved"). Thus, we are saved through the God of Abraham, Isaac, *and Jacob* (Genesis 50:24).

As a result of all of this, it is clear that Jacob was chosen *for sanctification*, set aside for a purpose *that could have been Esau's*, had he remained faithful to the birthright provided him by God in Deuteronomy 21:17.

In conclusion, this passage in Romans 9 has been wrongly interpreted and, thus, wrongly applied if it is believed it deals with justification. The error, again a *serious* error, is that an issue of justification has been wrongly substituted for an issue of sanctification. The passage, then, is not the *coup de grace* of freewill, as believed by Sproul; it is, in fact, its *fait accompli*.

Thus, if wrongly understood, embraced, and applied, the adverse effect on ministry will be impacting, adding to the *worst* worst-case scenario when this happens under the duress of the Great Tribulation.

CHAPTER 20

THE ACT OF FAITH

Now faith is the assurance of things hoped for, the conviction of things
not seen (Hebrews 11:1).

As a wrap-up to this Section, it is imperative to see what faith actually is.
The very definition, and what it connotes, will be telling.

The words "faith" and "belief" are the same word in the New Testament
Greek, *pistis*. It means to trust in, place confidence in, have reliance upon.
Vine's Expository Dictionary of New Testament Words defines it as a complete
"assurance"—a *guarantee* regarding something.[114]

So states Hebrews 11:1, which goes on to say it is "the conviction of
things not seen." The Greek word for conviction, *elegchos*, means "evidence."

There is only one place where trust can be discerned—whether it is
gained or lost: The mind. Trust is *always* an issue of decision. This is true
even if one is acting (or re-acting) off of emotions. The choice, the decision,
to trust or not to trust takes place in a person's mind... even if "felt in the
heart." (Who, on occasion, has not decided *against* an emotional leaning
and trusted anyway? Barnabas dealing with, trust in, John Mark in spite
of Paul's emotional response to Mark's desertion [Acts 13:13; 16:36-40]
comes to mind.)

For such decision-making, there is only one place that evidence for any
choice can be processed: The mind. Faith, then, *is an issue of our minds*.

A person's mind is made up of three elements: (1) intellect, our "thought

---

[114]   Vine, 76.

processes," the ability to "think"; (2) emotion, our "feelings"; and (3) will, our "ability to commit, to choose—and act on our choices." These three elements reveal to a person his or her own *self-consciousness*, and to the world one's *personality*. In biblical terms, this is, as we've previously seen, a person's "soul."

When, as an unbeliever who is identified in Scripture as being spiritually dead (Ephesians 2:1), our mind is the only capacity we have to act towards the physical world we inhabit. *And* it is the only way we can act towards the spiritual world to which we are, at best, ignorant, at worst, oblivious (John 3:3).

Because God is all-powerful—as Jesus said, "With God all things are possible" (Mark 10:27)—*it is through our minds that He works to bring us to salvation...* because our spirits are *dead* until we accept Jesus as our Savior (John 3:6). This is the clear message of Romans:

> How then shall they call upon Him whom they have not believed? And how shall they believe in Him whom they have not heard? And how shall they hear without a preacher? And how shall they preach unless they are sent?... So, faith comes from hearing; and hearing by the word of Christ. (vv. 10:14-15, 17).

It is through the Word being preached that the ear hears and the minds processes, either to accept or reject the Gospel message. But, *it is in the mind where that decision is made.* Because our spirits are still dead.

This brings us to the issue of "the heart." Wayne Grudem in his *Systematic Theology* defines it as "the center of our desires [will] and decision-making process [intellect]."[115] Because our desires and decision-making process are, at times, affected by our emotions, it is safe to say "the *heart* is the very center of who we are, that place where the three elements of our mind—intellect, emotion, and will—are most intense."

God Himself relates the heart with the mind: "I, the LORD, search the heart, I test the mind..." (Jeremiah 17:10).

The spiritual fact that must be acknowledged here is that until we believe in Jesus as our Savior, the heart is *always* intent on itself—even when doing "good deeds." Jeremiah continues:

---

[115] Grudem, 497.

The heart is more deceitful than all else and is desperately sick; who can understand it? (17:9).

Isaiah provides a Second Witness to this fact:

For all of us have become like one who is unclean [from sin], and all our righteous deeds [in our own eyes] are like filthy garments [literally, menstrual rags is how God sees our "good deeds"] (64:6).

Notwithstanding this horrific condition, it is through the mind that God approaches the sinner to call (*kletos*-"invite") him or her to salvation. We will turn to the renowned theologian, John Calvin (1509-1564), to confirm.

We shall now have a full definition of faith if we say that it is a firm and sure knowledge of the divine favour toward us, on the truth of a free promise in Christ, and *revealed to our minds*, and sealed on our hearts, by the Holy Spirit.[116]

Joseph C. Dillon in his book *The Reign of the Servant Kings: A Study of Eternal Security and the Final Significance of Man*, observed of Calvin's statement:

For Calvin faith is knowledge. *It is not obedience.* It is a passive thing received as a result of the witness of the Holy Spirit. It is "recognition" and "knowledge" (*Institutes* 3.2.14).... Calvin insists, "For, in regard to justification, faith is merely passive, bringing nothing of ourselves to procure the favor of God, but receiving from Christ everything we want" (*Institutes* 3.13.5).[117]

Let's explore this further.

Towering Christian theologian Jonathan Edwards (1703-1758) wrote in his *On the Freedom of the Will*, "The will always chooses according to

---

[116] John Calvin, Henry Beveridge Esq., trans., *Institutes of the Christian Religion*, 4th Ed. (London: Bonham Norton, 1581; Kindle Edition, (from 1964 trans. ed.), 3.2.7; emphasis added.

[117] Dillon, 249; references to *Institutes* in the original; emphasis added.

its strongest inclination at the moment."[118] R. C. Sproul in *Chosen by God* expounds on this and goes on to state,

> To have free will is to be able to choose according to our desires… This means that every choice is free *and* every choice is determined…. But "determined" does not mean that some external force coerces the will…. Coercion involves acting with some kind of force, imposing choices upon people that, if left to themselves, they would not choose…. Rather it refers to one's internal motivation or desire…: Our choices are determined by our desires… [and] we always choose according to our strongest inclination at the moment…. They remain our choices because they are motivated by our own desires. This is what we call *self-determinism*, which is the essence of freedom.[119]

We will "always choose according to our strongest inclination at the moment." This is a tremendously insightful statement! When confronted with the Gospel an individual of his or her own free will chooses to accept or reject it. Either choice is driven by that individual's "strongest inclination at the moment."

For those who choose to be saved because it makes sense immediately, the desire is instantaneous. For some, they have to "ponder it"—maybe over a period of years (decades?). But, for those who accept Jesus as Savior, there comes a point when they settle into agreement with the Gospel message.

Whether fast or slow, at the moment of decision, that moment that *is* their "strongest" inclination, they believe the Gospel facts. The choice is conducted *in their mind* and *of their own free will*.

Regarding this point Grudem asks, "Why did God choose faith as the means by which we receive justification?"…and then he answers:

> It is apparently because faith is the one attitude of heart that is the exact opposite of depending on ourselves. When we come to Christ in faith we essentially say, "I give up! I will not depend on myself or my own good works any longer. I know that I can never

---

[118] Ola Elizabeth Winslow, ed., *Jonathan Edwards: Basic Writings*, "Freedom of the Will" (New York: The New American Library, Inc., 1966), 201. Edwards treatise was written in 1754.

[119] Sproul, 54, 57; emphasis in original.

make myself righteous before God. Therefore, Jesus, I trust you and depend on you completely to give me a righteous standing before God."[120]

An individual is convinced—*in his or her mind*—that the Gospel is true... and responds accordingly. It is important to realize, in doing so *they choose* to act directly opposite that of Satan who attempted to usurp God's power. The new believer has chosen to relinquished power, giving authority back to God!

One final observation.

In Genesis 3 we have the First Mention of human decision. God had communed with Adam before this moment: "And God blessed them [Adam and Eve] and said to them..." (Genesis 1:28; cf. 2:16).

At the same time, God had commanded Adam to not eat of "the tree of the knowledge of good and evil" (Genesis 2:17). But, notice at the moment of Adam's decision, the Lord did nothing to influence Adam. God wanted the man to exercise the very freewill God had given him when Adam was created. For that reason, God does not make Himself present until after Adam has decided (Genesis 3:8ff). Note too, there is absolutely no mention that God in any way hardened Adam's heart so that he, Adam, would fail.

Thus, those Pre-destinarians who believe in double-predestiny, where God chooses ones to be saved and hardens the heart of the lost so they could never make that choice, is seriously weakened.

This is critical. If Adam had been "chosen" to failure by God rejecting him, hardening his heart, "before the foundation of the world," then Adam would have been nothing more than a proxy. Thus *God would have been the author of sin.*

But, because Adam had full opportunity for choice, it is Adam who is responsible. This pattern has continued throughout all human decision-making throughout Scripture... including Pharaoh (see chapters 19).

So, we have come full-circle. Having begun this Section with Adam in the Garden, we now end it there as well. In so doing, we have seen that faith, *an action of the mind exercising freewill* is done by the individual. Like the First Mention of the use of freewill by a human, God has not interfered in allowing us to choose.

---

[120]   Grudem, 730.

An understanding of this provides insights, many presented in the chapters above, of the weaknesses of the Pre-destinarianism beliefs. This should cause the Pre-destinarian, should that viewpoint prove wrong, to consider the worst-case scenario and prepare accordingly.

The *worst* worst-case scenario is linked to their perspective on Perseverance. A belief they will never fall away, when, in fact, that might occur, leaves them severely vulnerable if, as Jesus said, "many will." A wrong understanding could well lead to a wrong (spiritual) reaction.

The extent of such vulnerability will be explored in Section II.

SECTION 2

...IMPACTS THE KINGDOM OF GOD

CHAPTER 21

KINGDOM OF GOD

The kingdom of God suffers violence, and violent men take it by force
(Matthew 11:12).

A. INTRODUCTION

This opening verse from the Gospel of Matthew hardly sounds like the much less complicated (and less violent) "believe in the Lord Jesus Christ and you shall be saved" (Acts 16:31). Yet, it very succinctly lays the foundation to what we shall see regarding the Kingdom of God.

At the outset it should be noted not all Bible scholars are in agreement as to what the Kingdom of God is. There are two divergent perspectives on this issue of eschatology. The key concern that divides these scholars is centered on Revelation 20, which indicates a 1,000-year reign of Christ that will occur after the preceding events of the first nineteen chapters.

The concept of "a thousand years," rendered in the Latin as *mille* (thousand) and *annus* (years), produces the word *millennium*. The theological debate over this millennium is whether there will be a literal reign of Jesus Christ on earth for one thousand years, or whether the number should be interpreted figuratively, thus "spiritualized" into meaning a "complete" period of time.[121]

---

[121] Charles C. Ryrie, *The Basis of the Premillennial Faith* (Neptune, New Jersey: Louizeaux Brothers, 1953), 13-14.

The latter view, called *amillenialism,* was born out of the teachings of St. Augustine, a Christian writer from the North African city of Hippo, who wrote in the AD fourth century. Its tenets spiritualized the 1,000-year reign of Revelation 20, and assigned its fulfillment to the Church age.[122] Wholeheartedly embraced by the Roman Catholic Church, this view also found some Protestant adherents, the most ardent of which was Geerhardus Vos.[123]

Like St. Augustine, Vos saw no difference between the Kingdom of God and the Church herself,[124] hence Christ's "reign" existed "spiritually" within the Church. Writing in his book *The Kingdom and the Church,* he expanded on this,

> [I]t appears that every view which would keep the kingdom and the church (sic) separate as two entirely distinct spheres is not in harmony with the trend of our Lord's teaching. The church is a form which the kingdom assumes in result of the new stage upon which the Messiahship of Jesus enters with his death and resurrection.... The church actually has within herself the powers of [Christ].[125]

From this citation, it is easy to see why Vos would conclude that the millennium was already being fulfilled by the Church. So, as Ryrie noted of amillennialists, the one thousand was more a "number of perfection or completion, a symbolic reference to the complete period between the two Advents of Christ,"[126] i.e., the Church Age.

As a result of this reasoning, there would be no need for Christ to actually, physically reign on earth. Further, since the millennium is, as we have previously seen, preceded by the Great Tribulation, there was really no room in the amillennialist eschatology for such an event. As Walvoord

---

[122]   Ibid., 14; cf. Walvoord, *Rapture Question,* 16.

[123]   Charles L. Feinberg, *Premillennialism or Amillennnialism?* (Wheaton, Illinois: Van Kampen Press, 1954), 113.

[124]   Geerhardus Vos, *Biblical Theology* (Grand Rapids, Michigan: William B. Eerdmans Publishing Company, 1948), 427.

[125]   Geerhardus Vos, *The Kingdom and the Church* (Grand Rapids, Michigan: Wm. B. Eerdmans Publishing Company, 1951), 84, 85-86.

[126]   Ryrie, *Premillennial Faith,* 14.

observed, "Often [the Great Tribulation] is identified [by the amillennialist] with the troubles of Israel in connection with the destruction of Jerusalem in [AD] 70."[127]

In opposition to the amillennial view is that of the *premillennial*. This view interpreted the one thousand years of Revelation 20 literally, and holds that after the Great Tribulation described in the Book of Revelation (through chapter nineteen), Christ will reign upon the earth from the city of David, Jerusalem, in fulfillment of the Old Testament prophecies of such a kingdom.[128] Ryrie confirmed the premillennial position as:

> At the close of this [the Church] age, premillennialists believe that Christ will return for His Church, meeting them in the air (this is not the Second Coming of Christ), which event, called the rapture, will usher in [the Great Tribulation] on the earth. After this, the Lord will return to the earth (this is the Second Coming of Christ) to establish His kingdom on the earth for a thousand years, during which time the promises to Israel will be fulfilled.[129]

Important to the premillennial view is the Great Tribulation, a period of time preceding Jesus' return during which, literally, the Wrath of God — the most horrific judgments ever faced by mankind — will be inflicted upon the earth.

> Premillennialists generally believe that the return of Christ will be preceded by certain signs such as... a great apostasy, wars, famines, earthquakes, the appearance of the Antichrist and great tribulation. His return will be followed by a period of peace and righteousness before the end of the world. Christ will reign as King in person [during these 1,000 years].[130]

It should be noted that throughout the almost 2,000 years of the Church Age each of these views has had its time as predominate. But,

---

[127] Walvoord, *Rapture Question*, 16.

[128] Pentecost, *Things To Come*, 372.

[129] Ryrie, *Premillennial Faith*, 12; parenthesis in original.

[130] Robert G. Clouse, *The Meaning of the Millennium* (Downers Grove, Illinois: InterVarsity Press, 1977), 7-8.

as Clouse noted, "During the nineteenth... and twentieth centuries... premillennialism again attracted widespread attention."[131]

It is not for its current ascendancy, however, that premillennialism is championed in this writing. The reasons for choosing it over amillennialism are three:

1.) It is in keeping with the hermeneutical approach identified in this writing's Introduction: Where interpretation is applied, it is in the literal sense. If the Word of God says 1,000 years, literally it means 1,000 years. As an example, where the Jewish people were told their captivity in Babylon would last 70 years (Jeremiah 25:11), it, historically, turned out to be a literal 70 years.[132]

2.) It is so understood this way in some Jewish apocalyptic literature:

In the book of Daniel, [w]here it is said that "the God of heaven shall set up a kingdom... for whose coming God himself is responsible and in which his sovereignty will be acknowledged by "all the peoples, nations, and languages" (7:14).... It is to be given to "the saints of the Most High" *who will bear rule in it* with the full authority of God (7:13), 18, 27). *It is an earthly kingdom...* with *some* of the more illustrious dead who will be raised by resurrection to take part in it (12:2).[133]

3.) The issue of preparation demands it! One can only prepare *beforehand*. Once a person finds him- or herself in the midst of

---

131 Ibid., 11.

132 See Ryrie, *Study Bible*, "Introduction to the Book of Ezra: Historical Background," 693.

133 D. S. Russell, *The Method and Message of Jewish Apocalyptic* (Philadelphia: The Westminster Press, 1964), 286-287; emphasis added. Notice the elements described here: (1) All peoples [and] nations shall be ruled; this does not sound like the Eternal State where rule will be from a heavenly New Jerusalem. (2) the saints get to rule with the full authority of God. This will be pursued later when we look at the Kingdom in greater detail, but should be remembered for when we do. (3) It is an earthly kingdom; again, being different from the New Jerusalem. (4) Only *some* of the dead will be raised. This foretells of a future resurrection thereafter as found in Revelation 20 and, we would offer, separated by One Thousand Years.

a situation, they can no longer prepare; all they can do is *react*.[134]
With the Kingdom of God as a future event, preparation is still an available option.

So, the first thing to know about the Kingdom of God is that it is the Millennial Kingdom of Christ, the 1,000-years He will reign here on earth after the events of the first 18 chapters of the Book of Revelation. It is, in the sense expressed by Peter, "With the Lord one day is as a thousand years" (2nd Peter 3:8), the literal Day of the Lord. Keep in mind, though, it is *not* the Eternal State.

Jesus Himself made it clear what the Kingdom of God was:

> [Jesus said], "Our Father who is in heaven... Your kingdom come: Your will be done, on earth as it is in heaven" (Matthew 6:9-10).

The Lord's Prayer makes it clear that the Kingdom is God's will being done on earth as it is currently being done in heaven. Though many who are saved are living this today on earth, attempting to do God's will as best they can, during the 1,000-year reign of Jesus this will be done worldwide: "And the LORD will be king over all the earth..." (Zechariah 14:9).

A rare few Christian writers have seen this truth: In the Review of Literature for Pre-determinarianism in the writing's Introduction it briefly looked at J. Sidlow Baxter's quote from his book *The Strategic Grasp of the Bible*. Here is the full quote.

> When John and our Lord came preaching, "Repent ye; for the kingdom of heaven is at hand," they were referring to something publicly understood, namely, the long-promised Messianic kingdom which was the grand subject of Old Testament prophecy.... When our Lord interviewed Nicodemus (John 3) He spoke at once of the "kingdom of God" as a concern already familiar to Nicodemus' mind....

---

[134] And being in the midst of a situation for which you are unprepared is often as bad as it gets: As Blythe, *Blindsided*, 4, explains, *"There is little possibility of effective response without thoughtful preparedness"*; emphasis in original. If the Kingdom of God is not future, we are all, then, in trouble! And, as we shall soon see, the unprepared are, in fact, in *serious* trouble.

If by the "kingdom of heaven" our Lord meant the *Gospel*, as we now commonly use that word, meaning "the grace of God which bringeth salvation" to all who by faith appropriate the atonement of Christ, He would have been unintelligible, unless He had first explained that He meant this. For the Gospel of Calvary is "good news" of personal salvation to individual men and women everywhere ("whosoever"), not the proclamation of a "kingdom"...

THE KINGDOM OF HEAVEN IS THE KINGDOM PREDICTED IN (WHAT WE CHRISTIANS NOW CALL) THE OLD TESTAMENT SCRIPTURES; THE KINGDOM TO BE BROUGHT IN BY ISRAEL'S MESSIAH....

The "kingdom of heaven" which was offered and rejected [by the Jews] two thousand years ago is *not* on earth today in the form of the Church. The very word, "kingdom" (Greek, *basileia*), is a big inclusive term; whereas the word, "Church" (*ecclesia*), indicates a called out *minority*. Those very words should guard us against confusing the kingdom with the Church....

The kingdom will come when the King himself returns in the splendor of His second advent.... All history is fore-planned, *including* the present suspension of the Messianic kingdom and its yet future realization at the second coming of the now-ascended Lord Jesus....

...[It is] at the *end* of the Millennium, and the transition from it to the "eternal state," [that] our Lord's *Messianic* kingdom will [then] merge into that boundless, timeless, endless reign in which the triune God is "all in all" [1 Cor. 15:28].[135]

Nor is Baxter the only one to see this truth. David M. Panton (1870-1955) of the 19th century wrote in his *The Judgment Seat of Christ*:

The "Kingdom of God," or "of the heavens," a phrase drawn directly from Daniel, is a Kingdom which "fills the whole earth"

---

[135] Baxter, 234, 235, 236, 245, 249, 249; upper case emphasis in the original.

(Daniel 2:35,44), replaces all worldly empires, and is obviously the Messianic Kingdom: when the "Kingdom of the world is become the Kingdom of our Lord, and His Christ" (Rev 11:15). It is foreshadowed now by the Kingdom in Mystery (Matthew 13), or the Church... but its manifestation at the Second Advent, to which all Scripture prophecies refer it, proves it to be the Millennial.... Concerning the Everlasting Kingdom, prophecy reveals little, and that little perhaps solely in the last two chapters of the Apocalypse. In the only passage in which the Holy Ghost uses the phrase "the Kingdom" (1 Cor. 15:24), He means the Millennial.[136]

And this concept is not just relegated to archaic writers. Modern study Bibles have commented:

> *kingdom of heaven*: This is the rule of heaven over the earth. The Jewish people of Christ's day were looking for this Messianic or Davidic kingdom to be established on earth (Matthew 3:2, note, p. 1448). *kingdom of God*: This is the rule of Messiah on earth, promised in the Old Testament and earnestly longed for by the Jewish people... However, the people rejected rather than accepted Him, and the fulfillment of the kingdom promises had to be delayed until God's purpose in saving Jews and Gentiles and forming His church was completed. Then Christ will return and set up God's kingdom on this earth ([see] Acts 15:14-16; Rev. 19:15).[137]

> *Kingdom.* The kingly reign of Jesus Christ. This rule, which was initiated during his earthly ministry (Matt. 12:28), continues as He reigns from the Father's right hand during the present age (Acts 2:33-36), and climaxes in His thousand-year reign after His return (Matt. 16:28; 25:31-34), after which the Son, having completed His kingly task, will hand over the kingdom to the Father (1 Cor. 15:24-25).[138]

---

[136]   Panton, D. M. *The Judgment Seat of Christ* (Hayesville, North Carolina: Schoettle Publishing Co., Inc., reprint 1984), 36.

[137]   Ryrie, *Study Bible*, note on Mark 1:15, 1505.

[138]   W. A. Criswell, ed., *The Criswell Study Bible: Authorized King James Version* (New York: Thomas Nelson Publishers, 1979), Glossary note, 1539.

> What is the good news of the *kingdom of God?* These first words
> spoken by Jesus in Mark give the core of his teaching: that the
> long-awaited Messiah has come to… begin God's personal *reign
> on earth.*[139]

Once it is grasped that the passages in the New Testament dealing
with the Kingdom of God or Kingdom of Heaven are understood as Jesus'
Millennial reign *and not the Eternal State*, the verses come alive with insight
into the next age of God's plan. Insight that is critical for believers living in
this, the Church Age.

B. Gospel Of The Kingdom

It is important at this point to have a firm understanding of what the
Gospel of the Kingdom actually is. During Jesus' ministry of His First
Advent we are told that He

> …was going about… teaching in the synagogues, and
> proclaiming the gospel of the kingdom (Matthew 4:23).

> …was going about all the cities and villages, teaching in the
> synagogues, and proclaiming the gospel of the kingdom
> (Matthew 9:35).

What exactly was Jesus' "teaching" and "proclaiming"? The answer is
tremendously important as we are told that Paul followed Jesus' example:

> He was explaining to them by solemnly testifying about the
> kingdom of God, and trying to persuade them concerning
> Jesus… and he stayed two full years in his own rented quarters,
> and was welcoming all who came to him, preaching the kingdom
> of God, and teaching concerning the Lord Jesus Christ… (Acts
> 28:23, 30-31).

Paul preached—publicly proclaimed—the kingdom, and taught—gave
instruction—about the Lord Jesus, the Messiah. Again, this is exactly what

---

[139] Metzger, ed., *Life Application Bible,* note on Mark 1:15, 1681; emphasis added.

Jesus did. The only conclusion that can be reached is that although closely related, they are two different issues, and, thus, each with its own set of principles.

To understand the gospel—the good news—of the kingdom, then, it is important to understand its relationship to the gospel of salvation. Both are related to Jesus, the Messiah, but in different ways.

The full gospel, as we are about to see, has four components. Paul, writing to the Romans provides the "basic" three. Let's look at them first.

> Paul, a bond-servant of Christ Jesus... set apart for the gospel of God [the Father]... concerning His Son, who was born of a descendant of David according to the flesh, who was declared the Son of God... (1,3-4).

This is the *Gospel of the Father*. It declares that Jesus is both God, "concerning His Son," and man, "descendant of David." John writes in his gospel this is what must be believed for salvation: "...that you may believe that Jesus is the Christ—the anointed one (man)—[and] the Son of God; and that believing you may have life in His name" (20:31).

Jesus had to be God, because only God could save us: "I, even I, am the LORD, and there is no savior besides Me" (Isaiah 43:11; cf. Hosea 13:4). Hence, in order to redeem mankind, God had to be a man. As the *Ryrie Study Bible* states, "The... kinsman-redeemer [had to be] one who is related by blood to those he redeems, indicating the necessity for the incarnation"—God becoming man.[140]

And, the Father's good news continues: "This is My beloved Son, in whom I am well-pleased" (Matthew 3:17). If the Father were not well-pleased, i.e. if there was so much as one spot of sin with the Son, He could not have been the perfect sacrifice necessary to redeem us: "Your [Passover] lamb shall be an unblemished male" (Exodus 12:5). The Father's declaration here in Matthew confirms Jesus will be the perfect sacrifice that *will* take away our sins. Good news indeed!

Paul goes on to write about the Son's good news:

> For God, whom I [Paul] serve in my spirit in the preaching of the gospel of His Son... (Romans 1:9).

---

[140] Ryrie, *Study Bible*, notes on Isaiah 59:17-21, 1102.

For I [Paul] am not ashamed of the gospel, for it is the power of God for salvation to everyone who believes... For in it the righteousness of God is revealed from faith to faith (Romans 1:16,17).

The *Gospel of the Son* declares that salvation is for "everyone who believes" in the Son and it is received through faith. Notice, *not* obedience. The good news here is that we *can* be saved! Again, as the *Ryrie Study Bible* notes,

"righteousness of God. I.e., the restoration of right relationships between man and God, which proceeds from God... through His Son. *faith to faith.* I.e., faith from start to finish."[141]

Paul completes his writing on the gospel with its third part:

God... will render to every man according to his deeds... on the day when, according to my [Paul's] gospel, God will judge the secrets of men through Christ Jesus (Romans 2:5c, 6,16).

For we shall all stand before the judgment seat of God... [and] each one of us shall give account of himself to God (Romans 14:10b,12).

Paul refers to this as *my Gospel.* Because Paul is under inspiration of the Holy Spirit (2nd Timothy 3:16), this is really the *Gospel of the Holy Spirit.* However, as the Holy Spirit never draws attention to Himself, but only to Christ (John 16:13-14), He continues to do so here. With Paul identified as "an apostle of Jesus Christ by the will of God" (1st Corinthians 1:1), proclaiming this to be "my gospel," actually draws attention to Christ, whom Paul is representing here.

With that understanding, coupled with what we've previously seen, this judgment of which Paul writes is, again, good news... but only to those who are receiving reward, i.e., The Faithful (1st Corinthians 3:14; however, see the chapters on Understanding the Kingdom, for those who are not).

To re-cap, the gospel—good news—is that the Father is pleased with the Son whose sacrifice will redeem us and restore our relationship with

---

[141]   Ibid., note for Romans 1:17, 1702.

God and, as a result, we are eligible for not only salvation, but also rewards. Again, good news indeed!

This leads us to the *Gospel of the Kingdom*, proclaimed by Jesus Himself, as well as Paul, amongst others. What good news is that? It's what happens *in the kingdom*.

A full list would be space-prohibitive, but a partial list will provide insight into what awaits: Satan is bound for the 1,000 years (Revelation 20:2) and evil severely curtailed (Isaiah 65:25b), diseases will be cured (Isaiah 35:5-6a; cf. Matthew 4:23b, 11:5), war will cease (Isaiah 2:4b), the natural order will return to a pre-Fall status (Isaiah 65:25a; cf. Romans 8:19-22), and, possibly best of all, the glory of the LORD *will be seen* (Isaiah 35:2; emphasis added).

An important point must be made here. When Jesus was relating the conditions that preceded His return, notice what He said would be *the* condition signifying the end: "The gospel of the kingdom shall be preached in the whole world for a witness to all nations, and then the end shall come" (Matthew 34:14). *It is* not *the gospel of salvation*: the gospels of the Father and the Son and the Holy Spirit. *It is the gospel of the Son's kingdom.*

As at Jesus' First Advent, where the gospel of the kingdom was preached, so it is at the point preceding the Second Advent. This, thus, explains the absolute necessity for a thorough understanding of it, especially for those living in the Endtimes.

And what is the issue most related to the Kingdom?

> John the Baptist came, preaching... saying, "Repent, for the kingdom of heaven is at hand" (Matthew 3:1-2).

Jesus, in the very first recorded words of His ministry proclaimed this very message,

> "Repent, for the kingdom of heaven is at hand" (Matthew 4:17).

The issue of repentance is usually misunderstood by many Christians. It is *not* feeling remorse or being tearful. The original Greek word *metanoeo*, is a compound made up of *meta*, "afterwards," and *noieo*, "to exercise the mind," i.e. to comprehend. *Noieo's* root is *nous*, "the intellect, the mind." The word literally means, "to perceive afterwards," i.e, to *finally* come to see (perceive) the right course to take and, therefore, *to change your mind...* and do it.

Many of the Israelites of Jesus' day were not living according to the Law and, therefore, not living righteously—right in God's eyes. Living according to God's will, being obedient to Him, has direct impact on one's status in the Kingdom (see Understanding the Kingdom). Thus, John the Baptist and Jesus were trying to get the people to understand they needed to live according to God's principles. Once the Kingdom was begun, if they failed to do so (to "repent" as described above), it would be too late.

Because of the inordinate rise in evil just before Christ's return (Matthew 24:10-12, 21-22), this same message will need to be "preached in the whole world for a witness to all nations." At Christ's return, it will be too late to change one's mind and attempt to live righteously. Such failure has significant consequences, as we shall soon see.

C. THE KINGDOM AND THE APOSTLE JOHN

Unlike Matthew, Mark, and Luke, who speak extensively of the Kingdom, the Apostle John in his gospel directly mentions the Kingdom of God only twice, indirectly once, and with not one instance in his three letters! Even in the book of Revelation there are, surprisingly, only two references which deal specifically with the manner of the kingdom. Why so little attention to the Kingdom?

> These [things] have been written that you may believe that Jesus is the Christ, the Son of God; and that believing you may have life in His name (John 20:31).

John, in his gospel, is primarily interested in *justification*. The issues of the Kingdom are issues of *sanctification*.

But John does supply important information regarding the Kingdom in his rare occurrences writing about it.

> And the seventh angel sounded [his trumpet]; and there arose loud voices in heaven, saying, "The kingdom of the world has become the kingdom of our Lord, and His Christ... (Revelation 11:15).

> And I heard a loud voice in heaven saying, "Now... the kingdom of our God and the authority of His Christ have come... (Revelation 12:10).

> And I saw heaven opened; and behold, a white horse, and He who sat upon it is called Faithful and True; and in righteousness He judges and wages war.... And He is clothed with a robe dipped in blood; and His name is called The Word of God. And the armies which are in heaven, clothed in fine linen, white and clean—the fine linen is the righteous acts of the saints (v. 8)—were following Him on white horses. And from His mouth comes a sharp sword, so that with it He may smite the nations; and He will rule them with a rod of iron... And on His robe and on His thigh He has a name written "KING OF KINGS, AND LORD OF LORDS. (Revelation 19:11,13-16).

These passages indicate God's timing; and that the kingdom begins concurrent to the Lord's return to earth, which confirms that the kingdom deals with Christ's reign on *earth* not in heaven. (Note, Jesus will reign from the New Jerusalem in heaven only in the Eternal State [Revelation 21-22]).

With that as background, let's look at the two instances the Kingdom is discussed in John's gospel.

> Jesus answered and said to him [Nicodemus], "Truly, truly, I say to you, unless one is born again, he cannot see the kingdom of God (John 3:3).

The Greek word translated "see" is *eido*. It means *to be aware of*. John makes it clear that those who are unsaved are oblivious of the Kingdom. It is only those who have been born again, accepted Jesus as Savior and become justified, that are able to become aware of its existence. This is the result of the indwelling Holy Spirit (Romans 8:16) at the moment of our belief. Paul confirms this in his second letter to the Corinthians:

> [The] veil remains unlifted, because it is removed in Christ... whenever a man turns to the Lord, the veil is taken away (3:14,16).

So, John has told us the only way a person can become aware of the existence of the Kingdom. He then goes on to tell us how we can enter it.

> Jesus answered [Nicodemus], "Truly, truly, I say to you, unless one is born of water and the Spirit, he cannot enter the kingdom of God (John 3:5).

In relation to John 3:3, those born again are given the opportunity to become aware of the Kingdom. But *to enter it* has restrictions. As we shall confirm later, the implication is that all who are saved may not necessarily enter the Kingdom. Let's look at the restrictions.

One must be "born of the Spirit." John tells us that "God is Spirit... and that which is born of the Spirit is spirit (4:24; 3:6b). So, a restriction is that one be born again, thus justified unto salvation. The unsaved not only are oblivious to the Kingdom, they are restricted from entering into it.

But there is a second restriction: "born of water." Note that this concept is very often misunderstood. It does *not* refer to "natural birth" or undertaking the rite of baptism. Letting Scripture interpret itself we see that

> Christ also is the head of the church... [and] loved the church and gave Himself up for her; that *He might sanctify her by the washing of water with the word...* (Ephesians 5:23,25,26; emphasis added).

"Born of the water" is a reference to the "washing of water with the word." The *Ryrie Study Bible* comments that *"born of water... It [could] mean the Word of God as in John 15:3: 'You are already clean because of the word which I have spoken to you' "*[142] Thus, entrance into the Kingdom requires that a saved individual *also be sanctified*—which, as we've seen, requires repentance. This is exactly what Jesus (and Paul) preached.

Further, we shall see that entrance into the Kingdom *is a reward*. And, contrary to popular belief, *not all the saved will attain it*. Put simply, *if Christ isn't Lord of your life during your lifetime here on earth, He will not be your Lord during His 1,000-year reign here on earth.*

Let's let Scripture prove it.

---

[142]   Ibid., note for John 15:3, 1604.

D. Entrance Into The Kingdom

> From the days of John the Baptist until now the kingdom
> of heaven suffers violence, and violent men take it by force
> (Matthew 11:12).

"From the days of John the Baptist"—the time directly preceding Jesus'
ministry; thus, as John, and then Jesus, preached the Kingdom, those who
heard and understood began to "take it by force." Is there any mention here
of "believe," which is necessary for justification (Acts 16:31)? No. Further,
aren't those attempting to enter the Kingdom *working towards it*? Absolutely!
They are "taking it by force." The only conclusion to be drawn here is that
although salvation and entrance into the Kingdom are related, they are also
two different, distinct elements.

Further, this passage never tells us that Jesus condemns these people for
their "fighting to get in." In fact, Jesus speaks in a commendable tone as He
goes on to say, "And if you care to accept it, he [John the Baptist] is Elijah,
who was to come" (v. 14).

Malachi stated that Elijah would precede the Day of the Lord (4:5)—
when the Kingdom would be established. Again, Jesus is indicating that
those taking the Kingdom are doing the right thing if John the Baptist is
[in the spirit of] Elijah, because then "the Kingdom is at hand"—i. e., about
to begin (Matthew 3:2).

It is also clearly implied that *not all* are attempting to "take... the
Kingdom." And, as we'll see, not all will enter it.

> [Jesus said], "Not everyone who says to Me, 'Lord, Lord,' will
> enter the kingdom of heaven, but he who does the will of My
> Father who is in heaven will enter" (Matthew 7:21).

This is one of the most misunderstood verses in Scripture. The standard
understanding is that it is in reference to those who thought they were
saved, but subsequently, come to find out they are not.

The reason this understanding cannot be correct is that Scripture
states clearly, "No one can say Jesus is Lord except by the Holy Spirit" (1st

Corinthians 12:3). The people here *are* saying "Lord, Lord" in Matthew 7:21. They, then, *have to be saved.*

Why are they being excluded from the Kingdom? Obviously, they failed to do "the will of the Father"; they were disobedient. "If you love Me, you will keep My commandments… and he who loves Me shall be loved by My Father…" (John 14:15, 21). The issue here is one of obedience, *not belief.*

And how does one know what is commanded of them? Study of the Word:

> All Scripture… is profitable for teaching, for reproof, for correction, for training in righteousness… (2nd Timothy 3:16).

Those who are being sanctified are being prepared for The Kingdom. Those who are saved, but reject to be "washed in the Word," and, thus, disobey it, will not enter. *Jesus has said so. The Holy Spirit through Matthew's gospel has said so.*

> [Jesus said], "For I say to you that unless your righteousness surpasses that of the scribes and Pharisees, you will not enter the kingdom of heaven." (5:20).

Nor, as we've seen, is the process to enter an easy one. It is taken "by violence."

> [Paul and Barnabas were] strengthening the souls of the disciples, encouraging them to continue in the faith, and saying, "Through many tribulations we must enter the kingdom of God" (Acts 14:22).

The conclusion is inescapable, entrance into the Kingdom is related to *what we do.* Further, if entrance into the Kingdom is an "automatic" the moment we believe, as most Christians believe, than these verses make no sense. Yet, once a person sees the difference between Jesus as Savior—salvation—and Jesus as Lord (King)—sanctification, and that both relationships are entered into differently, these and other passages make perfect sense.

Additionally, it becomes absolutely clear why we must stay in—and encourage others to stay in—the spiritual battle. It's why Paul encourages us to "run the race to win" (1st Corinthians 9:24).

As an aside here, this understanding of the difference between being saved, justified, and being in the kingdom, sanctified, makes amillennialism untenable. We cannot be already *in* the kingdom (the amillennial view), and at the same time be *excluded from it* because we are being disobedient (Matthew 7:21).

One last issue before we move on.

> And Jesus said to His disciples, "Truly I say to you, it is hard for a rich man to enter the kingdom of heaven…. Again I say to you, it is easier for a camel to go through the eye of a needle, than for a rich man to enter the kingdom of God" (Matthew 19:23, 24).

> And Jesus, looking around, said to His disciples, "How hard it will be for those who are wealthy to enter the kingdom of God!… It is easier for a camel to go through the eye of a needle than for a rich man to enter the kingdom of God" (Mark 10:23, 25).

> And Jesus looked at him and said, "How hard it is for those who are wealthy to enter the kingdom of God!… For it is easier for a camel to go through the eye of a needle than for a rich man to enter the kingdom of God." (Luke 18:24, 25).

Three times we are told that rich people will find it most difficult to enter the Kingdom. As spiritual investigators (Proverbs 25:2b) we must ask: *Why?*:

> I know your deeds, that you are neither cold nor hot… because you say, "I am rich, and have become wealthy, and have need of nothing," and you do not know that you are wretched and miserable and poor and blind and naked…. (Revelation 3:15, 17).

They are *self-reliant*, "I… have need of nothing," which blinds them to their real spiritual condition. This self-reliance prevents them from turning to God and reliance upon Him and His Word. Sanctification, then, is near impossible. But, because God is so merciful, even for them there is some hope:

Again I say to you, it is easier for a camel to go through the eye of a needle, than for a rich man to enter the kingdom of God." When the disciples heard this, they were very astonished and said, "Then who can be saved?" And looking at them Jesus said to them, "With people this is impossible, but with God all things are possible" (Matthew 19:24-26).

If they can be saved, might not some yet be sanctified? "With God *all* things are possible." But money won't buy them in—love of it is the root of all sorts of evil (1ˢᵗ Timothy 6:10). The only way in is obedience.

As it is for *all* who wish to enter.

CHAPTER 22

UNDERSTANDING THE
KINGDOM: THE GUESTS

Seek ye first the kingdom of God, and His righteousness... (Matthew 6:33, KJV).

A. INTRODUCTION

Beginning in Matthew 5 and continuing to chapter 7, Jesus begins what is often referred to as The Sermon on the Mount. Let's look at how that sermon begins:

> And when He [Jesus] saw the multitudes, He went up on the mountain; and after He sat down, His disciples came to Him. And opening His mouth He began to teach them... (Matthew 5:1-2).

One of the first things that should be noticed is that the Sermon on the Mount is not for "the multitudes." Jesus actually escaped from them and, thus, provided this information to His disciples only. And, because just previously in Matthew 4 He began to choose The Twelve (actually those of the inner circle: Peter, Andrew, James, and John [4:18-22]), it is believed that "His disciples" (v. 5:1) is a reference to only those four. Here, again, is clear indication that The Chosen are for sanctification, not justification.

As part of the sermon, Jesus announces that they are to "seek... first the kingdom of God and His righteousness." He does not say the Father or the Holy Spirit will draw them to it. *They* are to seek it, an act of works on their part, and just the opposite of "No one seeks for God… [therefore] the Father will draw [you]" (Romans 3:11; John 6:44).

We seek God's kingdom through a study of His Word; the Sermon on the Mount being given to us in that Writing. It is, therefore, understandable that Kingdom principles are contained in that Sermon. It is these principles we should be living here because, as we've previously seen there are consequences when we—the saved—stand before Christ and His judgment at the Bema Seat. Again, all of this is the sanctification process. And some, as with the "inner circle" being told of the Kingdom principles at the Sermon on the Mount, are specifically chosen for that.

Regarding that judgment, Jesus goes on to provide further details:

> [Jesus said, "[T]hat slave who knew his master's will and did not get ready, or act in accord with his will, shall receive many lashes, but the one who did not know it, and committed deeds worthy of a flogging, will receive but few. And from everyone who has been given much shall much be required; and to whom they entrusted much, of him they will ask all the more (Luke 12:47-48).

This is a clear indication that the General Assembly, those who did not know all that had been revealed to The Chosen, will be judged less severely than those who *were* chosen. But those in the General Assembly *will* be judged (see below). And The Chosen? They will be judged more severely. In fact, some will face very severe discipline:

> Let not many of you become teachers, my brethren, knowing that as such we will incur a stricter judgment (James 3:1).

This shows the weight of responsibility in teaching God's Word to God's people. But, with faithful responsibility comes potential for greater rewards. The key word here is *faithful*.

B. The Penalty For Unfaithfulness: The Guests

We've seen that there will be those in attendance who have been called "guests." These appear to be those who make up the General Assembly as they are not identified as The Bride. Let's look at the information Jesus has provided, but this time with an emphasis on their judgment.

> [Jesus said], "The kingdom of heaven may be compared to a king, who gave a wedding feast for his son....and the wedding hall was filled with dinner guests. But when the king came in to look over the dinner guests, he saw there a man not dressed in wedding clothes, and he said to him, 'Friend, how did you come in here without wedding clothes?' And he was speechless. Then the king said to the servants, 'Bind him hand and foot, and cast him into the outer darkness; in that place there shall be weeping and gnashing of teeth.'" (Matthew 22:2, 10b-13).

These guests have responded to the invitation (call) and have shown up ready for the wedding feast. But, someone is not in the appropriate attire; they lack the "wedding clothes." It is important to understand in the Jewish culture of Jesus' day, one wore an outer garment, his or her finery, to the joyful occasion of a wedding. This person has failed to do that. What is this outer, wedding garment in spiritual terms? Let's first look at the inner garment:

> I will rejoice greatly in the LORD... for He has clothed me with garments of salvation; He has wrapped me with a robe of righteousness (Isaiah 61:10).

Notice the inner garment "of salvation." God puts that on us the moment we believe.

> Then he showed me Joshua the high priest standing before the angel of the Lord, and Satan standing at his right hand to accuse him. The Lord said to Satan, "The Lord rebuke you, Satan! Indeed, the Lord who has chosen Jerusalem rebuke you! Is this not a brand plucked from the fire?" Now Joshua was clothed with filthy garments and standing before the angel. He spoke and said to those who were standing before him, saying,

"Remove the filthy garments from him." Again he said to him, "See, I have taken your iniquity away from you and will clothe you with festal robes." Then I said, "Let them put a clean turban on his head." So they put a clean turban on his head and clothed him with garments, while the angel of the Lord was standing by (Zechariah 3:1-5).

The high priest, Joshua, is initially at Satan's side: Satan has control over him. Thus, the high priest wears "filthy garments," further indication he is unsaved (Isaiah 64:6). But when Joshua's iniquity (sin) is taken away from him—when he is saved—God Himself sees that he is dressed in "clean... garments." In fact, because Joshua has been chosen to be the high priest, he is given "festal robes" as well.

What is the outer garment? "It is a [festal] robe *of righteousness*": "Seek ye first... His *righteousness*..." This is sanctification. The wedding guests are expected to be obedient, even though they receive, and are responsible for, but a little.[143]

Notice, the wedding guest here is saved, but has done nothing towards his wedding garment. As Jesus said, once we are saved we are to abide in Him—"abide in Me... for apart from Me you can do nothing" (John 15:5).

Having failed to do this and, thus, "knit" his own wedding garment of righteous deeds,[144] he is confronted by the king. Notice this guest is speechless. An indication he is taken by surprise at this confrontation. So it will be with many on that day.

What is the guest's place during Christ's Millennial Kingdom?

> Then the king said to the servants, 'Bind him hand and foot, and cast him into the outer darkness; in that place there shall be weeping and gnashing of teeth.' "

---

[143] Acts 2:42, the "basics"—prayer, worship, study, and fellowship—are within the grasp of *all* who would avail themselves. It is through these four basic acts that one continues to abide in Jesus (see John 15:4a, 5), and is a demonstration of our love towards Him (John 14:21). Even the "wedding guests," with little knowledge and responsibility, are capable of doing these.

[144] As Revelation 19:8 states, "And it was given to her to clothe herself in fine linen [of the outer, seen garment], bright and clean; for *the fine linen is the righteous acts of the saints*"; emphasis added.

He is demoted from being a "guest" and becomes "an *outsider*"—a loss of reward, not a loss of salvation: The person *still remains in relation to the king*—he is not banished to some foreign location, like the Lake of Fire. He is merely prevented from enjoying the wedding feast, being "in" the Kingdom. To teach anything else is to be in error.

Notwithstanding, what *is* "the outer darkness." For there is much confusion about this.

> The "outer darkness" is *not* a description of hell or a place of punishment, like the Catholic's use of the term "purgatory," but a place of restoration, renewal, and re-instruction in the ways of the Lord. God does not punish His own; His desire is that *all* His children be re-established in holiness. The Millennium is the time the Lord will accomplish this.... "Fruit" *does* matter to the Lord. Again, the "salvation of our spirit" happens at our new birth where God imputes His righteousness to us by His shed Blood. This assures us that no matter how we live our Christian lives here and now, we will go to be "with Him..." At the Bema seat in heaven, however, our lives here on earth will be examined and our future role and position established. Those that have learned sanctification and how to produce Godly "fruit" in this lifetime will be used in a greater capacity than those who have not.[145]

None other than the eminent pastor Dr. Charles Stanley is in agreement:

> The final verse of this parable is so severe that many commentators assume it is a description of hell. It is not. The point of this parable is that in God's future kingdom, those who were faithful in this life will be rewarded and those who were not

---

[145] Nancy Missler. The Kingdom, Power, & Glory: How Secure Is Our Salvation? *Personal Update: The News Journal of Koinonia House*, January 2010, 31-32; emphasis in original. She goes on to observe God's actions to this unfaithfulness is actually for the benefit of the saved, but unfaithful person: "Revelation 3:19 confirms this: 'As many as I love, I rebuke and chasten.' Now, chastening is different than punishing. As we've said before: *God does not punish His own, He simply disciplines us*. And, there's a huge difference between these two. "To punish" means: to inflict harm; whereas "to chasten" means *something that is done for our profit and for our benefit*"; emphasis in original.

will lose any potential reward.... Therefore, the outer darkness refers to being thrown outside a building into the dark...[146]

This will be a place where there is "weeping and gnashing of teeth." Again, this must be the saved because the unsaved when confronted by God's judgment show no remorse:

> The rest of mankind who were not killed [by the previous six trumpet judgments of God's Wrath]... did not repent... so as not to worship demons and... idols... they did not repent... of their immorality... (Revelation 9:20-21).

Scripture goes on to tell us tells us the unsaved "blasphemed—[cursed]—the God of heaven because of their pains and their sores; and they did not repent of their deeds" (Revelation 16:11). The unsaved are *incapable* of remorse. They—wrongly—blame God for their judgment instead of accepting responsibility for it themselves. And, obviously, they are just as incapable of repenting.

The saved, on the other hand respond to disciplined-judgment with remorse (weeping) and the realization of their own wrong-doing (gnashing of teeth). Notice the only other place in the New Testament where the gnashing of teeth is named, apart from this discipline-judgment: Stephen in his speech to the Israelites who are about to stone him accuses them of being "stiff-necked and uncircumcised in heart and ears [and] are *always resisting the Holy Spirit*" (Acts 7:51; emphasis added).

What is the response of those hearing Stephen? "Now when they heard this, they were cut to the quick, and they began gnashing their teeth at him" (v. 54). They realized their wrong-doing and it affected them. But because they were unsaved, they stoned Stephen—they responded in anger.

What is the response of those sent to the outer darkness? *They weep.* D. Martin Lloyd-Jones in his book *Studies in the Sermon on the Mount* observes, "The man who truly mourns because of his sinful state and condition is a

---

[146] Charles Stanley. *Eternal Security: Can You Be Sure?* (Nashville, Tennessee: Thomas Nelson, 1990), 124-125.

man who is going to repent."[147] The discipline here will ultimately, eternally, pay off! As Nancy Missler has noted.

The "weeping and gnashing of teeth" is, as we've previously seen, then, the response at the Bema Seat by those who will *"suffer* loss" (1st Corinthians 3:15). The loss here is exclusion from the Kingdom. *This will be for the entire 1,000-years of Christ's reign* (see chapter 23).

> [Jesus said], "And I say to you, that many shall come from east and west, and recline at the table with Abraham, and Isaac, and Jacob, in the kingdom of heaven, but the sons of the kingdom [those who *should* have been in it] shall be cast out into the outer darkness; in that place there shall be weeping and gnashing of teeth" (Matthew 8:11-12).

A parable that provides insight is that of Matthew 25:1-12:

> [Jesus said], "Then the kingdom of heaven will be comparable to ten virgins, who took their lamps and went out to meet the bridegroom. Five of them were foolish, and five were prudent. For when the foolish took their lamps, they took no oil with them, but the prudent took oil in flasks along with their lamps. Now while the bridegroom was delaying, they all got drowsy and began to sleep. But at midnight there was a shout, 'Behold, the bridegroom! Come out to meet him.' Then all those virgins rose and trimmed their lamps. The foolish said to the prudent, 'Give us some of your oil, for our lamps are going out.' But the prudent answered, 'No, there will not be enough for us and you too; go instead to the dealers and buy some for yourselves.' And while they were going away to make the purchase, the bridegroom came, and those who were ready went in with him to the wedding feast; and the door was shut. Later the other virgins also came, saying, 'Lord, lord, open up for us.' But he answered, 'Truly I say to you, I do not know you.'" (Matthew 25:1-12).

The subjects here are ten *virgins*. Although many commentators state

---

[147]   D. Martin Lloyd-Jones. *Studies in the Sermon on the Mount* (Grand Rapids, Michigan: William B. Eerdmans Publishing Company, 1959-60), 49.

that half of these ten are saved and the other half are not, the fact that they are virgins indicates they are *pure*. All ten, then, are saved. What differentiates them is that half have "extra" oil. And this oil "costs" (v. 9). The wise virgins have purchased it *beforehand*. Note also that these are not identified as "the Bride." The clear implication is that they are "guests."

Oil in Scripture represents the Holy Spirit (Luke 4:18; Acts 10:38). As a person yields more and more to the Holy Spirit, the Spirit gains more and more control over his or her life. *They are being sanctified.* In a real sense, they have "more" Holy Spirit because of His control over their lives.

Notice, both sets of virgins have "oil"—the Holy Spirit given them when they believed, but the wise virgins paid the price for "more" oil. As a result, they were ready when the bridegroom [Jesus] arrived and took them into the wedding feast (the opening act of the Millennial Kingdom). Notice the wise were still not sure they "had enough": sanctification is a lifelong process... and we need to be "purchasing" the whole length of it!

The fact that the wise virgins were unsure is why it is called the *hope* of the inheritance. Until the judgment at the Bema Seat is complete, when one *hopefully* hears the exquisite words, "Well done thou good and faithful servant," there is no certainty they have done enough... they have won their individual race they were meant by God to run.

During this, the five foolish have gone away—into the outer darkness, to pay the required price–be disciplined–that they failed to pay prior to the arrival of the bridegroom. Notice, having paid that price, they now request entrance into the feast. But the bridegroom—the Lord (v. 11)—announces that he does not know them (v. 12). The word "know" here is *eido*, which can also be translated "see." They are on the outside. And having failed to prepare ahead of time, are not acknowledged and, thus, not allowed into the feast. For those who are the guests, this is the worst-case scenario.

So it shall be with those who are excluded, *disinherited*, from the Millennium. They will be disciplined, as they should have willingly been during their lives on earth, and even once the "price" is eventually paid, will still not be allowed into the Kingdom. Entrance into the Kingdom of God is part of the inheritance. Not all who are saved will receive it.

That is why the last verse of this parable is so impacting: "Be on the alert then, for you do not know the day nor the hour" (Matthew 25:13). We are not being commanded to be alert to Christ's return, we are being admonished to being alert—wise—*as we watch how we live.* Through sanctification we should be obtaining that extra "oil" *now.* This is how one prepares for entrance into the Kingdom.

It needs to be reiterated here, *this is an act of discipline, not a judgment of sins.* Thus, it is *not* a Protestant Purgatory. As Dr. Charles Stanley observed, and with whom famed eschatological scholar Nancy Missler, agrees:

> God's *grace* is extended to the worst sinner, but His *justice* moves Him to keep a record not only of those who are faithful, but also of those who are not… God's Love is such that He accepts us just the way we are [at salvation], but loves us too much to leave us that way [hence, the need for sanctification].[148]

In closing, as bad as the penalty for the unfaithful guests might appear, if you are one of The Chosen, it is far worse should *you* prove unfaithful. For some *very* far worse.

---

[148] Missler, 2010, 32; emphasis in original.

CHAPTER 23

UNDERSTANDING THE
KINGDOM: THE CHOSEN

From everyone who has been given much, much will be required;
and to whom they entrusted much, of him they will ask all the more
(Luke 12:48).

A. INTRODUCTION

We begin with this Gospel of Luke passage. It provides a critical insight.
Many consider Luke to be writing about one group of people. But the truth
is, he doesn't identify one group of people; he identifies two.

As Jesus had Disciples who were not part of the inner circle, but who
were indeed given much because of their position in The Twelve, much, we
are told, will be required of them. To those in the inner circle, not just given,
but "entrusted" with much, "all the more" will be required of *them*. "Each
according to his own [God ordained] ability" (Matthew 25:15).

There is a coming judgment of The Chosen. Some to great reward. But
there will be some, like Peter who denied Jesus, and Judas, who betrayed
Him, who will pay severe penalties for their disobedience. In the case of
Judas, *severe* penalties.

Scripture is clear on this. Yet, most Christians are oblivious.

Before we proceed, there is a need to recognize the issue of actually
"understanding the Kingdom." Not all will. But The Chosen *should*.

[Jesus continued], "When anyone hears *the word of the kingdom*, and does not understand it, the evil one comes and snatches away what has been sown in his heart. This is the one on whom seed was sown beside the road. And the one on whom seed was sown on the rocky places, this is the man who hears the *word*, and immediately receives it with joy; yet he has no firm root in himself, but is only temporary, and when affliction or persecution arises because of the *word*, immediately he falls away. And the one on whom seed was sown among the thorns, this is the man who hears the *word*, and the worry of the world, and the deceitfulness of riches choke the *word*, and it becomes unfruitful. And the one on whom seed was sown on the good soil, this is the man who hears the *word* and understands it; who indeed bears fruit, and brings forth, some a hundredfold, some sixty, and some thirty (Matthew 13:18-23; emphasis added).

Notice, this issue is "the word of the kingdom." This is not "the word of salvation." This does not deal with justification, it deals with sanctification. *Kingdom issues deal with sanctification.* The unsaved don't heed the word of salvation and, as we've seen previously, are thus *oblivious* to the Kingdom. Therefore, those spoken of here *must* all be saved individuals because the word of the Kingdom *is contained in the Word*, principally the New Testament, and *they are listening to it.* The unsaved don't listen; it is foolishness to them (1ˢᵗ Corinthians 1:18). Let's examine further.

The first person, "seed beside the road," at least "hears the word." They are open to receive it—which the unsaved can't do—but these hearers don't understand it. Paul writes of such people in his letter to the Ephesians.

Children [those immature in their Christian walk, are] tossed here and there by waves, and carried about by every wind of doctrine, by the trickery of men, by craftiness in deceitful scheming (4:14).

Notice also that although Satan, the evil one (v. 19), removes even the hint of knowledge of the Kingdom from this person, the Sower, God, makes no attempt to stop Satan. This person is part of the General Assembly, not chosen to receive "inside" information.

The second person, "seed on rocky places," hears it, and understands it—"receives it with joy." The message of sanctification is received *and understood*. In his initial joy this person begins to be sanctified.

The conclusion here is unmistakable, to understand the Kingdom *requires that one is part of The Chosen*. We cannot "unlock" Scripture on our own (1st Corinthians 2:14). It must be done by the Holy Spirit at the will of the Father (John 15:26; 16:13-15). Hence, he has been chosen to receive it.

As the parable continues, however, we are told this person easily falls away, "no firm root"—no real commitment to being sanctified—because of "affliction and persecution." As we've seen, we enter the kingdom "through many tribulations (afflictions)" (Acts 14:22). Not all will be willing to pay the price. A key element here is that *he* chose this, no one else.

The third person, "seed among the thorns," hears the word, but "becomes unfruitful." Notice he *becomes* unfruitful. This person had growth, he just didn't go on to completion, i.e. fruit-bearing; he didn't persevere. The reason? "Worry of the world and deceitfulness of riches" *choke the word*. Aren't we told "It is hard for a rich man to enter the kingdom"? (Matthew 19:23). Here is the reason why.

The Word *was* having an effect, but then is choked out. Like the church at Ephesus, this person has "left his first love" (Revelation 2:4). To have gotten even this far, not all do, tells us he has got to be part of The Chosen. God has made it possible for his growth, but he has squandered it.

This issue of riches needs to be examined in more detail, especially because of the wealth that exists amongst many Christians in the United States today. Jesus gives us insight from one of His most misunderstood teachings.

> [Jesus said], "Now there was a rich man, and he habitually dressed in purple and fine linen, joyously living in splendor every day. And a poor man named Lazarus was laid at his gate, covered with sores, and longing to be fed with the crumbs which were falling from the rich man's table; besides, even the dogs were coming and licking his sores. Now the poor man died and was carried away by the angels to Abraham's bosom; and the rich man also died and was buried. In Hades he lifted up his eyes, being in torment, and saw Abraham far away and Lazarus in his bosom. And he cried out and said, 'Father Abraham, have mercy on me, and send Lazarus so that he may dip the tip of his finger in water and cool off my tongue, for I am in agony in this flame.' But Abraham said, 'Child, remember

that during your life you received your good things, and likewise Lazarus bad things; but now he is being comforted here, and you are in agony. And besides all this, between us and you there is a great chasm fixed, so that those who wish to come over from here to you will not be able, and that none may cross over from there to us.' And he said, 'Then I beg you, father, that you send him to my father's house—for I have five brothers—in order that he may warn them, so that they will not also come to this place of torment.' But Abraham said, 'They have Moses and the Prophets; let them hear them.' But he said, 'No, father Abraham, but if someone goes to them from the dead, they will repent!' But he said to him, 'If they do not listen to Moses and the Prophets, they will not be persuaded even if someone rises from the dead'" (Luke 16:19-31).

Because Jesus does not begin with the "it is like," the first thing to notice is that *this is not a parable*. Jesus speaks of it as an actual event. Most commentators compare Lazarus with the rich man and proclaim the one is saved and the other not, because of where they wind up. Let's investigate.

First of all, the rich man goes to "Hades." This is often also translated "hell," which is part of the reason it leads to confusion. It is not *Gehenna* (see below). The Greek word is *ades*; (pronounced ah-dace, not āds [aides]). *There is no "h" in the Greek*; it is something added by English translators.

In Greek, "a" indicates a negative, such as does the prefix "un" in English, e.g. the negative of fit would be un-fit. The other half of the word *des* is from the verb *eido*, to be seen, know, understand. Thus *ades* is a place for people not seen, not known, *not recognized*. It is *not* "hell" in the sense of the final judgment in the Lake of Fire (Revelation 20:11-15). To make it so is incorrect; final judgment has yet to occur, especially in Jesus' day as he relates this incident. Therefore, this is a place for those *disinherited*, not recognized for the Kingdom (see below for a more expanded explanation).

Further, the word translated "torment" is the Greek word *basanos*. The *basanos* is a flint-like stone used to test metals *for genuineness*. The rich man *is being tested*. By what? *Flame* (review 1ˢᵗ Corinthians 3:10-15). And what is the rich man's reaction to "being tested by flame"? He is *in agony*. The Greek word is *odunao*, literally, *grief, sorrow*. The man has been sent to a place of "weeping (grief) and gnashing of teeth (sorrow)" (see below).

In this location he calls out to "father Abraham." Does Abraham rebuke the rich man for being incorrect in his address of Abraham as *father*, i.e. being an Israelite? Does Abraham rebuke the rich man telling him to not refer to him as *father*? No. The rich man is still recognized as a Jew, Abraham being his forefather.

Which leads to the place in Scripture, in the Old Testament, that both the rich man and Lazarus *as Israelites* should know. This passage places this entire rich man and Lazarus account in its correct understanding. Given in poetic form it reads:

> Keep deception and lies far from me,
> Give me neither poverty nor riches;
> Feed me with the food that is my portion,
> That I not be full and deny You and say, "Who is the Lord?"
> Or that I not be in want and steal,
> And profane the name of my God (Proverbs 30:8-9).

The wisdom in this proverb is that the rich should not be so self-satisfied—and thus become so self-sufficient—that they no longer turn to the LORD for their strength. Because, as David writes, "Oh LORD, you are my strength..." (Psalm 28:7). To ignore that and think one is self-sufficient is folly as it "denies" the LORD. (Those of the church of Laodicea [Revelation 3:14ff] take note!)

As a corollary, the accompanying wisdom of the proverb is that one not be in such want that it leads him or her to steal. Such an action would "profane the name of God."

So now, let's go back and examine the passage of the rich man and Lazarus. Does Lazarus, who is obviously in great want, steal from the rich man? The answer is No. Lazarus lives righteously according to God's Word: "Thou shalt not steal" (Exodus 20:15–the Law given to Moses). Having lived righteously, Lazarus goes to reward, "Abraham's bosom."

How about the rich man? He has the same Law given to Moses. He just hasn't lived it. Notice when he intercedes on behalf of his brothers Abraham admonishes "They have Moses and the Prophets [the Old Testament]; let them hear them." So, what does the Old Testament actually say about this?

> For the poor will never cease to be in the land; therefore I
> command you, saying, 'You shall freely open your hand to your

brother, to your needy and poor in your land (Deuteronomy 15:11).

The rich man has lived in unrighteousness. He has *disobeyed* the Law. With Lazarus at his doorstep, literally, the rich man *should* have provided for his destitute "neighbor." But he did not. The outcome? The rich man is on the *outside looking in*, as it were, and being disciplined for his failure to obey (see below). There can be no other conclusion. (As an aside, if this is "hell" in the sense of final judgment for the unsaved, where are the sinful, godless Gentiles?)

The last issue here is that the rich man intercedes for his brothers so that they will *repent*. They need to, as we've previously seen about the word repent, *change their minds* about how they are living. This deals with how they are living in relation to the Law. They are still children of Abraham ("*father* Abraham"), thus "chosen," but they are not living their faith (obeying the Law).

As we shall see, there are consequences for that. But what needs to be understood and stressed here is that this narrative is not about justification, believing; it is about obeying, *sanctification*.

It is extremely important to also note that being rich is *not* a sin. As we've seen, what it can do is have the potential to take one's focus off Christ. This is because being rich makes one *think* they are self-sufficient. Further, rich people tend to *pursue* money which has devastating effects: "For the love of money is a root of all sorts of evil..." (1st Timothy 6:10). Just ask Judas (John 12:6).

However, Paul makes is very clear that

> For everything created by God is good, and nothing is to be rejected *if it is received with gratitude* (1st Timothy 4:4; emphasis added).

If we give thanks to the Lord for the blessings of financial stability, being rich is not a drawback. Doing so demonstrates our hearts are still set on Him—not our money. In our gratitude, we realize that should He choose,

He can reverse the prosperity and take it away at any time.[149] We should, then, be *very* thankful He has provided us with *previous* financial blessings.

Further, because "faith without works is dead" (James 2:26), we demonstrate that we are thankful to the Lord for our financial blessings by giving a portion of them away; that portion referred to in the Old Testament as a *tithe*, a tenth of what is received. (Though for us in this, the Church Age, the Holy Spirit may call on us to give more, to which we need to be obedient.)

All of this leads us to the parable of Matthew 25:31-46, which is also usually misunderstood.

> [Jesus said], "But when the Son of Man comes in His glory, and all the angels with Him, then He will sit on His glorious throne. All the nations will be gathered before Him; and He will separate them from one another, as the shepherd separates the sheep from the goats; and He will put the sheep on His right, and the goats on the left.
>
> "Then the King will say to those on His right, 'Come, you who are blessed of My Father, inherit the kingdom prepared for you from the foundation of the world. For I was hungry, and you gave Me something to eat; I was thirsty, and you gave Me something to drink; I was a stranger, and you invited Me in; naked, and you clothed Me; I was sick, and you visited Me; I was in prison, and you came to Me.' Then the righteous will answer Him, 'Lord, when did we see You hungry, and feed You, or thirsty, and give You something to drink? And when did we see You a stranger, and invite You in, or naked, and clothe You? When did we see You sick, or in prison, and come to You?' The King will answer and say to them, 'Truly I say to you, to the extent that you did it to one of these brothers of Mine, even the least of them, you did it to Me.'
>
> "Then He will also say to those on His left, 'Depart from Me, accursed ones, into the eternal fire which has been prepared for the devil and his angels; for I was hungry, and you gave Me nothing

---

149   See Ecclesiastes 9:1; and for a recent personal testimony, see Chuck Missler and Nancy Missler, *Faith in the Night Season's: Understanding God's Will* (Coeur d'Alene, Idaho: Koinonia House, 1999), 27-35.

to eat; I was thirsty, and you gave Me nothing to drink; I was a stranger, and you did not invite Me in; naked, and you did not clothe Me; sick, and in prison, and you did not visit Me.' Then they themselves also will answer, 'Lord, when did we see You hungry, or thirsty, or a stranger, or naked, or sick, or in prison, and did not take care of You?' Then He will answer them, 'Truly I say to you, to the extent that you did not do it to one of the least of these, you did not do it to Me.' These will go away into eternal punishment, but the righteous into eternal life."

Most commentators take this to be the judgment at the beginning of Christ's Millennial reign and of those who survived the Wrath of God judgments (described in the Book of Revelation).[150] These people are now being judged for how they treated Israelis during that tribulation.

However, in Ezekiel 34:17, a parallel passage, we see "And as for you, *My flock*, thus says the Lord GOD, behold, I will judge between one sheep and another, *between the rams and the male goats*" (emphasis added). This judgment, then, is not of the Gentile nations, but of God's own, *My flock*. Daniel speaks of a 75-day period beginning after the return of Christ. He concludes with, "How blessed is he who keeps waiting and attains to the [end of this 75-day period]" (12:12).

Notice what the "blessed" sheep have done, that they have fed the hungry, gave drink to the thirsty, clothed the naked, etc., *even the least of them*. These people gave of their time and resources to even the least of them—the poor, thus fulfilling Jesus commandment: "A new commandment I give you love one another" (13:34).

Further, in the Matthew passage Jesus states, "You did it to one of these brothers of Mine." He is not referring to Israel; He is referring to the saved (Matthew 12:50). The "goats" failed to do this and are disciplined.

The other misunderstanding is the word translated "eternal." In the original Greek, used throughout this passage, it is *aion*, from which we get the English word "eon" (sometimes spelled "aeon"). The Greek word can also be translated *age*, as it is in Mark 10:30:

---

150   For example, see Pentecost, *Things To Come*, 284-285.

...but he shall receive a hundred times as much now in the present age [kairos–occasion, time]... and in the age [aion] to come eternal [aioinos–age] life.

What is eternal [aionios] life? "To know... the only true God, and Jesus Christ whom Thou [God the Father] has sent" (John 17:3). This speaks of *relationship*, not "living forever." That relationship will grow—*exponentially*, because sin is then behind us—*in the Kingdom*.

Another benefit, of course, is the inheritance! But for the unworthy, an age (*aion*) awaits them of discipline, from which they will *not* know such a deep, personal relationship of the Father and the Son.

Further, because reference is made to "the fire prepared for the devil and his angels" many, again, misunderstand this as *forever* in the Lake of Fire. As we shall see (below), Christians can also be subject to that "second death" (Revelation 2:11), hence the reference to that "fire." However, we will also see that exposure is not eternal—forever: *eis tous aionas ton aionos*: to the ages of the ages—it is limited to the 1,000-year period of the Millennium.

The clear message of this parable is to avoid the trap of riches, not riches themselves. To make that avoidance, we should be about sharing the financial blessings we receive. To reiterate the applicable cliché, "One should put their money where their mouth is." If you have faith in Jesus, demonstrate it! By sharing your financial blessings for furtherance of His Kingdom.

Returning to the Matthew 13 parable, the fourth person "hears the word and understands it" and—by applying it, being faithful—"bears fruit." Notice, some will bear "thirty, some sixty, some a hundredfold." No doubt, each according to his ability (Matthew 25:15).

What is interesting here is that we again have an outer (thirty), mid (sixty), and inner (a hundredfold) grouping as we saw with The Twelve. Out of this group—possibly the hundredfold—The Bride will be chosen; the others will be The Attendants.

There is a second issue that confirms this. In Matthew 18:3 Jesus states, "Truly I say to you, unless you are converted, become like children, you will not enter the kingdom of heaven." This verse has been badly mishandled in the past.

Let's let Scripture interpret itself. "Children, obey your parents in the

Lord, for this is right" (Ephesians 6:1). Jesus is saying that we are to be converted—Greek: *strepho*, turn around, i.e., stop doing the sinful things you are engaged in [i.e., akin to *repent*]—and *obey the Father* (the command for children). If you don't do that, you will not enter the Kingdom. The second and third person of The Chosen of the Matthew 13 parable obviously stop obeying.

With these as background, we realize The Chosen *should* go on to bear fruit for the Kingdom. But, clearly demonstrated in this parable, many will not.

Let's now look at their Bema Seat judgment.

B. THE PENALTY FOR UNFAITHFULNESS: THE CHOSEN

There are three main passages we are going to explore. Many expositors believe each one is merely a different view of the same judgment. We will see they are not. Each one has a direct application to a specific group of those who, from the saved, especially The Chosen, are unfaithful.

As we've seen, The Twelve have been so chosen because they have a specific purpose to fulfill. For this reason they are chosen to, in some way, *minister*. Here on earth they were to be Apostles—*apostolos*, literally one who goes forth; and in the Kingdom to rule—minister to—the twelve tribes of Israel.

> [Jesus said], "For it is just like a man about to go on a journey, who called his own slaves and entrusted his possessions to them. To one he gave five talents, to another, two, and to another, one, each according to his own ability; and he went on his journey. Immediately the one who had received the five talents went and traded with them, and gained five more talents. In the same manner the one who had received the two talents gained two more. But he who received the one talent went away, and dug a hole in the ground and hid his master's money. [As we've previously seen, the first two are faithful and receive reward.]
>
> "And the one also who had received the one talent came up and said, 'Master, I knew you to be a hard man, reaping where you did not sow and gathering where you scattered no seed. And I

was afraid, and went away and hid your talent in the ground. See, you have what is yours.' "But his master answered and said to him, 'You wicked, lazy slave, you knew that I reap where I did not sow and gather where I scattered no seed. Then you ought to have put my money in the bank, and on my arrival I would have received my money back with interest. Therefore take away the talent from him... [for] from the one who does not have, even what he does have shall be taken away. Throw out the worthless slave into the outer darkness; in that place there will be weeping and gnashing of teeth" (Matthew 25:14-30).

Again, although this person is described as "wicked (*poneros*–hurtful), *lazy*, and, thus, worthless [*achreios*–useless, unprofitable]," *he is still the master's slave.* (The unsaved are *enemies!* [James 4:4]). This individual is *saved*; that is why the master entrusts him with one talent, a portion of his, the master's, possessions. (As enemies, God entrusts the unsaved with *nothing!*) Hence, this slave is given responsibility that we do not see with The Guests. Yet the slave willingly, knowingly "went away"—he *fell away.* And his excuse? He was "afraid." But Paul writes,

> Now He who prepared us for this very purpose is God, who gave to us the Spirit as a pledge. Therefore, being always of good courage...[and] most of the brethren, *trusting in the Lord*... have far more courage to speak the word of God without fear (2nd Corinthians 5:5-6; Philippians 1:14; emphasis added).

We are not to be fearful. And if we are, we are still to be obedient. Certainly the two who were rewarded overcame any fear *they* might have had.

For his failure to obey, the worthless slave is thrown into the "outer darkness" along with the unfaithful Guests. There he will spend the Millennium "weeping and gnashing teeth." Because he only has one talent, the principle of divine judgment *by degrees* holds true (see below). As we shall see, he got off easy.

The second passage is from the gospel of Matthew.

> [Jesus said], "Who then is the *faithful* and *sensible* [*phronimos*–thoughtful, wise] slave whom his master put in charge of his household *to give them their food* (*trophe*–literally, nourishment)

at the proper time? Blessed is that slave whom his master finds so doing when he comes. Truly I say to you, that he will put him in charge of all his possessions. But if that evil [*kakos*—worthless (in character)] slave says in his heart, "My master is not coming for a long time," and shall begin to beat [*tupto*—to *thump* repeatedly] his fellow slaves and eat and drink with drunkards; the master of that slave will come on a day when he does not expect him and at an hour which he does not know, and shall cut (dichotomeo—to cut [by flogging]) him in pieces and assign him a place with the hypocrites; weeping shall be there and gnashing of teeth" (24:45-51; emphasis added).

There are a number of issues this passage presents. This slave (*doulos*—one who is subservient, a servant) is one amongst many: "his fellow slaves." They are all slaves of the master, thus saved. But he is given responsibility over them. To do what? "Give them their food at the proper time."

In the New Testament we are told that a deacon (*diakonos*—servant) is one who assists those ministering the Word (Acts 6:2-4) and whose qualifications are not as stringent as that of an elder (1ˢᵗ Timothy 3:1-7, cf. 8-13). They are a servant amongst many servants of the church who assist in various ways other than preaching and teaching, yet do so in order that the members get fed the Word by elders and teachers (Acts 6:2-4).

In this passage, the worthless slave does not do this. He was given (limited) authority in order that he would see that the others get fed. Instead, he "beats his fellow slaves." This is an abuse of the power given him.

Further, he "eats and drinks with drunkards." He is not safeguarding the meals, he's out partying, thus wasting time in disobedience... and, worse, wasting resources if he is using his masters food (and drink?) to supply the drunkards.

This is a greater violation, compared to the previous "fearful" slave, because the responsibility is greater. And so is the punishment. This slave is "flogged" (*suffer* greater loss) and placed with the hypocrites. As we shall see below this is worse than the outer darkness.

Let's investigate the issue of hypocrite first. Hypocrisy in Greek is *hypocrisis*. It was used of Greek and Roman actors who wore masks during a play. They appeared one way in the play, when, in fact, they were someone else in real life. A hypocrite, Webster defines as "one who demonstrates virtues or qualities he does not really have."[151]

So, let's look at what Jesus had to say about hypocrites.

> "Woe to you, scribes and Pharisees, hypocrites, because you shut off the kingdom of heaven from men; for you do not enter in yourselves, nor do you allow those who are entering to go in.... Woe to you, scribes and Pharisees, hypocrites! You... outwardly appear righteous to men, but inwardly you are full of hypocrisy and lawlessness... You serpents, you brood of vipers, how shall you escape the sentence of hell?" [Greek: *Gehenna*] (Matthew 23:13, 28, 33).

Jesus here defines hypocrisy, so there can be no misunderstanding as to what it is; a person appearing in public what he is not in private; a play actor for his own benefit—the literal meaning of the Greek word.

Notice that the spiritual hypocrite is not going to be in the Kingdom, but because he is not doing what he should, he is the cause of preventing others from entering. In the case of this worthless servant, because he is not doing what he should, the others aren't getting fed. In a spiritual sense, without being fed the Word, people are ignorant of what they should be doing to enter the Kingdom.

Finally, notice that his location, apart from the Kingdom, is *not* the outer darkness; it is a "place with the hypocrites." Where does Jesus state the hypocrites go? *Gehenna*.

The word *Gehenna*, most often translated "hell," was well-known to the inhabitants of Jerusalem in Jesus' day. It was in the valley of Hinnom, just outside the city—and it was where the rubbish was burned. Most expositors equate it with the place of final judgment. Let's investigate.

If the worthless slave is, as a hypocrite, destined for *Gehenna*, yet his reaction is one of weeping and gnashing of teeth, he is showing remorse. Again, as we've seen, this is not the reaction of the unsaved who curse God. Further, Scripture clearly states the destiny of the unsaved is a *lake* of fire. *Gehenna* is a *valley*.

Further, Jesus opens the parable under discussion with the words: "For *it* is just like a man about to go on a journey..." The "it" is identified in the first

---

151   Woolf, 564.

verse of this chapter, "Then the kingdom of heaven will be comparable..."
(Matthew 25:1). Jesus is referring to the Kingdom. When does this occur?
Matthew 24, which precedes these judgments and demonstrates what
occurs just before Jesus returns as King, demonstrates the Bema Seat occurs
just *before* the Millennial Kingdom.

When are those destined for the Lake of Fire judged? *After* the
Millennial Age (Revelation 20:7ff): "And when the thousand years are
completed... the books of [judgment] were opened... and if anyone's name
was not found written in the book of life, he was thrown into the lake of
fire." The *timing* is off: *Gehenna* can't be the Lake of Fire.

But it is a fire... and it will be painful, for just as in the valley of Hinnom,
in *Gehenna* the rubbish must be burnt off—"*suffer* loss," Paul writes in 1st
Corinthians 3:15. Notice also how Jesus speaks of a "furnace of fire":

> At the end of the age... the Son of Man will send forth His
> angels, and they will gather *out of His kingdom* all *stumbling
> blocks* and those who commit lawlessness, and will cast them
> into the furnace of fire; in that place there shall be weeping and
> gnashing of teeth (Matthew 13:40b-42; emphasis added).

Again, we see this occurs at the beginning of the Millennium, not at
its end, and these people are gathered "out of His kingdom," not out of "the
sea... and Hades" (Revelation 20:13). And the reaction is "weeping and
gnashing of teeth": remorse in the suffering.

The concept of *Gehenna*, burning rubbish away, will take place in that
furnace. Why? "Our God is a consuming fire" (Hebrews 12:29). And the
worthless slave has demonstrated he needs to be disciplined... severely.
"From everyone who has been given much, much will be required..."

Which brings us to our last passage. Luke 12:42-48 is often thought
to be a reiteration of the Matthew 24 passage just reviewed. It is not. There
are significant differences which set it apart.

> And the Lord said, "Who then is the *faithful* and *sensible*
> [*phronimos*—wise] steward, whom his master will put in charge
> of his servants, to *give them their rations* [*sitometron*—literally,
> grain-measure, i.e. allowance of food] *at the proper time?* Blessed
> is that slave whom his master finds so doing when he comes.

Truly I say to you, that he will put him in charge of all his possessions. But if that slave *says in his heart*, 'My master will be a long time in coming,' and begins to beat the slaves, both men and women, and to eat and drink and get drunk; the master will come on a day when he doesn't expect him, and at an hour he does not know, and will cut [*dichotomeo*] him in pieces, and *assign him a place with the unbelievers*. And that slave who knew his master's will and did not get ready, or act in accord with his will, shall receive *many lashes*, but the one who did not know it, and committed deeds worthy of a *flogging*, will receive but a few. And from everyone who has been given much shall much be required, and to whom they entrusted much, of him they will ask all the more" (Luke 12:42-48; emphasis added).

First, this person is not a slave (*doulos*), he is a *steward* (*oikonomos*, overseer). In the church, this is equivalent to an elder-pastor (*episkopos*—overseer [bishop]). This person has much greater authority as he has been "put *in charge* of the servants." He not only sees they get fed, but determines what food, and what amount, they will get: "allowance of food." Here is the person who actually delivers the Word (spiritual food), determining what and what amount will be "served." (If done correctly, under the guidance of the Holy Spirit. If done foolishly, under one's own authority.) The providing of the Word is a great responsibility!

But instead of doing what his master commanded, this person beats the slaves who are *under* him, a *severe* misuse of power. And worse, he beats the *women* as well, the mark of a contemptible bully, a disgusting misuse of power. *This person is a controller*, when he should be all-serving: "Whoever wishes to become great among you shall be your servant" (Matthew 20:26).

Further, he "eats and drinks," but apparently by himself as there is no mention, as with the previous worthless slave, of accompanying drunkards. This steward has isolated himself from the very people he was commanded to serve! And though the previous, worthless slave associated with drunkards, this steward *is* a drunkard. And the isolation may be an attempt to conceal from others what he really is. Further, we again see a misuse of time and resources, and worse, being drunk demonstrates his complete selfish self-absorption...

This man, though still owned by the master, and thus saved, and remains his master's throughout the parable, (and thus saved in spite of his actions), can only be described as *wicked*. Jesus has something to say about this.

> So it will be at the end of the age; the angels shall come forth, and take out the *wicked* from among the righteous, and will cast them into the furnace of fire; there shall be weeping and gnashing of teeth (Matthew 13:49-50).

Returning to the Luke passage, Jesus wraps up His parable by comparing judgments: "That slave who knew his master's will and did not get ready, or act in accord with his will, shall receive *many lashes*, but the one who did not know it, and committed deeds worthy of a *flogging*, will receive but a few." *What amount does the steward deserve?*

The answer is clear: Although the steward's place during the Millennium is also the furnace of fire, the indication is that the suffering will be more severe—"many lashes"—than that of the worthless slave. And *this* steward has demonstrated he needs to be disciplined… *most* severely: "… To whom they entrusted much, of him they will ask all the more" (Luke 12:48).

A closing side note: It is interesting that both the worthless slave and the wicked steward are not judged for any failures in their bringing people to Christ, i.e., evangelism. They are judged for how they acted with those who were already saved, those of the master, hence saved, entrusted to them. It is because they failed to shepherd—failed to see the entrusted got *sanctified by the Word*—as was required.

For pastors and teachers who fit this description, these outcomes are the *worst* worst-case for them!

CHAPTER 24

UNDERSTANDING THE KINGDOM: THE BETRAYERS

For it is not an enemy who reproaches me... But it is you, My companion and my familiar friend. We who had sweet fellowship together, walked in the house of God... (Psalm 55:12, 14).

A. INTRODUCTION

There is a last group that needs to be discussed. They are almost always overlooked. This group's actions are grounded in the example of Judas.

Most commentators, most *Christians*, write Judas off as unsaved. They look at The Betrayal as the unpardonable sin (Matthew 12:31-32). But, that very Scripture states the unpardonable sin is against the Holy Spirit, not Jesus.

> I say to you, any sin and blasphemy shall be forgiven people, but blasphemy against the Spirit shall not be forgiven.

It would seem that betrayal of Jesus is pardonable (see especially verse 32). So, let's investigate.

Here is what we know of Judas. He was chosen by Jesus.

> And He went up on the mountain and summoned *those whom He Himself wanted*, and they came to Him. And He appointed

twelve, so that they would be with Him and that He could send them out to preach... (Mark 3:13-14).

And Judas did preach. In fact, he cast out demons.

> And He called the twelve together, and gave them power and authority over all the demons and to heal diseases. And He sent them out to proclaim the kingdom of God and to perform healing (Luke 9:1-2).

> They went out... And *they were casting out many demons* and were anointing with oil many sick people and healing them (Mark 6:12-13; emphasis added).

And Judas was one of The Twelve at that time when he did this. Jesus clearly taught an unmistakable lesson:

> The Pharisees... said, "This man casts out demons only by Beelzebul the ruler of the demons." And knowing their thoughts Jesus said to them, "Any kingdom divided against itself is laid waste; and any city or house divided against itself will not stand. If Satan casts out Satan, he is divided against himself; how then will his kingdom stand? (Matthew 12 24-25).

It is clear that, at least initially, Judas was one of them.

There is a passage in the Psalms that, though written by David in poetic form in the original Hebrew about his own experience, is considered to be Jesus talking to Judas:

> For it is not an enemy who reproaches me,
> Then I could bear it;
> Nor is it one who hates me who has exalted himself against me,
> Then I could hide myself from him.
> But it is you, a man my equal,
> *My companion and my familiar friend;*
> *We who had sweet fellowship together,*
> *Walked in the house of God...* (55:12-14; emphasis added).

In Psalm 41, there is a similar statement:

Even *my close friend, in whom I trusted* [making Judas' action a
betrayal],
Who ate my bread [demonstrating their closeness],
Has lifted up his heel against me (v. 9; emphasis added).

If these indeed are the words of Jesus inspired by the Holy Spirit
through David regarding Judas, then, at some point, *Judas believed in Jesus*—
and Jesus knew it. That's why he, Judas, was chosen by the Lord: *"Those
whom He Himself wanted..."* we are told (Mark 3:13).

Many would object because in the Gospel of John we are told "Jesus
answered... '"Of those whom You have given Me I lost not one'" (18:9). But
the context is that of Jesus' arrest. Just previous Jesus tells his captors, "I told
you that I am He; so if you seek Me, let these go their way" (v. 8). The issue
here of "being lost" is in regard to them dying as a result of attempting to
defend Jesus (remember Peter's boast!), not an issue of salvation.

Others may offer John 16:64: "[Jesus said], 'But there are some of you
who do not believe.' For Jesus knew from the beginning who they were who
did not believe, and who it was that would betray Him."

First of all, Judas is differentiated from "those who do not believe."
Notice: "They (1) who did not believe and (2) who it was that would betray
Him." The first is plural, the second singular. Jesus is referring to two
different people. The "and" doesn't make it one group of two elements, it is
two "groups" each with their own specification(s).

Thus, this does not imply Judas didn't believe; he is separated from
"those" others. Further, the context; Jesus just prior stated: "It is the Spirit
who gives life; the flesh profits nothing; the words that I have spoken to
you are spirit and are life (v. 63). Thus, the reference is to *those who would
not believe that "the Spirit gives life; the flesh profits nothing."* This is an issue
of understanding—hence, *sanctification*—not of *believing*, justification: It
does *not* say they didn't believe *in Him*. It states clearly they rejected His
teaching regarding the Spirit.

The Scriptural evidence implies Judas once believed. But, like the many
who walked away from Jesus (John 6:66), so did Judas. (Possibly as a result
of the love of money, deceitfulness of riches: "[Judas] was a thief, and as he
had the money box, he used to pilfer what was put into it" [John 12:6].)

What is worse, though, than just walking away, or even denying Jesus as Peter did, *Judas turned on Jesus,* becoming a servant of Satan (Luke 22:3). There can be no other conclusion: Judas became an enemy of Christ.

This is the absolute *worst* worst-case scenario for those who are The Chosen. Let the Christian who is chosen take notice! (Yet, if salvation cannot be lost (Romans 8:38-39), then even this cannot remove an individual from God for eternity. Let the Christian take comfort!)

B. The Penalty For Unfaithfulness: The Betrayers

With that as prelude, note that Scripture does not directly relate the conditions of the Bema Seat judgment for those who have been chosen and, like Judas, turned on Christ and *betray* Him. However, there are indications. Let's investigate.

A great deal of thanks must go to Gary T. Whipple for his exposition of this subject. In his book *Shock & Surprise Beyond the Rapture,* he looks at the judgment of Christians at the Bema Seat. Whipple has clearly shown the *surprise* that will be experienced by Christians who are oblivious to the fact they *will* be judged and *shocked* at the unexpected severity of that judgment.

Whipple has built upon previous authors such as Robert Govett (1813-1901), and G.H. Pember (1837-1910). All of these Bible scholars draw our attention to a location, most often overlooked by other scholars, identified in Scripture as "the blackness of darkness" (Jude 13). Jude goes on to further identify those who will populate that region:

> Beloved, while I was making every effort to write you about our common salvation, I felt the necessity to write to you appealing that you contend earnestly for the faith which was once for all handed down to the saints. For certain persons have crept in unnoticed, those who were long beforehand marked out for this condemnation, ungodly persons who turn the grace of our God into licentiousness and deny our only Master and Lord, Jesus Christ (Jude 3-4).

These individuals are identified as saved by the fact they "turn the grace of our God"; the unsaved do not have God's grace—they are His enemies.

And what are the individuals of this Jude passage doing? They are turning that grace into licentiousness—loose, sinful living. Paul wrote of such men in 1st Corinthians 3 that they were living like "mere (unsaved) men" instead of being led by the Spirit, thus spiritual men (vv. 1, 3). Such sinful ways deny that Jesus is their "Master and Lord," *not* that He is their Savior. They are saved, but are betraying Jesus as they live lives more Satanic than godly. Though saved,

> these men... defile the flesh, and *reject authority*... Woe to them! ... autumn trees *without fruit, doubly dead*—["you have the name of being alive... but you are dead" (Revelation 3:1)]—uprooted... casting up their own shame... for whom the *blackness of darkness* has been reserved forever (vv. 7, 11-13; emphasis added).

They are destined for the blackness of darkness. For how long? The original Greek is *eis ton aionas*—"to the age." They are destined to remain there during the Millennial Age. Whipple clarifies:

> This is a place that is reserved for all those... apostates, the worst kind [being] apostate teachers. The "blackness of darkness" is in the region of "Gehenna" and includes the *grave* and the *pit* (Psalm 88; [denoting different, and more severe places of punishment]; cf. Ezekiel 32:18-32).
>
> The major difference between "the outer darkness" and the "blackness of darkness" is the degree of punishment that each represent. Whereas, the "outer darkness will be filled with *disinherited* believers just outside the light of the kingdom, the "blackness of darkness" will be filled with *disinherited* and *apostate* believers in a region far from any light....
>
> [However], apostates are not lost men. They will not be separated from God forever. They are the saved who have rebelled against God's Word [Jesus], [but who, in spite of that, cannot lose their salvation].[152]

Because Revelation 2:11 indicates The Chosen can be hurt by the second death, the person sentenced to the blackness of darkness gets to

---

[152]   Whipple, 152-153, 160; emphasis in original.

actually experience what he or she *should* have had happen to them for eternity, apart from the absolute mercy and grace of God. But they *do* get to experience it… for 1,000 years.

It is the place Peter writes of called *Tartarus* (also, unfortunately, translated as "hell"), which he describes as "the *pits of darkness*" (2nd Peter 2:4); the prison for fallen angels awaiting judgment. But like the treacherous Israelites who will one day be returned from exile, as we will see in our look at Ezekiel 39 (below), so too these betrayers will be released. Notwithstanding, this is not a place one wants to be… for a thousand years.

To more fully understand the coming judgments of all The Chosen, we will turn to examples from Jesus' own Twelve.

A. DISCIPLE: **JOHN**

EXAMPLE OF: **Loyalty**

KINGDOM LOCALITY: *In* **the Kingdom**

RELATIONSHIP AT JESUS' ARREST: **Followed Jesus (at own personal risk?)** (John 18:15)

FURTHER REFERENCE: **"The disciple whom Jesus loved."** (John 20:2; 21:7,20)

REVELATION REFERENCE: To the… church—The Chosen (3:7)… "I know your deeds. Behold, I have put before you an open door which no one can shut, because you… have not denied My name (3:8). I know your tribulation… do not fear what you are about to suffer… Be faithful and I will give you a crown of life. He who overcomes shall not be hurt by the second death" (2:9-11).

B. DISCIPLE: **ANDREW**

EXAMPLE OF: **Lack of commitment**

KINGDOM LOCALITY: **Outside, in the outer darkness with the fearful**

RELATIONSHIP AT JESUS' ARREST: **Did not accompany Jesus to pray with Him before His arrest, thus distant from Him at the moment of arrest** (Matthew 26:36-39).

FURTHER REFERENCE: **Now He who prepared us for this very purpose is God, who gave to us the Spirit as a pledge. Therefore,** [we should] be always of good courage... (2nd Corinthians 5:5-6). Through slackness the house leaks (Ecclesiastes 10:18).

REVELATION REFERENCE: To the... church—The Chosen (3:14)... "You are neither cold nor hot" (3:15); note, applies also to those of the General Assembly.

C. DISCIPLE: **JAMES** (amongst others)

EXAMPLE OF: **Drifting Away**

KINGDOM LOCALITY: **Outside, in the furnace with the hypocrites**

RELATIONSHIP AT JESUS' ARREST: **"Let these go their way": Left Him and fled** (John 18:8)

FURTHER REFERENCE: **We must pay much closer attention to what we have heard, less we drift away from it** (Hebrews 2:1). *drift away [pararrhueo*—to carelessly flow by].

REVELATION REFERENCE: To the... church—The Chosen (2:1; 3:14)... "You have left your first love" (2:4).

D. DISCIPLE: **PETER**

EXAMPLE OF: **Denial**

KINGDOM LOCALITY: **Further outside, deeper in the furnace with the unbelievers**

RELATIONSHIP AT JESUS' ARREST: **Denied Jesus** (Matthew 26:75)

FURTHER REFERENCE: **And he went out and wept bitterly** (Matthew 26:75) *Deny*: to disclaim connection with; DISAVOW; to back away from. **"Go tell His disciples... and Peter..."** (Mark 16:7). **Those who have once been enlightened... and then have fallen away...** (Hebrews 6:4,6). *fallen away [parapipto*–to fall aside; (to "drop out")].

REVELATION REFERENCE: To the... church—The Chosen (3:1)... "I know your deeds, that you have a name that you are alive, but you are dead... I have not found your deeds complete in the sight of My God" (3:1,2).

E. DISCIPLE: **JUDAS**

EXAMPLE OF: **Betrayal**

KINGDOM LOCALITY: *Way* **outside, in the blackness of darkness with fallen angels**

RELATIONSHIP AT JESUS' ARREST: **Betrayed Jesus** (Matthew 27:3)

FURTHER REFERENCE: *betray:* to deliver to an enemy by treachery; to desert, especially in time of need; [to change sides]. [Before the day of the Lord arrives] **the apostasy comes first** (2nd Thessalonians 2:3). *apostasy* [*apostasia*–defection (noun); from *aphestemi*–to revolt (verb)]. **And Satan entered into Judas** (Luke 22:3).

REVELATION REFERENCE: To the... church—The Chosen (2:12, 18)... "You have known the deep things of Satan...and eat things sacrificed to idols, and commit acts of immorality (2:24, 14).

C. Israel Our Example

Let's further confirm this issue of severe judgment of the saints. We are told in the New Testament that "whatever was written in earlier times— [the Old Testament]—was written for our instruction..." (Romans 15:4). Paul goes on to write to the Corinthians, "Now these things—[events in the Old Testament]—were written as examples for us..." (1st Corinthians 10:6).

So, what can we learn from God's dealings with the nation of Israel, His "chosen"? Hal Lindsey, writing in his book *Combat Faith*, observed that

> Israel is a picture of the believer's soul. God deals with us as individuals by the same principles He dealt with Israel or perhaps corporately—with the nation of Israel as a whole. The LORD sets up a clear typological model... through Israel's Exodus experience:
>
> (1) Israel in Egypt is a picture of unsaved humanity laboring in slavery to sin and Satan (typified by Pharaoh);
>
> (2) Israel's keeping of the Passover is a Divinely ordained passion play to illustrate salvation through the substitutionary sacrifice of God's greater lamb—Jesus the Messiah;

(3) Israel's deliverance at the Red Sea is a picture of redemption, by God's power, from the slave market of sin and the authority of Satan the slave-master;

(4) Israel's initial time in the Sinai portrays spiritual immaturity; Israel's return and continuance in the Sinai is a picture of the barren and unfulfilled life of a believer walking in unbelief and carnality; (There's nothing wrong with being a "spiritual baby" if you are a new believer, but if you continue to be one, you're in big trouble).

(5) Israel possessing the promised land demonstrates the victorious life of a Spirit-empowered believer who has cracked the faith barrier—[is being sanctified]—and entered God's rest by faith in God's promises.[153]

But the Israelites don't "crack the faith barrier"; they continue in their unbelief even though they've witnessed the LORD miraculously bringing them out of Egypt—a type of being saved. And what does God say of them?

> "[They] tested Me. They tried Me, though they had seen My work. For forty years I loathed that generation, and said they are a people *who err in their heart*, and they *do not know My ways*. Therefore, I swore in My anger, truly they shall not enter into My rest" (Psalm 55:9-11; emphasis added).

They were saved—brought out of Egypt—but they were disobedient: "erred in their heart… do not know My ways." Did God remove His promise that they were His "chosen"? Absolutely not!

But what did He do with them? They wandered 40 years in the wilderness just outside of the Promised Land. They lived in the outer wilderness, an outer darkness! For God's dealing with them was now one of disciplinary judgment for their disobedience (Hebrews 3:8-11).

In the book of Joshua we are told that the next generation—an *obedient* generation—was allowed to enter the Promised Land. This is a type of being allowed into the Kingdom. For the Jew, the land of Israel, like the Kingdom is for the Christian, is their *inheritance*:

---

153   Hal Lindsey. *Combat Faith* (New York: Bantam Books, 1986), 43-44; parentheses in original.

"We ourselves will cross over armed in the presence of the Lord into the land of Canaan, and the possession of our inheritance shall remain with us across the Jordan" (Number 32:32).

"'Surely the land on which your foot has trodden will be an inheritance to you and to your children forever, because you have followed the Lord my God fully'" (Joshua 14:9).

But the Israelites of a future generation are ultimately not faithful to the LORD. The prophets Isaiah, Jeremiah, and Ezekiel, amongst others, tell us they ultimately *rebel* against Him.

And how does the LORD react? God's "chosen" are deported, banished to Babylon—the place of Nebuchadnezzar (a type of Satan) and the evil Gentiles (a type of fallen angels), a place *spiritually* very much like Tartarus.

The house of Israel went into exile for their iniquity because they acted *treacherously—[they betrayed]*—against Me.... According to their uncleanness and according to their transgressions I dealt with them (Ezekiel 39:23-24; emphasis added).

The Israelite was removed from the promised land—*their inheritance*—and sent into exile, some Jewish families banished *for over 1,000 years*.[154] Has God, then, rejected His people forever? "May it never be!" writes Paul (Romans 11:1).

"I shall restore the fortunes of Jacob, and have mercy on the *whole house* of Israel... and they shall forget their disgrace and all their *treachery* which they perpetrated against Me.... I [will] bring them back from... the lands of their enemies.... I will leave *none of them* there any longer... And I will not hide My face from them any longer..." (Ezekiel 39:25-29; emphasis added).

And so it shall be at the end of the Millennium, when Christ hands the Kingdom over to the Father, and we enter into the Eternal State (1st Corinthians 15:24). Then those excluded from the Kingdom will return

---

[154] The northern tribes of Israel went into captivity in 722 BC and the southern tribes of Judah in 586 BC. To date, there are *still* Jews who have not returned to "the Promised Land."

and, as with the Israelites, "Then they will know that I am the LORD their God because I made them go into exile..." (Ezekiel 39:28). At this point God

> shall wipe away every tear from their eyes... and there shall no longer be any mourning, or crying, or pain; the first things have passed away.... Behold, I [God] am making all things new" (Revelation 21:4-5).

Can this be any clearer?

D. CONCLUSION

Entrance into the Kingdom of God is not automatic; it is a reward, part of the inheritance.

> [Jesus said], "But when the Son of Man comes in His glory, and all the angels with Him, then He will sit on His glorious throne... Then the King will say to those on his right, 'Come, you who are blessed of My Father, *inherit the kingdom* prepared for you from the foundation of the world (Matthew 25:34; emphasis added).

Few are being taught this. Yet, the Bema Seat awaits us; it is still a reality that looms in our future.

And the reward of that inheritance must be earned through the sacrifice of obedient sanctification. Those who reject that, for whatever reason, will be excluded from the Kingdom.

> Now the deeds of the flesh are evident, which are: immorality, impurity, sensuality, idolatry, sorcery, enmities, strife, jealousy, outbursts of anger, disputes, dissensions, factions, envying, drunkenness, carousing, and things like these, of which I forewarn you just as I have forewarned you those who practice [*prasso*—perform repeatedly or habitually] such *things shall not inherit the kingdom of God* (Galatians 5:19-21; emphasis added; see also Ephesians 5:5; cf. Ezekiel 18:4-5,9,20-32).

Yes, we will occasionally sin. This curse will not fully leave us until we are done with this life. That is why God has provided us with His Providential "Do Over": "If we confess our sins, He is faithful and righteous to forgive us our sins and to cleanse us from all unrighteousness" (1st John 1:9). If we are sensitive to our sinning, to confess it when we have, it is a good indication we are still "in the battle"—still "running the race to win."

But there are those who have stopped running. And they begin to "practice"—perform repeatedly or habitually—sin. It is clear their outcome: "such... shall not inherit the kingdom."

> Psalm 89:14 tells us that *justice and judgment* are the habitation of God's throne, but *mercy and truth* always go before Him. Consequently, just because we are "eternally secure," does not mean we have a license to sin. "Behold, therefore, the goodness and the severity of God; on them which fell severity; but toward thee goodness *if* thou continue in His goodness: otherwise thou also shalt be *cut off*" (Romans 11:22, KJV).

> Being born again is not all that matters... Everything we will be assigned to do in the future kingdom will have everything to do with what we have done here! We have a choice *here and now* what it will be like for us *there*. It will not be the same for every believer (Matthew 25:14-30; cf. Malachi 3:16).

> God's motive... is Love; but His Love is based upon His holiness and His Justice. Love without justice is partiality, and justice without Love is despotism. Therefore, everything God regarding us is based upon His Love, but in that Love is His justice.

> Revelation 3:19 confirms: "As many as I love, I rebuke and chasten." Now, chastening is different than punishing: **God does not punish His own; He simply disciplines us.** There's a huge difference between these two. "To punish" means: *to inflict harm*; whereas "to chasten" means *something that is done for our profit, for our benefit*.

> Yes, the Lord *scourges* (examines) every son whom He receives (Hebrews 12:6)! His absolute justice demands a review of our lives. This is what the Bema Seat of Christ is all about. We are

sinners "saved by grace" who need to be made holy.... There will be no godly wrath towards those who have been justified through faith. We can, however, expect chastening and discipline. But God's motive in this will always be Love. Chastisement seems to be God's highway to perfection....

Once we have made a commitment to believe in Jesus Christ, we are *eternally* saved... If, however, we choose to quench the Spirit and are not sanctified here on earth, we will run the risk of jeopardizing our place in the coming kingdom... Complete "salvation" means not only receiving God's Life in our spirit at our new birth (justification), but also renewing every part of our soul as well (sanctification) (Peter 1:9).[155]

Because it is the will of God...

It is a fearful thing to fall into the hands of the living God... [for] our God is a consuming fire... [and] everyone will be salted with fire... *Stern* discipline is for him who forsakes the way... (Hebrews 10:31; 12:29; Mark 9:49; Proverbs 15:10; emphasis added).

For many Christians the Bema Seat judgment will come upon them unexpectantly... and with a judgment more severe than they could have ever imagined. It is, indeed, the *worst* worst-case scenario for the unfaithful believer!

---

155   Missler, 2010, 32-34; all emphases in original.

CHAPTER 25

CONCLUSIONS

Jesus said to them, "...At that time... the end of the age... many will fall away..." (Matthew 24:3, 4, 10).

So, where does all of this take us? The key here is the Pre-determinarianism understanding that if one is truly saved, he or she will persevere in their faith to the end; they will never fall away.

As we have shown, there is weakness in that belief. And to demonstrate that is not the only weakness, other aspects of Pre-determinarianism were explored showing each has weaknesses.

Though the Pre-determinarian would think this is an attempt to sway them from their beliefs, the truth is the true intent is to show them the need to prepare should that belief, in fact, not prove true.

Let's look at two key questions. If one does not believe in the Pre-determinarianism tenet that one cannot fall away, that person will begin to prepare, to safeguard, him- or herself from that falling away. What is the harm to them if that proves false? The very acts of safeguarding are those of attempting to live righteously, a fulfillment of Matthew 6:33. It seems this provides a no-harm-no-foul situation.

On the other hand, if one believes that one can never fall away... and that proves to be an incorrect belief, what is the outcome? There is the potential of harm to one's faith should they actually, (unexpectedly to them), do fall away. For some (many?) this can lead them to quit, believing themselves to be an unsaved failure.

Even if this falling away proves to be temporary, the belief that they fell away at all can also lead them to conclude they were never saved to begin with. Thus, instead of picking up and pushing on, they return to (again) trying to be saved. Paul addresses this in his letter to the Hebrews.

> Let us press on to maturity, not laying again a foundation of repentance from dead works and of faith toward God (6:1).

The process of falling away, believing oneself to not be saved, then attempting "to (again) get saved," when, in fact, one is, can become a vicious cycle. Which can lead them to quitting.

And, as we have seen in reviewing the Kingdom of God, it is those who have given up on the sanctification process who are in jeopardy of potentially severe judgments at the Bema Seat. Every single person who is chastised in the parables we have looked at knew what they should have been doing, but chose to not do it. Had they pushed on, like the successful servants and slaves, reward awaited them.

And, as we have seen, that reward, the inheritance, includes being allowed into the Millennial Kingdom of Jesus Christ. A *worst* worst-case scenario is exclusion from that Kingdom.

Again, all of this hinges upon perseverance, which hinges upon the correct Biblical understanding of that concept.

Further, as we have seen, though disbarment from the Kingdom is a worst-case, there are *worst* worst-cases. These include the severe disciplines we have observed. When Paul, under inspiration of the Holy Spirit, writes that *believers* can "suffer loss" (1st Corinthians 3:15), he means that literally.

And the *absolute* worst worst-case is that of Christians, those like Judas, who not only fall away, but in doing so turn on Christ. Under the influence of Satan (Luke 22:3; John 13:27), they choose to return to being His enemy. They cannot lose their salvation, but, as Paul writes of them, they are "saved, yet so as through fire" (1st Corinthians 3:15).

With all of this in mind, the intent here has been to guide the Predeterminarian to see the risk that might exist in his or her view, and to adjust, and thus prepare, accordingly.

What would you do differently if there was, indeed, the very possibility of falling away from the faith? If it can happen to Peter, one of Christ's "inner circle," what makes one think it cannot happen to them?

It is hoped Pre-determinarians will ponder this... and act fittingly. Each of us should be preparing for the Great Falling Away in the Endtimes, of which Jesus said there would be "many" (Matthew 24:10). Those who are not preparing might one day find themselves in definite peril.

And, after that, the Bema Seat judgment...

PART III

BABYLONIALISM

Introduction

Babylon the Great... she has become a dwelling place of demons and a prison of every unclean spirit... (Revelation 18:2).

A. Background

Scripture states that in the Last Days, the period of time just prior to the Second Coming of Jesus Christ, a man identified as the Antichrist, under the power of Satan, will establish a One-World Government (Revelation 13:7b, "...authority over every tribe and people and nation was given to him" [the Antichrist]), which is linked to a One-World Economy (Revelation 13:17a, "...and he provides that no person should be able to buy or to sell, except the one who has the mark" [of the Antichrist, i.e. "666"]). Those who live close to this period of time should be able to see the indicators of such a coming evil government and economy.

This leads to the third issue that seems to be a strong stumbling block to preparation: The United States of America and her deep Christian roots. Many Christians, whether spoken overtly or held silently heartfelt, have the belief that America "is a Christian nation." Peter Marshall and David Manuel in their book *The Light and the Glory* succinctly expresses this view:

> We have seen how miraculously God would intervene to preserve and protect His covenant people.... At last all that God had purposed for His new Israel seemed to be within reach. America was now free to be that "city on a hill"...

God made certain that those same covenant promises which He made to our forefathers when He brought them here, would always be a viable possibility in the United States of America. We saw how He ensured that, no matter what happened in intervening generations, we Americans would still be able to avail ourselves of those promises, and re-enter a covenant relationship with *Him as a nation.... America, America, God shed His grace on thee...*[156]

Marshall and Manuel refer to United States in this passage as the "new Israel." Clearly, they see Americans as the "new covenant people."

What if, in fact, we are not? What if our "Christian roots" are not a guarantee of *"forever Christian fruit"*? What then would be the *worst* worst-case scenario for the United States? To identify that would provide insight into how to prepare.

Because much of what will be presented here is so foreign to many (most?) Christian readers, there is a need to document the concepts being present from reliable experts on the subject, and especially from those within, or having been within, the very organizations we are about to explore. This is being done to increase credibility as much of what is about to be presented is so nefarious, most will want to reject it otherwise. Such are the workings of Satan.

B. SATAN

The key to understanding *everything* about the conspiracy to set up a One-World Government, enslaving the populations of the world for a select elitist few, lies in the power behind the movement. This power has always been Satan.[157] So the issue here is to see how the evil spiritual actions of Satan and his demonic followers shows itself in the physical world, especially in the areas of economics and politics.

---

[156] Peter Marshall and David Manuel. *The Light and the Glory: Did God Have a Plan for America?* (Old Tappan, New Jersey: Fleming H. Revell Company, 1977), 336, 337; emphasis in original.

[157] Revelation 13:2b: "And the dragon [Satan] gave him [the Antichrist] his power, and his throne and great authority."

Here is an overview of Satan taken from Scripture:[158]

Satan = a Hebrew word meaning "one who contends [struggles in opposition with], opposes, ADVERSARY" (see Job 1:6-12); his basic nature is to oppose God's Person, Plan, and People (see 1 Peter 5:8).

Devil = a Greek word meaning "slanderer, liar" (John 8:44b).

Dragon = the Greek root means "to see"; it indicates in the sense of farseeing (Rev. 12:9)

Deceiver = [Greek], causes to roam, to lead astray; translated *seduce* in Rev. 2:20, KJV

WHO/WHAT/WHERE — deceives the whole world (Rev. 12:9; cf. "nations" 20:3,8)

WHY — to be worshiped as God (Isaiah 14:14; see also Luke 4:7)

HOW — through lies and murders (John 8:44)

WHEN — from the beginning (1 John 3:8)

ACCOMPLISES: (1) Fallen angels (Rev. 12:4,9)

(2) Evil World Powers (Daniel 10:12-13, 20)

(3) Antichrist (Rev. 13:3-7 [vv. 2, 4, *dragon* gives authority to]; v. 10 [by *murder*]; cf. Daniel 8:23-25)

Lucifer = a Hebrew word meaning *lightbearer* or *illumined one*; it is not surprising, then, his followers would call themselves "illuminated ones"—*illuminati*

With this as background, how do you think Satan would demonstrate

---

158 All the definitions taken from Vine, 992, 298, 328, 272, except *Lucifer*, taken from Strong, #1966.

himself to the world? And establish his government and economy? Would his actions be easy or difficult to identify?

God Himself draws back the spiritual curtain for us to see:

> In the third year of Cyrus king of Persia a message was revealed to Daniel... and the message was true and one of great conflict.... In those days, I, Daniel, had been mourning for three entire weeks. I did not eat any tasty food, nor did meat or wine enter my mouth, nor did I use any ointment at all until the entire three weeks were completed. On the twenty-fourth day of the first month, while I was by the bank of the great river, that is, the Tigris, I lifted my eyes and looked, and behold, there was a certain man dressed in linen, whose waist was girded with a belt of pure gold of Uphaz....
>
> Then he said to me, "Do not be afraid, Daniel, for from the first day that you set your heart on understanding this and on humbling yourself before your God, your words were heard, and I have come in response to your words. But the prince of the kingdom of Persia was withstanding me for twenty-one days; then behold, Michael, one of the chief princes, came to help me, for I had been left there with the kings of Persia. Now I have come to give you an understanding of what will happen to your people in the latter days, for the vision pertains to the days yet future." When he had spoken to me according to these words, I turned my face toward the ground and became speechless....
>
> Then he said, "Do you understand why I came to you? But I shall now return to fight against the prince of Persia; so I am going forth, and behold, the prince of Greece is about to come. However, I will tell you what is inscribed in the writing of truth. Yet there is no one who stands firmly with me against these forces except Michael your prince." (Daniel 10:1,2,3-5,12-15,20-21).

Arlen Chitwood, in his book *The Spiritual Warfare*, provides insight into what has taken place in this Daniel passage.

> Daniel chapter ten presents insights into how the present kingdom of Satan is structured, along with the location of

those administering authority in that kingdom. In this chapter, a heavenly messenger has been dispatched to Daniel on the earth from the heavens where God resides and was detained en route. This messenger was detained in the heavens above the earth by "the prince of the kingdom of Persia." Then Michael was dispatched from heaven [and he]... fought with the prince of Persia for [the messenger's] release (v. 13).

The picture presented is that of powerful angels in the kingdom of Satan ruling the earth from a heavenly realm through counterparts in the human race on earth. There was a prince (ruler) of Persia in the heavens, and there was a prince (ruler) of Persia on the earth. Then, in the heavens, there were lesser rulers associate with Persia (the kings of Persia); and the same would have been true on earth.

Then beyond that "the prince of Greece" is mentioned – another heavenly ruler over the Grecian kingdom on earth (v. 20). Daniel, throughout his book, deals with the kingdom of Babylon, from the days of Nebuchadnezzar to the days of Antichrist; and Daniel 10:20 ("... the prince of Greece shall come") anticipated that day when Alexander the Great in the Grecian kingdom on earth would conquer the kingdom of Babylon under the Medes and the Persians.

Thus, there is not only a breakdown of powers in the heavenly kingdom under Satan corresponding to a breakdown of powers in various earthly kingdoms under fallen man, but there is also a shifting of powers in the heavenly kingdom corresponding to a shifting of powers in the earthly kingdoms. In this respect, any person occupying a position of power in any Gentile earthly kingdom during the present age is merely occupying a position of power under Satan and his angels, as they rule from the heaven through counterparts on the earth.

Note that the nation of Israel is the lone exception among nations on earth whose rulers presently hold positions of power and authority under fallen angels in the kingdom of Satan. The prince over Israel is Michael (10:21), an angelic prince in the heavens who is not numbered among those ruling in Satan's kingdom, as Israel is not numbered among the nations (Numbers 23:9).[159]

The evil power—and evil personality—of Satan has not only been passed down to the fallen angels, now called "demons" (Matthew 8:28, 31, et al), who rebelled with him in eons past, but it also has control over the nations of the earth. The Apostle John writes: "The whole world lies in the power of the evil one" (1st John 5:19), which confirms Chitwood's observation of Satan's control of every "Gentile nation."

At this point one must ask the key question: If John literally means "the whole world," which would include every Gentile nation, how could America, then, avoid being included? A point to ponder as this is investigated.

Let's see how Satan has caused influence on the governments of the world. He has already been described as a liar and deceiver. It would, then, be by that method he would conduct himself.

---

[159] Arlen L. Chitwood, *The Spiritual Warfare* (Norman, Oklahoma: The Lamp Broadcast, Inc, 2012), 6-8; on-line http://www.lampbroadcast.org/Books/TSW.pdf (accessed November 24, 2017).

Chapter 26

SECRET SOCIETIES

The prudent man sees the evil and hides himself, but the naïve go on,
and are punished for it (Proverbs 22:3).

A. Introduction

Secret Societies, we are about to discover, are patterned after the Ancient Mystery Religions, quoted not only in the Old Testament, but found in the ancient writings of past civilizations discovered by archeologists. If Satan is in control of the Secret Societies, as he was in the Ancient Mystery Religions, then by looking at these past religions will provide an insight into the more modern Secret Societies.

> The Luciferian plot to overthrow the worship of Jesus has always worked in secret using camouflage to remain hidden. It has not come upon the world suddenly, but little by little. Likewise, we must also trace this history of the great Luciferian Conspiracy little by little....

> As Lucifer was the chief leader that led the angelic host to rebel against God, so did Nimrod cause the early descendants of Noah to rebel against God.... Nimrod tries to unite the whole known world of his day into a One World Government that would be against (anti-) God [cf. Anti-Christ]. God wanted

the sons of Noah to eventually replenish the earth by traveling abroad on the earth and settling in colonies. This would have kept in check wickedness that has always derived out of the cities. In the beginning it was not intended that man be crowded together in large cities.

[Nimrod built the first great city after the flood]: The city of Babel would become the metropolis of the world and unite its inhabitants under the dictatorial rule of Nimrod.... Th[e] Tower of Babel, the building of which Nimrod supervised ... was to be a monument to man to stand as a symbol of the wisdom [enlightenment] of its builders. By building the city of Babel, Nimrod hoped to prevent the people from scattering abroad into the colonies as the Lord intended.

[After God intervened and confounded the peoples' speech, which caused them to scatter] Nimrod built Nineveh [where he] was worshipped by its early inhabitants under his deified name "Ninus." He was the first to incite people to war with their neighbors after the confusion of tongues had scattered [them].... Hence, Nimrod was celebrated at Nineveh as a war-god, and his epics as a hunter [of men], a warrior, and his death were later imitated in the Assyrian, Babylonian, Egyptian, Greek, Roman, and American Indian Mysteries.[160]

The core of the Ancient Mystery Religions was Pantheism:

Pantheism...originated in the ancient city of Babylon and from there spread rapidly in all directions to cover the face of the earth.... [It] is Satan's religion. Although direct Satan worship [Satanism] has drawn some followers, most people will not embroil themselves in it because of its blatant evil overtones. Instead, something more subtle – such as pantheism – developed to draw in the masses. [In pantheism] God is the sum total of all that exists [not that He is *above* all He created]. There is no

---

[160] William Josiah Sutton. *The New Age Movement and the Illuminati 666*. (The Institute of Religious Knowledge, 1983), 16-20; cf. Rev. Alexander Hislop. *The Two Babylons* (Neptune, New Jersey: Loizeaux Brothers, 1916, 1959), 23.

personal God; instead, [God is] really a god-force or life-force.... Since this life-force is in us, we must therefore be gods or at least part of God [and, thus, we will never die – being reincarnated – as this life-force within us forever continues.]

[Another aspect of] the Ancient Mystery [Religion is that it] had an occult priesthood which ruled the country. In order to enter the priesthood, one always went through a series of secret occult rituals and initiations. When an Initiate reached the highest level [the "inner circle"] of the priesthood, the secret doctrine was revealed. It *always* included the worship of Lucifer, more frequently referred to as the God of Hades, or God of the Underworld, and usually was symbolized by a serpent or dragon. The highest priests took their orders directly from Satan or his demon messengers in altered states of consciousness. The techniques for achieving these states [through mind altering drugs, hypnosis, etc.] were once the deepest, best kept secrets of the high priests. Later, they would be kept alive and carried forward by the Secret Societies, [because the men in the highest levels knew they worshiped Lucifer], this should have sent a clear message to the[se] people that their [actions] were satanically inspired.[161]

The core of the Ancient Mystery Religions included witchcraft, use of magical, i.e., supernatural, powers, especially to communicate with the devil or demons; sorcery, the use of drugs; divination, the foretelling the future, such as through the stars (astrology), cards (tarots), or devices (ouija board, etc.); spiritism, the calling back of the dead or other spirit-like beings from the "world beyond." Especially note astrology:

The Babylonians taught that the fate of *everything* was dependent upon the sky. The Babylonians, as most ancient peoples, believed that each mortal, like the gods, had his own star in the sky. Here we can see why primitive men believed their chief gods inhabited the planets as the homes of their gods [hence worship of the sun and moon as well].... This will also help to understand the

[161] Gary H. Kah. *En Route To Global Occupation: A High Rankin Government Liaison Exposes the Secret Agenda for World Unification* (Lafayette, Louisiana: Huntington House Publishers, 1992) 69-70, 74.

cosmic religion of Astrology, and how astrology ties in with the Sun-worship [i.e. worship of the devil].[162]

Now that we understand astrology is inspired by Satan, this raises another key question: How much has astrology permeated our own world today, especially here in the U.S.?

With this as background, let's see how these secret religions and their practices began to play out in Scripture.

B. KABBALSIM

The Jews were constantly being deceived into worshipping of the foreign gods of the nations that surrounded them. Take for example, Jezebel's influence on the northern kingdom of Israel.

> [Jezebel] would attempt to change Israel into the image of Phoenicia [from where she came].... Her goal was to eradicate Israel's faith and replace it with the cult and worship of the Phoenician gods.[163]

Many of these were cosmic gods of nature. They would, in part, be the cause for the Jewish people to slip into idolatry. Ultimately, the Jews would be sent into captivity by God to Babylon as punishment for that idolatry.

While there, certain Jewish priests would be exposed to the Ancient Babylonian Mysteries. The deep study of these mysteries by the priests would, over time, produce what became known as a philosophy call Kabbal, from the Hebrew word meaning "that which is received."

> The Kabbala's central doctrine deals with the unfolding of the hidden and unknowable God not the fullness of the manifest [demonstrated] God, known by His works. In other words, they try to explain that which is hidden that the Lord has not revealed. The scientific name for this is "metaphysics." The Hebrew word Kabbal means "to receive" and implies that

---

162 William Sutton, 31.

163 Jonathan Cahn. *The Paradigm* (Lake Mary, Florida: Charisma House Book Group, 2017), 33.

> this [hidden knowledge] was received in the form of special revelation [*enlightenment*] to a few elect who were especially chosen for the privilege....

> The Kabbal teaches that man can reach the magnitude of the Omnipotent God [i.e. become God]. The method of the Kabbal can be summed up in one word: *magic*, [whose] roots are found in [ancient] Babylon.[164]

Notice the blasphemy here: "man can reach the magnitude of the Omnipotent God." This was the desire of Satan at his fall (Isaiah 14:14b). And is the lie presented to Eve in the garden of Eden (Genesis 3:5). The same deceitful tactics had seeped into the Jewish "faith."

C. GNOSTICISM

As Kabbalism was to the Jewish people of the Old Testament, Gnoticism became a New Testament movement which prospered in the early Christian period. Its name comes from the Greek work *gnosis*, "knowledge, to know." It combined portions of ancient Oriental mysticism with elements of Greek philosophy.

The result was a seeking of human wisdom to understand the ways of God in His relations with man. The heresy that was produced attempted to avoid what seemed to them to be the stigma of the cross, that of the deity of the human Christ. The Gnostics vehemently rejected this. Notice though, that is what John writes as the very core of an antichrist spirit.

> Who is the liar but the one who denies that Jesus is the Christ? This is the antichrist, the one who denies the Father and the Son (1 John 2:22).

To the Gnostics, salvation (justification) was obtained through the revealed knowledge of God that was, in reality, only given to a few. Thus, the Gnostics believed only *they* "knew" the great secrets of religion and life. In essence, it was, as Gary Kah noted

---

[164] William Sutton, 90-91.

a further development of Kabbalism taking into account Satan's "new problem" posed by the risen Christ.... [Kabbalism's basic] belief: God, the Supreme Father, has two sons, the elder Satanael [note the "el" ending, signifying "God"], the younger, Jesus. To Satanael, who sat on the right hand of God, belonged the right of governing the celestial world, but, filled with pride, he rebelled against his Father and fell from heaven. Then, aided by the companions of his fall, he created the visible world, image of the celestial, having like the other its suns, moon, and stars, and last he created man and the serpent his minister. Later Christ came to earth in order to show men the way to Heaven, but His death was ineffectual, for even by descending into Hell He could not wrest the power of Satanael, i.e. Satan. This belief in the impotence of Christ and the necessity for placating Satan, not only the "prince of this world," *but its creator*, led to further doctrine that Satan, being all-powerful, should be adored.[165]

These Satanic influences would continue throughout the first millennium of Christianity and on into the second. In the second, however, they would begin to become more refined, ultimately becoming focused on control of politics and economics.

D. Knights Templar

The Knights Templar was a combined military and religious order established around AD 1118. Their stated mission was to protect pilgrims on their way to the Holy Land during the many crusader wars. Concurrently, they also fought in various battles of the crusades themselves. In these battles they demonstrated extreme bravery for which they became legendary.

By their participation in the crusades the Templars became extremely wealthy and powerful through gifts of both land and money. Their enormous wealth and eventual political organization actually led them to become bankers of Europe. Their overpowering desire was to become wealthy in order to buy the world.

The Templars, who embraced the religious beliefs of the Gnostics,

---

[165] Kah, 99-100; quoting, in part, Nesta Webster. *Secret Societies and Subversive Movements* (Hawthorne, California: Christian Book Club of America, originally published in 1924), 32-34, 63; emphasis added.

represented the first widescale attempt to organize and mobilize forces of occultism for the purpose of gaining control of the world.

Satan had begun in earnest his long-held desire to create a One-World Government. It would be based upon control of the economy. Its fulfillment will occur in the Endtimes (Revelation 13:7,17).

Probably the greatest occultic perversion of the Templars was their Holy Blood, Holy Grail heresy:

> According to the [Templars who are the] guardians of the Grail, Jesus, [prior to His death], was supposed to have married Mary Magdalene [who had children by Him]. Mary Magdalene reportedly fled Jerusalem in A.D. 70 with her "sacred" children. She sailed across the Mediterranean to France, bringing the cup from which Christ drank the Last Supper and in which her alleged uncle, Joseph of Arimathea, had caught the blood of Christ.... In an esoteric [limited to a small circle of "knowledgeables" – those who know] sense, the womb of Mary Magdalene becomes the Grail – preserving the bloodline or lineage of Jesus. [In this sense], Mary Magdalene is linked with the Babylonian goddess of fertility whose name was Istar.[166]

This perversion, begun in the early second millennium of the Christian faith would gain new ground in that millennium's mid-point.

E. ROSICRUCIANS

The history of the Rosicrucian order is obscure, partly because of the secrecy it always maintained. Some claim it began in Egypt in 1500 B.C., linking it with the Ancient Mystery religions.

Notwithstanding, after the Knights Templar plot of world domination was discovered, and allegedly destroyed by the governments of its day in about A.D. 1420, like the Phoenix of lore, a new sect arose from its ashes.

This new sect was allegedly founded by Christian Roesenkreuz (Rose Cross). However,

---

[166] J. R. Church. *Guardians of the Grail* (Oklahoma City, Oklahoma: Prophecy Publications, 1989), 73, 75-76, 78.

in 1629, when Rosicrucian interest in Europe was at its zenith, a man named Robert Denyau composed an exhaustive history of the Rose-Croix [Rose Cross, in which] he states explicitly [it] was founded by Jean de Gisors, a Knights Templar [as far back as] 1188.[167]

Regardless of its starting date, this offshoot of the Knights Templar was a secret society that studied the mysteries of life and nature by intuitive mystical means. Though they believed in a latent sixth sense which, when developed would enable one to investigate the realm of the dead, it is Astrology that figures largely in their "studies."

There was one additional element that played heavily in its beliefs.

Rosicrucism is a mixture of both Christianity and Witchcraft.[168]

As we have seen, Rosicrucism became one more stepping stone between the Ancient Mystery religions of the past and the more modern emanations of Satanic control.

F. FREEMASONRY

The link between the Knights Templar and Rosicrusism with their more modern ancestor, Freemasonry, is really not hard to find. Any interested person need only look at the names of the last three degrees of the Freemasonry York Rite – the Knight of the Red Cross, Knight of Malta, and Knight Templar – and the eighteenth degree of the Scottish Rite – Sovereign Prince of Rose-Croix, which together with the seventeenth degree is known as the Chapter of Rose Croix.

Once that link is established, it becomes important to see two features. First, is the strategy the Freemasons would employ.

If the Rosicrucians were to progress toward their goal of establishing a New World Order, they would eventually have to go public to enlist the support of more people to carry out their task. In the tradition of Knights Templars, they decided to take

---

[167]   Ibid., 97.

[168]   William Sutton, 92.

on the outer appearance of a benevolent organization of good works in order to continue their occult traditions within. They merged with and finally took over the stonemason guilds of Europe, retaining many of their symbols from the building trade. The stone masons became referred to as Operative Masons, as they were actually employed in the building profession [i.e., they really did build things]; unlike the occult adepts who took over their guilds, who became known as Speculative Masons....

The transition from Operative to Speculative Masonry took several decades to complete.... The "new" Order expanded rapidly. By the late 1700s, it had become firmly established as an organization known for its good works, and was, for the most part, viewed favorably by the public. With the groundwork successfully laid, the Adepts were once again free to pursue their age-old ambition of re-establishing the Luciferic World Order.[169]

The second feature is to see the power behind their movement. Because Freemasonry is a modern-day organization, something to be dealt with in our own day-and-age, it is critical to confirm that their power is not limited to the mind of man, but is, in fact, being moved upon by a spiritual force.

Albert Pike, the leader of the Freemasons in the 1800s, wrote the Masons' "bible," a code of their established opinions, entitled *Morals And Dogma*. Pike's background is something to be noted.

Very few Masons [much less outsiders] know that Albert Pike, th[e] highest authority of Freemasonry, the Prince Adept Mystic, Scholar of Freemasonry, was also head of the Palladist, another secret society which openly worshipped Lucifer and was bent on destroying Christianity, replacing it with worship of Lucifer himself. Albert Pike, the head of Freemasons was also an Apostle of Lucifer.[170]

The theological dogma of Freemasonry was explained in the "Instructions" issued by Albert Pike in 1899 to that organization's twenty-three Supreme Councils of the world. His words were recorded:

---

[169] Kah, 106-107.

[170] William Sutton, 114.

If Lucifer were not God, would Adonay [Hebrew for "the Lord," used in Scripture as a term for the God of faithful believers] whose deeds prove His cruelty, perfidy [treachery], and hatred of man, barbarism and repulsion of science, would Adonay and his priests, calumniate [utter false charges against] him?

Yes, Lucifer is God, and unfortunately Adonay is also God. For the eternal law is that there is no light without shade, no beauty without ugliness, no white without black, for the absolute can only exist as two Gods: darkness being necessary to light to serve as its foil, as the pedestal is necessary to the statue....

Thus, the [Scritptural] doctrine of Satanism is a heresy; and the true and pure philosophical religion is the belief in Lucifer, the equal of Adonay; but Lucifer, God of Light and God of Good, is struggling for humanity against Adonay, the God of Darkness and Evil.[171]

If one is still not convinced of the spiritual underpinning of Freemasonry, there are the writings of Pike in his book *Morals and Dogma*:

The true name of Satan, the Kabalists say, is that of [Jehovah] reversed; for Satan is not a black god, but the negation of God. The Devil is the personification of Atheism or Idolatry. For the [Freemason] Initiates, this is not a person, but a force [i.e., the "life-force" of Pantheism] created for good, but which may serve for evil; it is the instrument of liberty and free will. They represent this force, which presides over the physical generation [physical creation, especially the earth; cf. John 12:31 – "prince of this world"; 2 Cor. 4:4 – "God of this age"; Eph. 2:2 – "prince of the power of the air"] under the mythological and horned form of the god Pan; thence came the He-Goat...brother of the ancient serpent, and the Lightbearer...of which poets have made the false Lucifer legend....

---

171 Edith Starr Miller, *Occult Theocrasy* (Hawthorne, California: The Christian Book Club of America, 1933). 220-221; quoted in Kah, 124. Notice this very attribute of Satan is identified by Scripture: "And no wonder, for even Satan disguises himself as an angel of light" (2nd Corinthians 11:14).

Lucifer, the Lightbearer! Strange and mysterious name to give to the Spirit of Darkness! Lucifer, the Son of the Morning! It is he who bears the light, and with it splendors intolerably blinds feeble, sensual, or selfish souls! Doubt it not![172]

As has been the process we have observed here over the many thousands of years of human history, Freemasonry would also morph into an offshoot. A new ultra-secret society would form, enlisting in its ranks members from the highest degrees of the Masonic Order. This new Order-within-an-Order would increase the intensity towards establishing the Luciferic ideal of a One World Government and Economy.

It would come to be known as the *Illuminati*.

G. ILLUMUNATI

The Masonic historian, Albert G. Mackey, described the Illuminati as a "secret society, founded May 1, 1776, by Adam Weishaupt, then a professor of canon [religious] law at the University of Ingolstadt."[173] He was born a Jew, converted to Catholicism where he became a Jesuit priest, only to break away from that order to form his own secret organization.[174]

Weishaupt planned a world take-over by using the Fraternal Order of Freemasonry. His plan was to penetrate into the high levels of the Order, then take control in directing the affairs of nations into an eventual One World Government. The plan was to operate under cover as long as possible, and when the gullible world finally found out, it would be too late to stop him.

The Illuminati was to be a Secret Society within the Secret Society of the Freemasons. He adopted the Jesuits' system of espionage[175] in which every member spied on every other member. Each month the Novice had

---

172 Albert Pike. *Morals and Dogma of the Ancient and Accepted Scottish Rite of Freemasonry* (Washington, D.C.: House of the Temple, 1966), 102, 321; also quoted in Kah, 116-117.

173 Kah, 107.

174 Kirban. 147.

175 William Sutton, 175, 178-179.

to deliver to Weishaupt a sealed letter which revealed every aspect of his relationship with his superior.[176]

Weishaupt introduced Witchcraft to his followers, using it to brainwash his new Initiates into becoming anti-Christian. He recruited indirectly an army of international terrorists and propagandists to win others to his movement, and help in his struggles to overthrow *all* religions and *all* governments.

However, before the people of the world would accept the Luciferian Government, which Weishaupt, an apostle of Lucifer, hoped to eventually offer them in its stead, there would have to be a culture change within the societies of the people first, along with a spirit of unrest and riots in the air. The people of the world would have to be reduced into a godless society.

Atheism, then, was a front, it was just a tool to destroy Christianity. Weishaupt and his "Inner Circle" were not *atheists; they believed in a god.* However, this god was not Jesus Christ, but Lucifer.[177]

On July 16, 1782, at the Masonic Congress of Wilhelmsbad, Austria, an alliance between Illuminism and Freemasonry was finally sealed. John Robison, a Professor at Edinburgh University, and recognized by Weishaupt as one of the truly great intellectuals of his day, was entrusted with top secret Illuminati documents and was thus able to scrutinize the inner workings of the secret society from close range.

It was Robison who exposed the Illuminati conspiracy, noting that by the time a member had reached the "inner circles," his oath of absolute secrecy and unquestioning obedience had become deadly serious. Only at this stage was he finally allowed to see the ultimate aims of the Order: (1) the abolishing of all ordered governments, (2) abolishing of private property+, (3) abolishing of inheritance, (4) abolishing of patriotism, (5) abolishing of all religion+, (6) abolishing of the family+ (impacting morality, marriage [see 1 Tim. 4:3], and the proper education of children), and (7) the creation of a New World Order, i.e. a One World Government.[178]

Adam Wieshaput died in 1830 at the age of 82. It is believed he rejoined

---

[176]   Kirban, 147.

[177]   *The Illuminati 666*, pp. 216, 198.

[178]   Des Griffin. *Fourth Reich of the Rich* (Clackamas, Oregon: Emissary Publications, 1976, 1992), 54, 44, 46, 52; note those elements with a plus sign (+) are also Communist objectives as well.

the Catholic Church with a death-bed repentance. After his death Giuseppe Mazzini, an Italian revolutionary leader, was appointed as Director of the Illuminati, serving from 1834 to 1872. He, in turn, selected Albert Pike, previously mentioned as the author of the Masons' "bible," to head the Illuminati activities in the United States beginning around 1859 and lasting until Pike's death in 1891.[179]

In an effort to centralize the authority of Universal Freemasonry a new ultra-secret governing body was established on September 20, 1870. This represented the first major restructuring of illuminized Freemasonry. At the center of this creation was Albert Pike.[180]

The restructuring appears to be, in part, preparation for the actualization of the expected New World Order. In a remarkable letter dated August 15, 1871, which had been on display at the British Museum Library in London up until approximately 1975, Pike gave Mazzini details of the Luciferian plan for world conquest. In graphic detail he outlined plans for three world wars.[181]

The First World War was to enable Communism, already expressed by Karl Marx's "Manifesto" in 1848, to destroy the Czarist government of Russia and replace it with militant atheism. The Second World War would begin by manipulating the governments of Great Britain and Germany to start a war. Hitler, however, accomplished this by himself, bringing in World War Two.

After this war, so the plan went, Communism would then be in a position to destroy governments and weaken religions. This, as we have seen over the last 100 years, also has come to pass.

The Mazzini-Pike blueprint also called for a World War Three. This would begin by stirring up the controversy between Judaism and the Moslem world. Mazzini and Pike hoped that the Zionists and Moslems would destroy each other and bring the rest of the world into a final conflict.

This fake Armageddon would bring complete social, political, and economic chaos[182] — and set up the Illuminati "answer." Strife, and fear that a conflict somewhere could escalate into a nuclear war, was hoped to

---

[179] Kirban, 151, 157.

[180] Kah, 111-112.

[181] Griffin, 70.

[182] Kirban, 162-163.

play on peoples' minds psychologically, wearing them down. It was expected this would cause them to desire world peace above all else.[183]

As all of this was pre-planned, it was expected to play perfectly into the Illuminati's hand to create a One-World Government run by them as the hands of Satan in this world. And their strategy to accomplish all of this has been working successfully over the past centuries.

> When Adam Weishaupt formed the New Order for the Ages [in the late 1700s], the Illuminati, [he] infiltrated the high levels of the nations of Europe through Freemasonry. Through this [he] hoped to be able to fill the top positions in the Old World Governments so [he] could legislate bills that would connect the countries according to [Illuminati] plans. Using social issues and humanitarian causes, the Illuminati of today have in their ranks untold millions promoting this same Luciferic scheme, and many in it are completely unaware. Millions upon millions of sincere people think they are doing the world a great service by joining this international Luciferic movement...[184]

This attempt to control mankind would begin with the infiltration of European governments and economies. It was Europe's nations that were colonizing, and thus controlling, the world at that time, so this made perfect sense. The processes that worked in Europe for the Illuminati could then be extended to the rest of the world.

This would, then, include the American colonies.

---

[183] Kah, 119.

[184] William Sutton, 204.

CHAPTER 27

THE MONEY MANIPULATORS

There is a power so organized, so subtle, so watchful, so interlocked, so complete, so persuasive, that prudent men had better not speak above their breath when they speak of it.

— Woodrow Wilson

A. INTRODUCTION

The *process* of infiltrating the governments and economies of Europe will lay the foundation for what we are about to explore.

> In 1782, at the Masonic Congress of Wilhelmsbad... Weishaupt also succeeded at forging an alliance between illuminized Freemasonry and the growing Rothschild banking network, thereby giving the Order the financial means to begin to carry out its plans.[185]

> [While] Adam Weishaupt produced the blueprint for...a one world government whose ruler is Lucifer ... the Rothschild international banking family, who for some 200 years had great influence on the economic and political history of Europe... provided the money...[186]

---

[185] Kah, 108.

[186] William Sutton, 173, 192.

The place to begin, then, is to look at money.

B. Facts About Money

> "Give me the power to coin money and set its value,
> and I care not who makes the laws."
> – Meyer Amschel Rothschild

Fact 1 – Paper Money is not real wealth; it only represents something of value.

To begin with, the paper money we so easily use today is, as we shall see, actually the creation of international bankers. This paper money creation has been done with the full support of governments who, on the surface, appear to be in control of it.

Prior to paper money, people used a simple barter system. Once a swap was agreed upon, each party would receive what he or she needed. The problem here is that one cannot "make change" if the barter was one-sided.

Eventually gold and silver coins were produced. These means of trade have had the longest record of purchasing power in human history. They are reliable as these metals have actual value... and can be physically held. This, however, creates the problem.

Gold and silver eventually became *the* means of purchasing. Unfortunately, in large quantities, they are cumbersome... and heavy. They are also openly available for thieves.

From this, modern banking developed. People who were considered trustworthy would actually hold the gold and silver for someone else, charging them a slight fee for that safe-keeping. They would issue "paper receipts" indicating that the money was, in fact, actually available. Paper money was born.

Using this paper, a prospective purchaser could show that there was actual gold or silver available at a certain location if the merchant wanted to collect it. The purchaser would write a script (creating more paper), which the merchant could take to the holder for his, the merchant's, portion of the gold or silver being held.

These "holders" eventually saw that the owners were actually reluctant to give away all of their gold and silver at once (if ever) and so that metal sat around "collecting dust." It was at this point that the more business-like realized they could easily *lend* the money. They would do this with an "interest" charge, and so make further money off of the money they were "protecting."

Of course, once the real owners found out, they would want a portion of those profits, but the "holders" made sure *they* got the lion's share. This process has continued into modern banking today.

The key concept here is that the paper is not real wealth; it is only paper. It does, however, represent real wealth... the actual gold or silver.

Fact 2 –The Rothschild Family of Europe developed this system best.

Though, no doubt, a number of people became very successful at these new monetary procedures, inevitably someone does it best. Meyer Amschel Rothschild of Germany not only developed his system well locally, but also realized it could be expanded by him throughout Europe. This would give him access to untold financial wealth, which he could leverage into political control as well. He could then use the political to safeguard his financial! This became all the easier as the most wealthy individuals who wanted to store gold and silver were the kings, princes, lords, and ladies. So, he already had an "in."

Rothschild also came to see that local notes at one location might not be so acceptable somewhere else, especially between different countries.

> Thus, Meyer conceived the idea of international banking for the Europeans and their leaders. He set his son Carl over the Bank of Naples in Italy, his son James over the Bank of France, and his son Edmund over the bank of Germany, his son Solomon over the bank of Vienna, and his son Nathan over the Bank of England. The Rothschild family thus controlled international banking in Europe for a long time.[187]

It is offered, and will soon be seen, that the Rothschilds *still* control international banking. And not just in Europe.

---

[187] Doug Clark. *The Greatest Banking Scandal in History* (Eugene, Oregon: Harvest House Publishers, 1981), 20.

Fact 3 – Wars are expensive and so Governments (Kings) need money for them.

Because human history is riddled with war, kings and other nobles are known to be fond of them. But, they are expensive. Eventually, leaders became aware that they too could "borrow" to help pay for them. This change from being the investor, putting their gold and silver *in* to a holder (banker), to being a borrower, taking money on-loan (i.e., with interest) *from* a bank, would change the very fiber of politics and finances.

> It wasn't long until one nation warring against another ran out of gold and silver from the national treasuries, or else ran precipitously short. It was then the governments learned that they too could borrow from the holders. The bankers soon learned that to loan to the king meant big loans and thus big profits on the interest charge. It became an overnight revelation to the Rothschild family that *the way to unfathomable riches was through financing the kings' need in war and peace.* But it was also instantly evident that the kings could usually finance their own needs in times of peace through heavy taxation on the people or else through business that the government might be into. So it became expedient for the bankers to encourage war, that they would be called upon to finance the warring governments.[188]

It became obvious that manipulating economic and political events that promoted war was a financial dream for the Rothschilds. The loaning of money to governments also helped them secure the political end. It provided them with leverage over those governments which allowed the insertion of Rothschild proxies, even at the highest levels.

It is at this point that we must reflect back on the opening quotes in the Introduction to this section. Adam Weishaupt's Illuminati, like the kings of nations, also was in need of finances to carry out his conquest of the world. They too turned to the Rothschilds for financing. And like with the European kings, the Rothschild banking interests began to guide, then control, the Illuminati.

Those who worshipped Satan, the Illuminati, were now wed with

---

[188] Ibid., 20-21.

those who worshipped money—the root of all evil (1st Timothy 6:10)—the international bankers.

> Multinational Bankers... hold allegiance to no flag and constitution and pay no homage to any political leaders. They are their own nationality and breed. They worship money and power.... Their... end goal [is] their [world] government domination.[189]

This produced, for the first time in man's history since the scattering from the tower of Babel (Genesis 11:9), the Satanic means for total control of mankind.

Fact 4 – Total control of a nation lies in creation of, and control over, a Central Bank

As Meyer Amschel Rothschild once said about governments and power, "Give me the power to coin money and set its value, and I care not who makes the laws." Money is power. And, as we noted above, if an international banker could succeed in loaning money to a government through the king or prime minister, (or even a president), he could exercise greater control over the policies of the regime to which he loaned that money.

Thus, it was always preferable for the bankers to have "their men" in key positions in the king's cabinet. Once this was accomplished, the Rothschilds had, literally, almost total control over a nation. Almost.

The last piece was to create a Central Bank for a nation which was controlled by the Rothschilds. They then had control over private banking, the nation's government, and, finally, that nation's finances.

With this in mind, the Rothschilds would inevitably turn their gaze to the growing wealthiest nation on the earth, America.

> The House of Rothschild was also a powerful influence in early American banking. President Jackson abolished the early effort at establishing a central bank in 1836, but even after that European Central Bankers had a long record of influencing banking procedures in the U.S. Because of this control in [America], a series of panics were arranged so that the final blow

---

[189] Ibid., 58, 72.

to centralized banking would be acceptable to the leadership [of the U.S.]. Problems were created in the United States that were used to convince bankers and the authorities that centralization was the only way to go…. They got it in 1913 in establishing the Federal Reserve System, with their own men controlling it.[190]

Though International bankers had wanted control of the American money supply (as they had in Europe), they did not get it immediately. They did, as Doug Clark noted, eventually get it in 1913 in the establishment of the Federal Reserve.

America now had a Central Bank, the last piece to controlling a nation. With the manipulated 1929-33 stock market crash[191] they have attained even more power. Their power base has expanded throughout the world during the last century. This has been largely due to its organizations such as the Royal Institute of International Affairs (RIIA), in England, and its American counterpart, the Council on Foreign Relations (CFR), headquartered in New York City. To the uninitiated, that power would be found to be unbelievable.

C. America's Shadow Government

Control of the nations of the world through a world government, one-world money, and a one-world government board of governors has been the goal of several groups down through the last 200 years. As we have seen, the principle group, a secret society, was started by Adam Weishaupt in 1776 called The Order of the Illuminati. When that group became known, it

---

[190] Ibid., 36.

[191] See especially, Tal Brooke, *When the World Will Be As One: The Coming New World Order in the New Age* (Eugene, Oregon, Harvest House Publishers, Inc., 1989), 254, where Brooke, quoting noted 20th century, Harvard economist, John Kenneth Galbraith from his *The Great Crash, 1929*, (New York: Time Inc., 1954) p. 102: " 'Sir Winston Churchill [was] walked out on the floor of the New York Stock Exchange the morning it fell. Churchill was brought to witness the crash firsthand on October 24, 1929, because it was desired that he see the power of the banking system at work.' " Brooke goes on to say, "This presumes plenty of lead time for Winston to take the ship from England to the United States, hang out for a while, maybe start the day with a good breakfast at the Waldorf, and make it there in time to see the floor open up."

was apparently crushed in 1786 by the very governments it was attempting to destroy.

In reality, the group was not destroyed but went underground. Later they re-surfaced calling themselves the League of Just Men.

Still later, in the days of the Rothschilds and their financial backing, the League of Just Men evolved into the Round Table Group in England. This organization would branch into the Royal Institute of International Affairs (RIIA), which, as we previously noted in the United States, became the Council on Foreign Relations (CFR).

According to Professor Carroll Quigley, former professor emeritus at Harvard and Princeton Universities, the Royal Institute of International Affairs and the Council on Foreign Relations were originally planned and drawn up in secret meetings in Paris.[192]

Quigley went on to say that the secret meetings to set up these power groups

> all happened in 1919, and was led primarily by the European banking groups, who wished to establish themselves more clearly in the United States in order to work on government policies here as well. Many of these same original families, which promoted the Council on Foreign Relation in the U.S.A., were involved in promoting the Federal Reserve in 1913.[193]

> Their aim is nothing less than to create a world system of financial control in private hands able to dominate the political system of each country and the economy of the world as a whole.[194]

---

[192] Carroll Quigley, *Tragedy and Hope: A History of Our Time* (New York: The Macmillan Company, 1966), 950; see also Brooke, 251, where Brooke noted, "Quigley, who confessed to being an insider and confidant of this elite group, [wrote in] *Tragedy and Hope* [a] 1,300-page book naming major insider power groups attempting to manipulate a world socialist order. Quigley ardently supported The Plan, but said that it should no longer be under cover. His book was a triumphalist announcement of the inevitable, since The Plan had virtually reached completion. He had been among the intellectual brain-trust rubbing shoulder with the Insiders. The problem was that he said too much. The Macmillan first edition of 1966 suddenly disappeared almost overnight, even from publishers' libraries."

[193] Ibid.

[194] Brooke, 253.

Before he became saved, Christian author Gary H. Kah was once an inside member of the plot for a one-world government. In his book *En Route to Global Occupation*, he stated:

> During the early 1980s, I was on the fast track of a successful government career, which took me around the world dealing with American embassies, foreign governments officials, international business leaders, and, at times, member of the press and media…from Taiwan to Israel to the Soviet Union…. Through my travels and job-related contacts, I became aware of plans being laid worldwide for the establishment of a one-world government, most frequently referred to by insiders as the New World Order….
>
> Most American's live in a false reality. We think that because we had the right to vote and choose candidates that we, the people, were somehow in control. But the fact is, we aren't.[195]

As we have seen, the Council on Foreign Relations (CFR) has direct links to the Rothschild-Illuminati group. The extent of the involvement of that organization in American politics can be seen in CFR members within the United States Federal Government.

> From the time of Franklin D. Roosevelt, the influence of the Council on Foreign Relations in the executive branch of government has continued to grow. By the Nixon administration, at least 115 CFR members held positions within the executive branch. And during the Carter years, more than a dozen were appointed to top positions in the administration…. The tradition continued during the Reagan years. Even though Reagan campaigned against the group; once elected, he appointed no less than seventy-five CFR members to key posts. The Bush [senior] administration, however, would shatter all previous records, as more than 350 CFR members held positions with the executive branch.[196]

---

[195] Kah, 6, 51.

[196] Ibid., 51ff.

George W. Bush would continue in his father's footsteps. Such CFR members as Vice President, Dick Cheney; Secretaries of State, Colin Powell and Condoleezza Rice; Defense Secretary, Robert Gates; and Treasury Secretary, Henry M. Paulson, Jr., would help dominate his government.[197]

In the intervening administration of William Clinton, he too would rely heavily on CFR members at senior command posts. These would include Vice President, Albert Gore, Jr.; Warren Christopher, Secretary of State; Anthony Lake, National Security Advisor; James Woolsey, Director of Central Intelligence Agency; Les Aspin, Secretary of Defense; Colin Powell, then Chairman, Joint Chiefs of Staff; and Madeleine Albright, Secretary of State.[198]

President Clinton's fellow Democratic Party successor, Barak Hussein Obama, would not rely as heavily on CFR members. But, there would still be a CFR presence in his administration. They included John Kerry, Secretary of State; Jeh Johnson, Secretary of Homeland Security; and Penny Pritzker, Secretary of Commerce.[199]

Gary Kah made an insightful observation of this:

> I soon realized that the New World Order was not only economic in nature, but also contained a political dimension... If these same leadership positions were held by evangelical Christians belonging to a particular church denomination, we could rest assured that the media would cry conspiracy every day until something was done to correct the situation. Yet chances of 80 percent of our leaders consistently coming from a single church denomination without the manipulation of the political process are far greater than these same leaders coming from the Council on Foreign Relations – since many church denominations have hundreds of thousands, or even millions of members, while the

---

[197]   The White House Archives: President Bush's Cabinet, https://georgewbush-whitehouse.archives.gov/government/cabinet.html; Council on Foreign Relations: Membership List, https://www.cfr.org/membership-roster; both accessed November 25, 2017.

[198]   The Council on Foreign Relations. *Annual Report 1991-1992* (New York: Pratt House, 1993).

[199]   The White House: President Barak Obama: The Cabinet, https://obamawhitehouse.archives.gov/administration/cabinet; Council on Foreign Relations: Membership List, https://www.cfr.org/membership-roster; both accessed November 25, 2017.

CFR has less than *three thousand* members. In fact, the chances of a majority of leaders consistently coming from such a small group as a matter of coincidence are so remote as to not even warrant serious consideration….[200]

More chilling, Kah also found

a spiritual motivation. I found the inter-connections between the three [politics, economics, and spiritual] to be extensive…. I am convinced that America's purpose in the overall plan was to lay the necessary groundwork for the world government; and then, having accomplished this mission, to lead humanity to the threshold, if not actually into, the New World Order.[201]

Which leads us to the *worst* worst-case scenario.

D. AMERICA'S SHADOW SHADOW GOVERNMENT

Gary Kah's last observation may be more correct than he realizes. In 1990, William T. Still published *New World Order: The Ancient Plan of Secret Societies*. He offered much of the information already presented above, but he went one step further:

Most people believe that the legend of Atlantis is only a myth. Yet the similarities between the account of the destruction of Atlantis and the biblical account of the flood of Noah are really quite remarkable. They appear to be the same event. The difference may be just one of perspective. From the vantage point of secret societies the destruction of Atlantis was a tragedy. Manly Hall, [a Freemason writing in his books *The Lost Keys of Freemasonry* (1923) and *The Secret Destiny of America* (1944)], claimed that the Atlantean legend is central to the philosophy of all secret societies. He describes Masonry as, "…a university, teaching the liberal arts and science of the soul…. It is a shadow of the great Atlantean Mystery School, which stood with all its splendor in the ancient City of the Golden Gates [on Atlantis]."

---

[200] Kah, 6, 55-56.

[201] Ibid, 6, 62.

[In contrast], from the biblical point of view its destruction was a necessity because the pre-flood world had become so corrupt....

[Hall] claimed...secret societies have existed in most, if not all nations throughout history, [and] that a super-secret society superior to the Masonic order was the backbone of...the ancient civilizations of Greece and later Rome... Where did this ancient order originate? Hall claimed that it originated in the legendary Atlantis. He claimed that the Atlanteans devised a plan – a "Great Plan" – which would guide world events for millennia to come, and that it included a mysterious blueprint of what would later become America... long before it was "discovered" by Columbus.

Hall maintained that the unifying goal of these secret societies was to create a "New Atlantis" in America....[202]

As fantastic as this may sound, Still goes on to show that there is further underlying evidence that America has been actually claimed for Satan.

Even the name "America" may be the product of ancient American secret societies. In an 1895 edition of a magazine called *Lucifer*, published by the occult-promoting Theosophical Society [i.e. an organization of occultist Alice Bailey], [it] gave an interesting insight into the meaning of the word "America." [The article] said that the supreme god of the Mayan culture of Central America was known...in Peru as Amaru "from [which] comes our word America. Amaruca is, literally translated, 'Land of the Plumed Serpent.' "...Most historians attribute the name America to explorer Amerigo Vespucci, but Manly Hall claims that since the serpent is frequently symbolic of Lucifer, it is not an exaggeration to extrapolate from this that America may well mean "Land of Lucifer."...

---

[202] William T. Still. *New World Order: The Ancient Plan of Secret Societies* (Lafayette, Louisiana: Huntington House Publishers, 1990), 6, 41, 45-46, 54.

If one man can be singled out as the person most responsible for the colonization of America, the honor would certainly fall to the head of both Masonry and Rosecrucianism [sic] of his era, Sir Francis Bacon. In the early 1600s Bacon...born only sixty-nine years after Columbus "discovered" America...authored a novel entitled *New Atlantis*, which laid out the idea for a utopian society across the ocean from Europe where mankind could build a new civilization based upon the principles he believed to be those of the legendary lost continent of Atlantis.... Manly Hall claims that a Baconian secret society was [eventually] set up in America while Jamestown was still floundering....

Although secret societies played a significant role in the British colonization of America, [albeit a hidden one], with colonization came a [visible] force that was to bedevil their well-laid plans for the New World Order — Christians.... Today, as then, it is Christians who are the major stumbling block to the plans for the rise of their New World Order. Through the years, this concept has remained the same: to unite all nations under a single sovereign world government.... [However,] the secret architects of this "Great Plan" are not benign humanitarians, as they would have us believe, but are men in the service of evil. Their "government of nations" is a deception, hiding, in reality, an iron-clad, world dictatorship.[203]

And America, covertly, is being used — ultimately by Satan — as their tool!

———— ✦✦✦✦✦ ————

What has been presented here is the *worst* worst-case scenario. There is evidence, which many will want to discard as being too incredible, that America is the Endtime Babylon. And that the tentacles of that Babylonialsim is spread worldwide. No nation has had an influence upon the world like the United States. Rome, in its day, never had the political, military, and economic influence that America has now. In fact, there

---

[203]   Ibid., 45-46, 54.

is every indication that Rome had no idea portions of the world, where America holds sway, even existed!

We have tracked the activities of Satan in and through the secret societies over which he has had power these many millennia. These secret societies have infiltrated into the United States. Once that is understood, it becomes easier to see the cause of the anti-Christian activities of our government. If America is Endtime Babylon, this trend will continue and the evil within its borders will accelerate.

Few Christians believe in their heart they are living in the very land that will prove so anti-Christ. Yet, those who do not see this possibility and ignore the *worst* worst-case it causes will be blindsided should it occur. Preparation, then, is a must. But only the wise will do so.

CONCLUSIONS

CHAPTER 28

THE FOURTH TURNING

"Of that day and hour no one knows, not even the angels of heaven, nor the Son, but the Father alone... [Notwithstanding], can [you] not discern the signs of the times? When you see these things happening, recognize that He is near, right at the door. Behold, I have told you in advance!" (Matthew 24:25, 36; 16:3; Mark 13:29).

In the verses above, Jesus makes it clear that the day and hour of His return was only known by God the Father. At that time, not even Jesus knew these.

But, previously, He has chastised the Pharisees for not knowing the signs of the times, i.e., the events that pointed to Him being their Messiah, confirming His First Advent. The message here is equally as clear: We may not know the day or hour, but we should certainly know we are in the "season."

Then, in the verse recorded by Mark, Jesus tells us that when we see the signs he has given, we should immediately take notice: His return is imminent.

The wrap-up is the implication that Jesus stresses all this information He has provided is for a purpose – "I have told you in advance." What has been offered throughout this writing is that the purpose is for us to prepare for these events.

In 1997, William Strauss and Neil Howe's book *The Fourth Turning* was published. The title doesn't provide much of an insight into what the book is about. But the subtitle does: *An American Prophecy: What the Cycles of History Tell Us About America's Next Rendezvous with Destiny.*[204]

It was a follow-up to the authors' 1991 groundbreaking book *Generations: The History of America's Future, 1584 to 2069.*[205] This book's references, contained in *51 pages* of endnotes, help verify its conclusions, and can only be described as *overwhelming*. Strauss and Howe alleged a forthcoming American Apocalypse, described in both books and now seemingly appearing on America's horizon. They repeatedly stressed that their warning should not be disregarded.

Strauss and Howe begin by presenting substantial evidence that there are four generations that make up the bulk of a generational cycle. Each generation is passing through four stages of life, "Youth (0-21 years), Rising Adult (22-43 years), Midlife Adult (44-65 years), Elderhood (66-87 years)."[206] As each generation moves into the next stage, they are replaced by the generation behind them.

The combined timeframe of these four generations making up a generational cycle are "the length of a long human life, roughly eighty to one hundred years, a unit of time the ancients called a *saeculum*."[207] Each of these four generations, contain "a common collective persona,"[208] i.e. characteristics that are unique to each. Further, in Strauss and Howe's examination of "'Twenty-Four Anglo-American Generations,'"[209] these four generations re-cycle *in the exact same order* – and have been doing so *since 1433* (with one exception caused by the American Civil War).

These authors identify the order of the four stages as being peopled by what they call "Prophet, Nomad, Hero, and Artist."[210] Again, this order replicates itself: As the Elder Prophet is dying off and being replaced in

---

[204] William Strauss and Neil Howe. *The Fourth Turning: An American Prophecy: What the Cycles of History Tell Us About America's Next Rendezvous with Destiny* (New York: Broadway Books, 1997).

[205] William Strauss and Neil Howe. *Generations: The History of America's Future, 1584 to 2069* (New York: Harper Perennial, 1991).

[206] Ibid., 73.

[207] Ibid. 4.

[208] Ibid. 16.

[209] Ibid, 71.

[210] Ibid., 19.

Elderhood by the Nomad, the up-coming Youth constitute a new generation with the characteristics of a Prophet. Each fifth generation, then, replicates the generation dying-off.

Each generation is further identified with those characteristics of its era. Hence, each "turning is an era with a characteristic social mood, a new twist on how people feel about themselves and their nation."[211]

> The *Prophet* is born into the *First Turning*, which is identified as a *High*, an upbeat era of strengthening institutions and weakening individualism, when a new civic order implants and the old values regime [regular pattern of doing things] decays.

> The *Nomad* is born into the *Second Turning*, which is identified as an *Awakening*, a passionate era of spiritual upheaval, when the civic order comes under attack from a new values regime.

> The *Hero* is born into the *Third Turning*, which is identified as an *Unraveling*, a downcast era of strengthening individualism and wakening institutions, when the old civic order decays and the new values regime implants.

> The *Artist* is born into the *Fourth Turning*, which is identified as a *Crisis*, a decisive era of secular upheaval, when the values regime propels the replacement of the old civic order with a new one.[212]

It is the Crisis that "ends one *saeculum* [generational cycle] and launches the next.... [It is] history's winter solstice... [because it contains] a cycle-ending war [that causes] decisive social and political consequences [which] end an era."[213]

It should be noted that *every* Crisis contains the same order of generations: Prophets in Elderhood, Nomads in Midlife, Heroes in Rising Adulthood, and Artists in Youth.

Not by happenstance, respected Christian financial analyst Donald

---

[211] Strauss and Howe, *Fourth Turning*, 3.

[212] Ibid., 99.

[213] Ibid., 37, 39.

S. McAlvany in his "The McAlvany Intelligence Advisor" makes reference to *The Fourth Turning* in its recent February 2017 intelligence newsletter:

THE FOURTH TURNING AND THE CYCLES OF WAR – After spending some time watching the recently concluded intelligence briefing to the US Senate, **one of the most disturbing and ominous conclusions one comes to is that the Establishment seriously wants war.** One of the most discomforting aspects of Neil Howe and William Strauss' seminal work on generation cycles, *The Fourth Turning* (1997), is the fact that as far as American history is concerned, they all climax and end with massive wars.

To be more specific, the first "fourth turning" in American history culminated with the **Revolutionary War** (1775-1783), the second culminated with the **Civil War** (1861-1865), while the third ended with the bloodiest war in world history, **World War II** (1939-1945). The number of years between the end of the Revolutionary War and the start of the Civil War was 78 years, and the number of years between the end of the Civil War and the start of World War II was 74 yours (76 years if you use America's entry into the war as your starting date). **Therefore, if Howe & Strauss' theory has any validity, we're due for a major conflict somewhere around 75 years from the end of World War II. That brings us to 2020.**

And now there are a growing number of signs that the world is headed into another major conflict. **From an unnecessary resurgence of a Cold War with Russia to increased tensions in the South China Sea and complete chaos and destruction in the Middle East, the world is a gigantic tinderbox. All it will take to transform these already existing conflict zones into a major conflagration is <u>another severe global economic downturn</u>,** which can be expected to happen within the next 1-2 years. This puts us on a perfect collision course with the 2020 timeframe.[214]

---

214   Donald S. McAlvany, "The Establishment Powers-That-Be Want War," The McAlvany Intelligence Advisor (February 2017), 8-9; all emphases exactly as in original.

If McAlvany is correct, then the trigger to the next "major conflict" is "another severe global economic downturn."

With this in mind, let's return to Strauss and Howe. They observe that the period before an era-ending major war is called the Unraveling. In this period "cynical alienation hardens into a brooding pessimism.... [It is] a downcast era... when the civic order comes under attack from a new values regime."[215]

Are not the "old values" of the current "civic order" coming under attack here in the United States? The riots in the streets are tearing up the once-held, absolute legal-worthiness of the Constitution. Those who support the "*archaic* Constitution," are thus seen as outdated neo-nazis. This, by the upcoming, midlife, power-entering generation of "alientated" Nomads. These Nomads are led by Elder Prophets who profess "new spiritual agendas and social ideals."[216]

As an example, notice these Elder Prophets and their near-fanatical support of Planned Parenthood. Such an agenda is a rejection of the "old" biblical value of the sanctity of life, which they demonstrate by their unwavering support of the murder of the unborn. Here is an unmistakable anti-Christ spirit, for murder is of Satan (John 8:44).

And, in these Elder Prophets' "new social agendas," they demand "free stuff," when, in fact, nothing is "free"; someone has to work to produce and distribute it. This explains why the "old values" of Capitalism, which helped produce the greatness of our nation's economy, are now "evil" and are strongly being rejected. The demand has become the "new value" of socialism.[217]

Joining with these Prophet and Nomad generations in enthusiastic support ("energetic hubris") of these "new" agendas and ideals are the

---

[215] Strauss and Howe, *Fourth Turning*, 3, 103.

[216] Ibid., 84, 102.

[217] For example, see Shawn Langlois, "Millennials: Communism Sounds Pretty Chill," Market Watch, https://www.marketwatch.com/story/millennials-communism-sounds-pretty-chill-2017-11-01 November 9, 2017, (accessed November 27, 2017).

younger adult generation, the Heroes.[218] It is these Millennials who will shoulder the worker-bee tasks.

So, if we are indeed in the Unraveling, the Crisis, Strauss and Howe would argue, cannot be far away. Those who understand these things will be looking for it.

And, it appears not long in coming: "A Crisis era begins with a *catalyst* – a startling event (or sequence of events) that produces a sudden shift in mood…. It arises in response to sudden threats that previously would have been ignored or deferred, but which are now perceived as dire."[219]

It is offered that terrorism, which, up through the summer of 2001, was most often viewed as some distant threat—"on somebody else's shore"—created a crisis environment here in the U.S. on September 11th of that year. There was a distinct, and sudden, mood change here in America. The Crisis Era had begun!

If this is a correct assessment, look for an economic upheaval, coming in the not-to-distant future. No doubt caused by the Elites' banks, such as the Federal Reserve, but blamed on others (maybe, with Satan the spiritual force behind it, even evangelicals!).

A war of unparalleled proportion will follow the economic collapse. Probably nuclear; *limited* nuclear, but nuclear nonetheless: "[History has shown] Crisis ending wars were all large, deadly, and decisive…. Wars in the Fourth Turning find the broadest possible definition [of *war*] and are fought to unambiguous, [i.e., *final*] outcomes…. [They] are fought with fury and for maximum result."[220]

In the Book of Revelation at the end of the Bible there is a progression of event characteristics in Chapter 6. Most Bible scholars see this progression as chronological. If that proves correct, it should be noted that the "third living creature" indicates economic scarcity: "A quart of wheat for a day's pay, and three quarts of barley for a day's pay…" (v. 6; NRSV). Could such a condition be caused by a concurrent economic upheaval? If so, the next prophesied event is chilling.

---

[218] Strauss and Howe, *Fourth Turning*, 84. Yet, if we are indeed in the Endtimes, it will eventually be seen that these are really *anti*-Heroes. Their enthusiasm will enthrone the Anti-Christ.

[219] Ibid., 103, 256.

[220] Ibid., 103, 104, 119.

"When he opened the fourth seal, I heard the voice of the fourth living creature call out, 'Come!' I looked and there was a pale green horse! Its rider's name was Death, and Hades followed with him; they were given authority over a fourth of the earth to kill with sword [war], famine, and pestilence [resulting disease]..." (vv. 7-8; NRSV).

This resulting war will wreak havoc over one-quarter of the earth! And, because the world then will want *established* peace, cause the enthronement of the Antichrist.

Note, these events occur *before* the enthronement of the Antichrist. Well before a Pre-tribulational Rapture, should it occur. What will that do to faiths of those not expecting it? Cause a falling away, even from those who believe that could never happen to them? Occurring here in the United States and from which, rising from its ashes, becomes the Endtime Babylon?

> The spirit of America comes once a *saeculum*, and only through what the ancients called *ekpyrosis*, nature's fiery moment of death and discontinuity.... What it doesn't kill, it reminds of death. What it doesn't wound, it reminds of pain.... History's periodic eras of Crisis combust the old social order and give birth to a new. A Fourth Turning is a solstice era of maximum darkness, in which the supply of social order is still falling but the *demand for order is still rising.*[221]

It will be this "demand for order" from which the Antichrist will rise to power. The horrors of the fourth living creature's dreadful war, destruction of a quarter of the earth, will cause people to *demand* him to take power.

The next developing event beyond the predicted war in Revelation 6 confirms this. It is the foretold Antichrist's persecution of believers: "And when He broke the fifth seal, I saw underneath the altar the souls of those who had been slain because of the word of God, and because of the testimony which they had maintained" (v. 9).

Jesus Himself provides the confirmation: "You will hear of wars and rumors of wars [a period of on-going conflict, long enough to effect one-quarter of the earth].... *Then* they will deliver you to tribulation, and will kill you, and you will be hated by all nations on account of My name," i.e. being called *Christian* (Matthew 24:6, 9; emphasis added).

---

[221] Ibid., 225; emphasis added.

John the Apostle, the writer of Revelation, continues: "And the beast [the Antichrist], it was given to him to make war with the saints and to overcome them; and authority over every tribe and people and tongue and nation was given to him" (13:2, 7).

This is the "new spiritual agenda and social ideals" that will then be pandered by those in support of the Antichrist. *Many*, "every tribe and people and tongue and nation," will consider this the culmination of the Fourth Turning. But they will be wrong. For the battle of Armageddon, which lies ahead, is the real climax.

Strauss and Howe have clearly identified the process. Once the Crisis catalyst has occurred, "a society achieves a *regeneracy* – a new counter-entropy that reunifies and re-energizes civic life."[222] This stage is the enthronement of the Antichrist, where he is lauded because of the "re-energized civic life" of the fourth creature's war survivors.

At that point "the regenerated society propels toward a *climax* – a crucial moment that confirms the death of the old order and birth of the new."[223] For the Antichrist and the unsaved who follow him, the "new regenerated society," will cause the extermination (martyrdom) of believers; they will firmly believe they are ridding themselves of the "evildoers" who cause problems for the new (Antichrist) regime.

Because of their rejection of Jesus, they will be unprepared for the real climax: The revealing of Christ as He returns from heaven to fight the battle of Armageddon and administer judgment on those unbelievers.

"The climax culminates in a *resolution* – a triumphant or tragic conclusion that separates the winners from losers, resolves the big public questions, and established the new order."[224]

For the believer, the resolution, Christ's return, is *triumphant*; for the unbeliever, *tragic*. This ultimate Fourth Turning will produce the rule of the King of Kings and Lord of Lords, Jesus Christ. And the New Order will be that of the Kingdom of God!

In his book *Spectacular Sins*, pastor John Piper offers a sobering observation followed by three equally as sobering questions.

---

[222] Ibid., 256.

[223] Ibid.

[224] Ibid.

The times are changing.

Hard times are coming.

Catastrophes are coming.

Global cataclysms and personal catastrophes are coming.

I need the tough warning that the Beast will win. For a season.

Who is prepared to meet the Agony that is coming?

Where are Christians being prepared for global sorrows?

Where is the shepherd who is preparing the saints for this kind of future?[225]

It is hoped that this book has begun the process of answering John Piper's questions.

---

[225] John Piper. *Spectacular Sins: And Their Global Purpose in the Glory of Christ* (Wheaton, Illinois: Crossway Books, 2008), 13-16.

CHAPTER 29

PREPAREDNESS

The prudent man sees the evil and hides himself, but the naïve go on, and are punished for it (Proverbs 22:3).

The issue of preparedness begins with the question: What is the worst that can happen? This begins to produce the answer(s) as to why one needs to prepare. If the first response to that question is "I don't need to prepare because (fill in the blank)," any discussion about preparing is pretty much ended. As we recently noted, denial is the first, and hardest, barrier to overcome if actual preparation is to begin.

Throughout this writing we have attempted to develop a *worst* worst-case scenario from the three most prevalent "barriers" encountered by this writer. Each of the issues raised herein has been supported by some pretty staunch devotees. For that reason, the weaknesses of each have been reviewed in detail.

Again, if the response is to defend any of these positions, any preparedness discussion is over before it begins. As we have seen, a humble heart will realize because there are different views on the issue, one's own view is not 100-percent assured. If it were, there would be chapter-and-verse that would be cited and from which no one could dispute.

Let me offer an insight here: If there is so much as only a one-percent possibility of being wrong, Murphy's Law (at the least) says a worst-case scenario needs to be assessed... and planned for.

The intent of this writing has been to get a person to consider that possibility. The Endtime events described throughout the Old and New Testament identify a period that will require the greatest of preparation. Jesus Himself described it as the worst period in human history (Matthew 24:21).

So, what has been present here is a beginning. Hopefully, the need has been seen. Those who, then, realize the danger will want to take action and prepare. If you are interested, please access the author's ministry website, The Bible-based Emergency Preparation Ministry, at http://bibleemergencypreparation. org/home.html. All of the material on the site is free.

As an individual is made up of body, soul, and, spirit (1st Thessalonians 5:23), each of these aspects is separately addressed. In the "Articles" menu on the site's righthand click for the article. An introductory note will follow. At its bottom, click on the "Outline Notes PDF," which will take you to the full discussion. You will see these are clear, understandable outlines, with information that is easily grasped.

If you have not yet accepted Jesus Christ as your Savior, ETERNAL SURVIVAL is the first place you want to start. Without that, the rest are pretty much moot. Once you have accepted Jesus as Savior, or if you already have, SPIRITUAL PREP is where you want to look next. EMERGENCY PREP is a step-by-step approach to physical preparation. DEEP SURVIVAL looks at mental preparation. SPIRITUAL SURVIVAL looks at deepening your walk with Jesus so as not to "fall away."

A closing reflection:

> It has been found that just thinking about the unthinkable prior to its occurrence makes one much more able to think on one's feet and hence to recover from a crisis once it has occurred. The fact that one has anticipated the unthinkable means that one is not paralyzed when it occurs.[226]

Whether in reading this material you have accepted the need for preparation or decided to reject it, by having reached this far you have at least considered the possibility. That alone is a good preparation!

MARANATHA!

---

[226] Mitroff and Anagnos, 37; some believe if you have done nothing more than think about the unthinkable, you have increased your survivability by upwards of 50-percent. They also agree that with no pre-crisis reflection, survivability can be reduced to zero!

CHAPTER 30

THE NEED: A SURVEY

Pilate [asked Jesus], "What is truth?" (John 18:37).

Having looked at issues critical to survival in the Last Days, these become merely theory if they, in fact, have no practical application. But, to what extent are they practical?

To answer that question, to determine the truth of whether these are, indeed, matters of consequence, a Survey (found at the end of the chapter) was conducted during the period November 2017 to January 2018. A total of 140 Christians participated, almost equally split between Men (48%) and Women (52%). Mainline Denominations included Baptists, Episcopalians, Lutherans, Methodists, Presbyterians, and Roman Catholics. Non-denominational churches included Acts 29, Calvary Chapel, (Independent) Bible, Christian and Missionary Alliance, Evangelical Free, and one identified as a "Multi-Denominational" church. The Survey also included a local (Jersey Shore) Pentecostal church. Participants spanned eight states: California, Colorado, Florida, Kansas, Maryland, New Jersey, Pennsylvania, and Utah.

Because of the subject matter of this writing, the Survey was specifically targeted for committed, mature, decision-makers, those who would impact their own local church. To accomplish that, most of the Surveys were done by small groups in "fellowship" or Bible study settings, an indicator the participants were committed to more than "just a Sunday morning" Christian walk. Further, to reinforce the issue of decision-makers, those who self-identified as Pastors (12%), Elders (7%), and Deacons (9%) accounted for 28-percent of the participants, almost one-in-three.

As to maturity, 60-percent were 50-years of age or older.

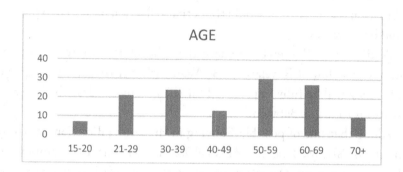

And as a whole, the participants were well-educated with 78-percent having some college experience or higher (up to Ph.D.). Of this group, 62-percent had a college degree of which fully 26-perecent, over one-in-four, held a Masters or Doctorate.

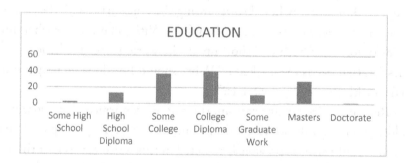

The Survey results were impacting!

Apart from the Pentecostal church, which will be discussed separately below for reasons that will become apparent there, those participants who identified their perspective in the timing of the Rapture were almost evenly split with 55-percent being Pre-tribulational. Interestingly, two participants identified the Rapture as being "None" or "Doesn't Exist."

However, especially in light of the material in this dissertation, although over half believed in a Pre-tribulational Rapture, with 64-percent believing they will never personally see a Divine judgment of the United States, fully 95-percent believed such a judgment would be "Significant" or worse, with 66-percent believing that judgment would be "Catastrophic"! These numbers alone should cause American Christians to consider "What if my belief that I will be raptured before a judgment of America or the Great Tribulation *is wrong?*" One would think that reflection on a need to prepare would begin to dawn!

Additionally, 78-percent believe that the United States is *not* the Endtime Babylon of Revelation 18. Again, what if they are wrong? No doubt, they will be fully unprepared for the judgments described there if America *is* Endtime Babylon.

Along that line of possibly "looking in the wrong direction," a strong majority (83%) viewed the "he" of Daniel 9:27 as a reference to the Antichrist. A lesser majority saw Daniel's reference to the 70th Week as being a 7-year period (60%), with a vast majority (93%) rejecting the 70th Week having only 3½-years remaining. Again, if they are wrong, it might impact them by catching them unaware of events indicating they are nearing the judgments of the Endtimes and, thus, unprepared for them.

As to belief that there will be a real, in-the-flesh Antichrist and False Prophet, 92-percent believed so regarding the Antichrist, with 84-percent believing so regarding the False Prophet. With such an overwhelming majority for belief both will show up on the world stage, it is believed the question that needs to be asked is "What should I be doing in preparation to deal with such evil individuals?"

Regarding Pre-destinarianism, the Survey confirmed that those who hold to such view do so with a deep commitment to its principles. What was also confirmed, as previously indicted in this writing, was that there is not a real consensus for *all* of its principles for each individual.

One-in-three (32%) believe that salvation occurs at the moment they freely choose to believe Jesus died for them. This is in contrast to the tenet that God chose them before the foundation of the world.

Similarly, 27-percent believe that a sinful person can choose Jesus by his or her own free will. The Pre-destinarianism principle is that a person is incapable of choosing God if He hasn't chosen them first.

The third principle that one cannot resist God if he or she has been previously chosen also proved problematic. Almost half (43%) believed one *can* resist God.

The fourth principle that Jesus' death was limited in its scope, being made available to only those previously chosen, proved stunning by the Survey's responses. Fully 66-percent believed Jesus' death had been made available to all!

(As an aside, this wide diversity from acceptance of the major tenets of Pre- destinarianism has to be frustrating to the pastors of Pre-destinarianist churches.)

Having presented the results of these four principles, it is really the fifth that concerns us the most. A vast majority (94%) believed that salvation cannot be lost. Implicit within this perspective is the fifth tenet of Pre-destinarianism, that one will persevere until the end; that one can never "fall away" and be unable to return. (For, they believe, if one fell away and remained there, he or she was not really saved to begin with.)

What, then, will be the perspective of church leaders, of the person him- or herself, who has fallen away as Jesus indicated "many" would? What will be the response to such a person, especially under the stress of on-going Endtime events occurring around all the individuals involved? A wrong "diagnosis" has the grave potential to lead to a wrong "cure." Especially under such duress as the Great Tribulation.

This leads us to the issue of Jesus' 1,000-year Millennial Kingdom. A vast majority (87%) believed this will come to pass. One can conclude the low 13-percent of those identifying themselves as Amillennialists demonstrates the significant impact the late 20th century Evangelical church teachings have had on this subject.

With the belief that an actual 1,000-year reign on earth is to be expected, an overwhelming 90-percent believe a saved person "automatically" gets in, and 73-percent believe they "automatically" get to rule and reign with Jesus in that Kingdom. It is safe to say these respondents have never read (probably, not heard of) writers such as Robert Govett, D.M. Panton, et al. If these writers are correct, there will be "shock and surprise" as each Christian stands before Christ at the Bema Seat.

The last issue looked at in this writing is that of secret societies and their impact on the United States and the world. The results were surprising: 83-percent believed both that Satan-controlled secret societies exist on earth today *and* are here in the United States. Additionally, 77-percent believed these secret societies wanted to create a one-world government.

Couple these statistics with the 92-percent who believe in a real Antichrist and one can conclude the material presented in this writing will be more easily understood and accepted than I would have originally considered!

In contrast, however, only 37-percent believed the secret societies were controlled by international bankers. The material presented herein, therefore, may come as a shock to them.

There is one more interesting side-note to this issue of international bankers involvement in control of secret societies. Although every issue raised on the Survey had at least one participant who did not respond to it (checking *no* choice offered), this international banker issue was bypassed by a whopping 15-percent! Again, the material presented herein of this issue may be even more shocking to *them*!

What the Survey has done, then, is to confirm the need for the issues raised in this writing. In the belief the data developed by the Survey is representative of American Christians as a whole, these issues are, indeed, critical to a large number of these Christians. It is not overstating to say many will otherwise be caught unawares and be partially, if not totally, unprepared for the life-or-death events of the Last Days.

Which leads us to the Pentecostal church... for which there will be little, if any, surprise.

Almost *to a person* they agreed that the Rapture will *not* be Pre-tribulational (93%; almost half [47%] believing in a Post-tribulational Rapture). They also believed there will be a Divine judgment of America in their lifetime (87%), they will see it (90%), and it will be significant or worse (96%), with 48-percent of the latter believing it will be catastrophic.

Here is an issue for further study. Is this perspective that of only this local church? Or is it a general perspective of Pentecostals universally? Notwithstanding, *this* New Jersey church has been preparing to face the issues raised in this writing. It's sister churches may want to take note.

Speaking of further study, 94-percent believed that a saved person throughout the ages of mankind will spend eternity in heaven. Those with a more theological-bent may want to pursue this issue. Nowhere in the Old Testament are the saved prior to the New Covenant promised heaven. There are indications of a resurrection (much, I'm sure, to the disappointment of the Sadducees). But, to what location is not distinctly indicated.

Further, the pre-New Testament Jew is told their inheritance... forever (Genesis 18:8, et al) is the earthly national boundaries of Israel, not heaven.

No Old Testament person, no Old Testament Jew, no person in their natural bodies who enter or are born in the Millennial Kingdom is told they are not of mankind. Only the New Testament person who is saved is told he or she is a "new creature" (2nd Cor 5:17; cf. Galatians 3:28) and destined for heaven (John 14:2-3).

If the earth has been created for mankind's habitation (Genesis 1:28; 2:8), one would think the new earth (Revelation 21:1) would be so inhabited also. As an indicator, why would Jeremiah purchase land he knew in his lifetime he would not inhabit (Jeremiah 32:6ff)? Might he not have had the belief that he would get it "in the future"?

As stated, an eschatological issue worth a theologian's future pursuit![227]

---

[227] As an aside, if this proves the case and only Church Age believers inhabit the New, Heavenly Jerusalem of Revelation 21-22, then Hebrews 12:22-24 should also be revisited. In that passage, the General Assembly would more likely fit The Called; the Church of the First-Born, the Chosen; and the Spirits of Righteous Men Made Perfect (fully mature), the Faithful. Again, no doubt a *very* interesting pursuit of study for a theologian!

Christian Belief Assessment Survey

Gender:
- o Male
- o Female

Your State:
_____

Age:
- o 15 - 20
- o 21 - 29
- o 30 - 39
- o 40 - 49
- o 50 - 59
- o 60 - 69
- o 70+

Education:
- o some high school
- o high school diploma
- o some college
- o college diploma
- o some graduate work
- o Masters degree
- o PhD or equivalent

I consider myself a
(choose only one):
- o Pastor
- o Elder
- o Deacon
- o Lay Person

The church I attend is *best* described as:
- o Baptist
- o Episcopal
- o Lutheran
- o Methodist
- o Presbyterian
- o other Reformed
- o Pentecostal
- o Roman Catholic

Non-denominational:
- o Acts 29
- o Alliance
- o Calvary Chapel
- o Other (specify)

_____
- o Other (specify)

_____
- o I currently don't attend any church

I believe salvation occurred (chose only one):
- o because of *God's sovereign choice* "before the foundation of the world"
- o At a moment in time when *I freely choose* to believe Jesus died for me

I believe salvation:
- o can be lost
- o can never be lost

Jesus' death was:
- o only for a limited amount of people (the "chosen")
- o made available to all

I believe:
- o a person is incapable of choosing Jesus without God choosing him first
- o when presented with the Gospel, a sinful person can choose Jesus by his own freewill

I believe:
- o a person cannot resist God if that person has been chosen by God
- o a person has freewill to resist, and therefore reject, God

America will undergo God's divine wrath *in my lifetime*:
- o Never happen
- o Not likely
- o Possibly
- o Probably
- o Dead certain

The severity of God's divine judgment will be:
- o None
- o Minor
- o Significant
- o Severe
- o Catastrophic

But I personally will *not* see that judgment occur:
- o agree   o disagree

I believe the Rapture is:
- o Pre-tribulational
- o Mid-tribulational
- o Pre-Wrath
- o Post-tribulational
- o Huh?

Without looking at the reference, this very second I believe the United States is the nation described in Revelation 18: o Yes o No o Huh?	*Without looking at the reference*, this very second I believe the "he" in Daniel 9:27 refers to the Antichrist: o Yes o No o Huh?	I believe in Jesus' 1,000-year reign here on earth, often called the Millennial Kingdom: o Yes o No o Huh?
Now, having looked at the reference, this very second I believe the United States is the nation described in Revelation 18: o Yes o No o I didn't look	*Now, having looked at the reference*, this very second I believe the "he" in Daniel 9:27 refers to the Antichrist: o Yes o No o didn't look	I believe that if you are saved you are/will be "automatically" in Jesus' Millennial Kingdom: o Yes o No o Huh?
Regarding the Endtimes, there are seven (7) years left on God's timeclock, i.e. Daniel's 70th "week": o Yes o No o Huh?	No, there are actually only 3½ years left on Daniel's 70th "week": o Yes o No o Absolutely o Huh? Not	If you are saved you will "automatically" rule and reign with Jesus' in His Millennial Kingdom: o Yes o No o Huh?
I believe there are Satan-controlled secret societies that exist on the earth today: o Yes o No	These Satan-controlled secret societies exist here in the United States: o Yes o No	These Satan-controlled secret societies want to create a one-world government they rule: o Yes o No
These Satan-controlled secret societies are controlled by the elite international bankers: o Yes o No	In the Endtimes, I believe Satan will raise up an evil world ruler (who is referred to as the Antichrist): o Yes o No	In the Endtimes, I believe Satan will raise up an evil religious leader (who is often referred to as the False Prophet): o Yes o No

Every **saved** person throughout all the ages of mankind will spend eternity in heaven: o Yes o No	The **unsaved** from all the ages of mankind will spend eternity in a lake of fire: o Yes o No

BIBLIOGRAPHY

General Reference

Baker, Warren, and Eugene Carpenter. *The Complete Word Study Dictionary Old Testament*. Chattanooga, Tennessee: AMG Publishers, 2003.

Criswell, W. A., ed., *The Criswell Study Bible: Authorized King James Version*. New York: Thomas Nelson Publishers, 1979.

Falwell, Jerry, ed., Edward E. Hindson, and Woodrow M. Kroll. *Liberty Bible Commentary*. Nashville, Tennessee: Thomas Nelson, Inc., 1983.

Halley, Henry H. *Halley's Bible Handbook*. Grand Rapids, MI: Zondervan Publishing House, 1927 (24th ed., 1965).

Langlois, Shawn. "Millennials: Communism Sounds Pretty Chill," Market Watch, https://www.marketwatch.com/story/millennials-communism-sounds-pretty-chill-2017-11-01, November 9, 2017, (accessed November 27, 2017).

Metzger, Bruce M., ed., *Life Application Bible: New Revised Standard Version*. Iowa Falls, Iowa: World Bible Publishers, Inc, 1990.

McAlvany, Donald S. "The Establishment Powers-That-Be Want War," *The McAlvany Intelligence Advisor* (February 2017), 8-9.

Piper, John. *Spectacular Sins: And Their Global Purpose in the Glory of Christ*. Wheaton, Illinois: Crossway Books, 2008.

Ramm, Bernard. *Protestant Biblical Interpretation*. Grand Rapids, Michigan: Baker Book House, 1970.

Radmacher, Earl D., Ronald B. Allen, and H. Wayne House, eds., *The NKJV Study Bible*, 2nd Edition. Nashville, Tennessee: Thomas Nelson Publisher, 2008.

Rickards, James. "The Coming Big Freeze." Agora Financial, LLC. https://pro.agorafinancial.com/AWN_icenine_0117/

LAWNT1AN/?h=true, released via e-mail on February 9, 2017, (last accessed November 27, 2017).

Ryrie, Charles C. *The Ryrie Study Bible: New American Standard Translation*. Chicago: Moody Press, 1978.

Stein, Robert H. *A Basic Guide to Interpreting the Bible*. Grand Rapids, Michigan: Baker Books, 1994.

Strauss William, and Neil Howe. *Generations: The History of America's Future, 1584 to 2069* (New York: Harper Perennial, 1991.

———. *The Fourth Turning: An American Prophecy: What the Cycles of History Tell Us About America's Next Rendezvous with Destiny*. New York: Broadway Books, 1997.

Strong, James. *Strong's Exhaustive Concordance of the Bible*. Nashville, Tennessee: Abingdon Press, 1890.

Vine, M. E. *An Expository Dictionary of New Testament Words*. Nashville, Tennessee: Royal Publishing, Inc., 1939.

Woolf, Henry Bosely, ed., *Webster's New Collegiate Dictionary*. Springfield, Massachusetts: G. & C. Merriam Company, 1975.

Zuck, Roy B. *Basic Bible Interpretation*. Colorado Springs, Colorado: Chariot Victor Publishing, 1991.

Emergency Management

Blythe, Bruce T. *Blindsided: A Manager's Guide to Catastrophic Incidents in the Workplace*. New York: Penguin Putnam, Inc., 2002.

Fink, Steven. *Crisis Management: Planning for the Inevitable*. New York: American Management Association, 1986.

Mitroff, Ian I., with Anagnos, Gus. *Managing Crises Before They Happen: What Every Executive and Manager Needs to Know About Crisis Management*. New York: American Management Association, 2001.

Schwartz, Peter. *The Art of the Long View: Planning for the Future in an Uncertain World*. New York: Doubleday Publishers, 1996.

Silberman, Mel. (1998). *Active Training: A Handbook of Techniques, Designs, Case Examples, and Tips*. San Francisco: Jossey-Bass Publishers, 1998.

Pre-tribulationalism

Anderson, Robert. *The Coming Prince*. London: Hodder and Stoughton, 1909.

Barnes, Albert. *Barnes' Notes on the Book of Daniel*. New York: R. Worthington, 1881.

Barnhouse, Donald Grey. *Revelation: God's Last Word*. Grand Rapids, Michigan: Zondervan Publishing House, 1971.

Beechick, Allen. *The PreTribulational Rapture*. Denver, Colorado: Accent Books, 1980.

Benware, Paul N. *Understanding End Times Prophecy: A comprehensive Approach*. Chicago: Moody Press, 1995.

Bloomfield, Arthur E. *The End of the Days: The Prophecies of Daniel Explained*. Minneapolis, Minnesota, 1961.

Byers, Marvin. *The Final Victory*. Shippensburg, PA: Companion Press, 1991.

DeHaan, Richard W. *Israel and the Nations in Prophecy*. Grand Rapids, MI: Zondervan Publishing House, 1967.

Grudem, Wayne. *Making Sense of the Future*. Grand Rapids, Michigan: Zondervan, 1994, 2011.

Gundry, Robert H. *The Church and the Tribulation: A Biblical Examination of Post-Tribulationaism*. Grand Rapids, Michigan: Zondervan Publishing, 1973.

Jeffrey, Grant R. *Armageddon: Appointment with Destiny*. Toronto, Ontario, Canada: Frontier Research Publications, 1988.

LaHaye, Tim. *The Beginning of the End*. Wheaton, Illinois: Tyndale House Publishers, 1972.

———. *Revelation: Illustrated and Made Plain*. Grand Rapids, Michigan: Lamplighter Books, 1973, 1975.

———. *The Coming Peace in the Middle East*. Grand Rapids, Michigan: Zondervan Publishing House, 1984.

———. *How To Study Bible Prophecy For Yourself*. Eugene, Oregon: Harvest House Publishers, 1990.

Lindsey, Hal, *There's a New World Coming: An In-depth Analysis of the Book of Revelation*. Eugene, Oregon: Harvest House Publishers, 1973, 1984.

Lindsey, Hal, with C.C. Carlson, *The Late Great Planet Earth*. Grand Rapids, MI: Zondervan Publishing House, 1970.

MacArthur, Jr. *The Second Coming of the Lord Jesus Christ*. Panorama City, CA: Word of Grace Communications, 1981.

McKeever, Jim. *Christians Will Go Through The Tribulation: And How to Prepare for It*. Medford, Oregon: Alpha Omega Publishing Company, 1978.

Odom, Robert Leo. *Israel's Prophetic Puzzle*. Washington, DC: Israelite Heritage Institute, 1987.

Packer, James I., ed., Merrill C. Tenney and William White, Jr. *The Bible Almanac*. Nashville, Tennessee: Thomas Nelson Publishers, 1980.

Pentecost, J. Dwight. *Things to Come: A Study in Biblical Eschatology*. Grand Rapids, Michigan: Zondervan Corporation, 1958.

Rosenthal, Marvin. *The Pre-Wrath Rapture of the Church*. Nashville, Tennessee: Thomas Nelson Publishers, 1990.

Van Impe, Jack. *Israel's Final Holocaust*. Nashville, TN: Thomas Nelson Publishers, 1979.

———. *Revelation Revealed: Verse By Verse*. Mount Pleasant, Michigan: Enterprise Printers, Inc., 1982.

———. *11:59 and Counting*. Nashville, Tennessee: Thomas Nelson Publishers, 1987.

———. *Your Future: An A-Z Index to Prophecy*. Troy, Michigan: Jack Van Impe Ministries, 1989.

Walvoord, John F. *The Revelation of Jesus Christ*. Chicago: Moody Press, 1966.

———. *The Rapture Question*. Grand Rapids, Michigan: Zondervan Corporation, 1979.

Pre-destinarianism

Barnhouse, Donald Grey. *The Invisible War*. Grand Rapids, Michigan: Zondervan Publishing House, 1965.

———. *Revelation*. Grand Rapids, Michigan: Zondervan Publishing House, 1971.

Baxter, J. Sidlow. *The Strategic Grasp of the Bible*. Grand Rapids, MI: Zondervan Publishing House, 1968.

Calvin, John, Henry Beveridge Esq., trans., *Institutes of the Christian Religion*, 4th Ed. London: Bonham Norton, 1581; Kindle Edition, from 1964 trans. ed.

Chafer, Lewis Sperry. *Satan: His Motives and Methods*. Grand Rapids, Michigan: Zondervan Publishing House, 1919 (11th ed. 1975).

Chitwood, Arlen L. *Salvation of the Soul*. Norman, Oklahoma: The Lamp Broadcast, Inc. 2003.

———. *Selected Writings of A. Edwin Wilson*. Hayesville, North Carolina: Schoettle Publishing Co, Inc., n.d. (however, Printing Date 1981, 1982, 1996).

Clouse, Robert G., ed., *The Meaning of the Millennium*. Downers Grove, Illinois: InterVarsity Press, 1977.

Dillow, Joseph C. *Reign of the Servant Kings: A Study of Eternal Security and the Significance of Man*. Hayesville, North Carolina: Schoettle Publishing Company, 2006.

Feinberg, Charles L. *Premillennialism or Amillennnialism?* Wheaton, Illinois: Van Kampen Press, 1954.

Govett, Robert. *Entrance Into The Kingdom*. Conley & Schoettle Publishing Company: Miami Springs, Florida, 1978.

———. *The Jews, the Gentiles, and the Church of God, in the Gospel of Matthew*. Schoettle Publishing Company: Miami Springs, Florida, 1989.

———. *Govett On Revelation* (Volumes 1 and 2). Hayesville, North Carolina: Schoettle Publishing Company, 2010.

Grudem, Wayne. *Systematic Theology*. Grand Rapids, Michigan: Zondervan, 1994.

Hill, Charles E. *Regnum Caelorum: Patterns of Millennial Thought in Early Christianity*. Grand Rapids, Michigan: Wm. B. Eerdmans Publishing Co., 2001.

Hunt, Dave. *What Love Is This? Calvin's Misrepresentation of God*. Bend, Oregon: The Berean Call, 2013.

Lindsey, Hal. *Combat Faith*. New York: Bantam Books, 1986.

Lloyd-Jones, D. Martin. *Studies in the Sermon on the Mount*. Grand Rapids, Michigan: William B. Eerdmans Publishing Company, 1959-60.

McClain, Alva J. *Romans: The Gospel of God's Grace*. Chicago, Illinois: Moody Press, 1973.

Missler, Chuck, and Nancy Missler, *Faith in the Night Season's: Understanding God's Will.*(Coeur d'Alene, Idaho: Koinonia House, 1999.

Missler, Nancy. 2010. The Kingdom, Power, & Glory: How Secure Is Our Salvation? *Personal Update: The News Journal of Koinonia House,* January, 31-32.

Nee, Watchman. *The King and the Kingdom of Heaven.* New York: Christian Fellowship Publishers, Inc., 1978.

Panton, D. M. *The Judgment Seat of Christ.* Hayesville, North Carolina: Schoettle Publishing Co., Inc., 1984

Pentecost, J. Dwight. *Thy Kingdom Come.* Wheaton, Illinois: Victor Books, 1990.

Radmacher, Earl D. *Salvation.* Nashville, Tennessee: Word Publishing, 2000.

Russell, D. S. *The Method and Message of Jewish Apocalyptic.* (Philadelphia: The Westminster Press, 1964.

Ryrie, Charles C. *The Basis of the Premillennial Faith.* Neptune, New Jersey: Louizeaux Brothers, 1953.

Seiss, J. A. *The Apocalypse: Letures on the Book of Revelation.* Grand Rapids, Michigan: Zondervan Publishing House, 1957.

Sproul, R. C. *Chosen By God.* Wheaton, Illinois: Tyndal House Publishers, Inc., 1986.

Stanley, Charles. *Eternal Security: Can You Be Sure?* Nashville, Tennessee: Thomas Nelson, 1990.

Vos, Geerhardus. *Biblical Theology.* Grand Rapids, Michigan: William B. Eerdmans Publishing Company, 1948.

―――. *The Kingdom and the Church.* Grand Rapids, Michigan: Wm. B. Eerdmans Publishing Company, 1951.

―――. *The Eschatology of the Old Testament.* Phillipsburg, New Jersey: P & R Publishing, 2001.

Whipple, Gary T. *Shock & Surprise Beyond The Rapture.* Hayesville, North Carolina: Schoettle Publishing Company, 1992.

―――. *The Matthew Mysteries.* Hayesville, North Carolina: Schoettle Publishing Company, 1995.

Winslow, Ola Elizabeth ed., *Jonathan Edwards: Basic Writings,* "Freedom of the Will." New York: The New American Library, Inc., 1966.

Babylonialism

Anderson, Roy Allan. *The New Age Movement and the Illuminati 666.* Alta Loma, California: The Institute of Religious Knowledge, 1983.

Brooke, Tal. *When the World Will Be As One: The Coming New World Order in the New Age.* Eugene, Oregon: Harvest House Publishers, Inc., 1989.

Cahn, Jonathan. *The Harbinger.* Lake Mary, Florida: Front Line, Charisma House Book Group, 2012.

———. *The Mystery of the Shemitah.* Lake May, Florida: Front Line, Charisma House Book Group, 2014.

———. *The Paradigm.* Lake Mary, Florida: Front Line, Charisma House Book Group, 2017.

Clark, Doug. *The Greatest Banking Scandal in History.* Eugene, Oregon: Eugene House Publishers, 1981

Chitwood Arlen L. *The Spiritual Warfare.* Norman, Oklahoma: The Lamp Broadcast, Inc, 2012; on-line http://www.lampbroadcast.org/Books/TSW.pdf (accessed November 24, 2017).

Council on Foreign Relations: Membership List, https://www.cfr.org/membership-roster, (accessed November 25, 2017).

Cuddy, Dennis L. *Now is the Dawning of the New Age New World Order.* Oklahoma City, Oklahoma: Hearthstone Publishing, 1991.

———. *The Globalists: The Power Elite Exposed.* Oklahoma City, Oklahoma: Hearthstone Publishing, 2001.

Church, J. R. *Guardians of the Grail.* Oklahoma City, Oklahoma: Prophecy Publications, 1989.

Fortner, Michael D. *The Fall of Babylon the Great America.* Lawton, Oklahoma: Trumpet Press, 2016.

Griffin, Des. *Fourth Reich of the Rich.* Clackamas, Oregon: Emissary Publications, 1976, 1992.

———. *Descent into Slavery.* Clackamas, Oregon: Emissary Publications, 1980.

Hislop, Rev. Alexander. *The Two Babylons.* Neptune, New Jersey: Loizeaux Brothers, 1916, 1959.

Hunt, Dave. *Peace, Prosperity, and the Coming Holocaust: The New Age Movement in Prophecy.* Eugene, Oregon: Harvest House Publishers, 1983.

Jeffrey, Grant R. *Prince of Darkness: Antichrist and the New World Order.* Toronto, Ontario, 1994.

———. *Final Warning: Economic Collapse and the Coming World Government,* Toronto, Ontario, 1995.

Kah, Gary H. *En Route To Global Occupation: A High Rankin Government Liaison Exposes the Secret Agenda for World Unification.* Lafayette, Louisiana: Huntington House Publishers, 1992.

Katz, Howard S. *The Paper Aristocracy: America's Money System.* New York: Books In Focus, Inc., 1976.

Kirban, Salem. *Satan's Angels Exposed.* Chattanooga, Tennessee: AMG Publishers, 1980.

Marrs, Jim. *Rule By Secrecy: The Hidden History that Connects the Trilateral Commission, the Freemasons, and the Great Pyramids.* New York: Harper Collins Publishers, 2000.

Marrs, Texe. *Millenium: Peace, Promises, and the Day They Take Our Money Away.* Austin, Texas: Living Truth Publishers, 1990.

Marshall, Peter, and David Manuel. *The Light and the Glory: Did God Have a Plan for America?* Old Tappan, New Jersey: Fleming H. Revell Company, 1977.

McAlvany, Donald S. *Toward A New World Order: The Countdown To Armageddon.* Oklahoma City, Oklahoma: Hearthstone Publishing, Ltd., 1990.

Miller, Edith Starr. *Occult Theocracy.* Hawthorne, California: The Christian Book Club of America, 1933.

Pike, Albert. *Morals and Dogma of the Ancient and Accepted Scottish Rite of Freemasonry.* Washington, D.C.: House of the Temple, 1966.

Quigley, Carroll. *Tragedy and Hope: A History of Our Time.* New York: The Macmillan Company, 1966.

Still, William T. *New World Order: The Ancient Plan of Secret Societies.* Lafayette, Louisiana: Huntington House Publishers, 1990.

Sutton, Antony C. *America's Secret Establishment: An Introduction to the Order of Skull & Bones.* Billings, Montana: Liberty House Press, 1986.

Sutton, William Josiah. *The New Age Movement and the Illuminati 666.* The Institute of Religious Knowledge, 1983.

Webster, Nesta. *Secret Societies and Subversive Movements*. Hawthorne, California: Christian Book Club of America, originally published in 1924.

White House Archives: President Bush's Cabinet, https://georgewbush-whitehouse.archives.gov/government/cabinet.html, (accessed November 25, 2017).

White House: President Barak Obama: The Cabinet, https://obamawhitehouse.archives.gov/administration/cabinet, (accessed November 25, 2017).

Yallop, David A. *In God's Name: An Investigation into the Murder of Pope John Paul I*. New York: Bantom Books, 1984.

ABOUT THE AUTHOR

Rick Young is a deeply committed Christian with over four decades devotion to Jesus Christ. He is a retired senior special agent with almost twenty-nine years of experience in Federal law enforcement. This included an extended tour of combat duty in Vietnam (May 1968-December 1969) as a military policeman, and subsequently, civilian criminal investigations for various Cabinet-level agencies, to include the U.S. Department of State. Trained by the Secret Service in dignitary protection, he also served as a team leader of the U.S. Secretary of Labor protection detail.

More recently, as the director of the Bible-based Emergency Preparation Ministry, he developed, and over-saw while in Kabul, Afghanistan; the Kaisut Desert of Kenyan Africa; and other missionary journeys, an anti-terrorist (security) program for teams he accompanied to those locations.

Rick received an Associate of Arts in pre-law political science from Pasadena City College, a Bachelor of Science in investigative criminal justice from California State University at Los Angeles, and a Master of Science in organizational leadership, with an emphasis in emergency preparation and management, from Philadelphia Biblical University. He is also a graduate of the 3-year program at the Liberty Home Bible Institute, a division of Liberty University, Lynchburg, Virginia, receiving a certification in Advanced Bible Studies.

As one who enjoys writing, Rick is the author of *Combat Police: U.S. Military Police in Vietnam*, currently in the U.S. Library of Congress; co-author with Michael E. Bolyog of three fantasy adventure novels under the title, *Aiden's Cauldron Trilogy*; and co-author with Bob Salomon of the children's picture book, *Beyond The Laces*.

In *Matters of Consequence: Critical Eschatological Issues Impacting Endtime Preparation*, his dissertation for a Doctor of Philosophy in Eschatology from the Luder-Wycliffe Theological Seminary, Endicott, New York, Rick applies the proven methods of emergency pre-planning and crisis management to better prepare Christians for the prophetic, Endtime events foretold in the Bible. By means of developing the worst-case scenario concept, he challenges the reader to think through counter-measures for that vital preparation. In this way, eschatology actually becomes practical!

Rick is married to his wife of forty-eight years, Linda. They have two sons and four grandchildren.

Printed in the United States
By Bookmasters